RETHINKING SEXUALITY

ONE WEEK LOAN

RETHINKING SEXUALITY

Diane Richardson

SAGE Publications
London • Thousand Oaks • New Delhi

First published 2000

SAGE Publications Ltd
6 Bonhill Street
London EC2A 4PU

SAGE Publications Inc
2455 Teller Road
Thousand Oaks, California 91320

SAGE Publications India Pvt Ltd
32, M-Block Market
Greater Kailash – 1
New Delhi 110 048

British Library Cataloguing in Publication data

A catalogue record for this book is available from the British Library

ISBN 0 7619-6708-7
ISBN 0 7619-6709-5 (pbk)

Library of Congress catalog record available

Typeset by M Rules
Printed in Great Britain by Biddles Ltd, Guildford, Surrey

For Hazel

CONTENTS

ACKNOWLEDGEMENTS

I would like to thank a number of people for their help and support during the writing of this book. Thanks to all those who have made comments on drafts of the chapters or responded to sections of them: to reviewers and Lisa Adkins, Peter Aggleton, Magdalene Ang-Lygate, Diane Bell, Jean Carabine, Chris Corrin, Lesley Doyal, Millsom Henry, Janet Holland, Renate Klein, Hazel May, Jennie Naidoo,Vicki Robinson, Tom Shakespeare and Tamsin Wilton. Thanks, too, to Nicki Gillies, Maria Panagos and Brad Robinson in the Department of Sociology and Social Policy at the University of Newcastle, all of whom, in a variety of ways, contributed to getting the book in on time. Val Ashforth has also been an important source of support, and thanks also go to her. While I was working on this book a friend of my family since childhood, Susan Groves, and her partner David, died. I would like to remember them here. Finally, my thanks as ever to family and friends who have provided friendship and warmth, and helped keep me going. The book is dedicated to Hazel May as a small token of my deepest thanks for the support, patience and encouragement that she has given me. The Betty Nation award goes to you.

Some of the essays have been published previously, although most have been edited, updated and revised. Chapter 1 was originally published in *Theorising Heterosexuality*, ed. Diane Richardson (Buckingham: Open University Press, 1996); Chapter 3 is a significantly revised version of an essay that appeared in *Desperately Seeking Sisterhood: Still Challenging and Building*, eds Magdalene Ang-Lygate, Chris Corrin and Millsom S. Henry (London: Taylor & Francis, 1997); Chapter 4 was first published in *Sociology*, 32 (1) (1998); Chapter 6 initially appeared in *Critical Social Policy*, 20 (1) (2000); Chapter 8 is based in part on a chapter in *Sex, Sensibility and the Gendered Body*, eds Janet Hollands and Lisa Adkins (Basingstoke: Macmillan, 1996); and Chapter 9 draws on some of the material contained in an article published in *Culture, Health and Sexuality*, 2 (1) (2000). I am grateful to the publishers for permission to revisit this previously published material.

INTRODUCTION

In the second half of the twentieth century there have been enormous transformations of sexuality. The 1960s was a particularly significant period of social change, despite the fact that the vast majority of people did not experience it as the 'sexual revolution' that it is often characterised as being. Reform of the divorce law took place in 1969, in the context of increasing marital breakdown, leading to a new Divorce Act and an immediate increase in divorce. The Sexual Offences Act, which liberalised legislation on male homosexuality, became law in 1967, as did the Abortion Act, which introduced the possibility for social as well as medical grounds for a legal termination, resulting in a rapid rise in the number of abortions. Alongside increased access to abortion, the 1960s saw important changes in attitudes to contraception. The 1967 Family Planning Act enabled local authorities to set up family planning clinics, which for the first time made no distinction between married and unmarried women. Not only could single women get information about contraception, but also during the 1960s a highly reliable contraceptive, 'the pill', became widely available, and its use spread quickly.

A more 'permissive' attitude to cultural representations of sexual themes was also apparent, aided by changes such as the abolition of the Lord Chamberlain's censorship of the theatre in 1968, which allowed more explicit references to sexuality on stage. In addition, there was a (re)emergence of social movements concerned with sexuality. The rise of the women's and gay liberation movements became a major social and political influence. Feminists emphasised how sexuality, commonly regarded as something that was private and personal, was a public and political issue. Lesbian and gay movements challenged negative understandings of 'homosexuality' and emphasised positive self-definitions, which enabled more and more people to come out and declare that they were 'glad to be gay'.

The 1960s also saw important developments in the theorisation of sexuality, which have had significant implications not just for how we think about sexuality, but also for social and cultural theory more generally. It seems rather trite to claim nowadays that sexuality is socially constructed. Yet this certainly was not the case thirty or even twenty years ago, when essentialist understandings still held sway; not that these have entirely disappeared from view. When, for example, Mary McIntosh suggested in 1968, pre-Foucault, that we might think of homosexuality as a 'social role' rather than as a particular type of person, it was a major breakthrough. Such an idea was revolutionary in terms of the discourses of sexuality that were dominant at the time. However, it is now widely accepted by sociologists and social historians that the categories homosexual and heterosexual persons are a relatively recent social 'invention', deriving from the late seventeenth to the beginning of the eighteenth century in Europe (McIntosh, 1968/1996; Weeks, 1990).

It is this emphasis on the 1960s as a decade of social change, which often dominates our thinking about the transformations in sexuality that have taken place in the second part of the twentieth century. However, we ought not to exaggerate the extent of the changes that took place then, nor should we underestimate the dramatic shifts in the social meanings and organisation of sexuality that have taken place since. Over the last thirty years, divorce rates have risen dramatically in many parts of the world. In the 1970s in Britain, after divorce was made more easily available, divorce rates doubled, and current trends suggest it is likely that almost half of all marriages will now end in divorce (Jackson, 1997). The traditional nuclear family comprising a married heterosexual couple with dependent children is no longer the (hetero)norm of social living arrangements that it once was. More and more people are living together rather than getting married. More fundamentally, 'the couple' as the basic unit of society appears to be threatened, as more women are staying single, and the predictions are that the dominant trend will be to live alone. Reflecting these changes, there has been a steady increase in the number of children born outside marriage, as well as in the number of children being brought up by one parent. For example, by 1991 about a third of all children in Britain were born to women who were unmarried and a fifth of families with children were headed by lone parents, most of whom were women (Central Statistical Office (CSO), 1995). If the social context in which people are bringing up children is changing, then so too are the ways of having them as a result of access to new reproductive technologies such as in vitro fertilisation (IVF) and the freezing of eggs, embryos and sperm. If contraception enables us to have (hetero)sex without reproducing, then new reproductive technologies are allowing more and more people to reproduce without having sex. This represents a further disruption of the reproductive model of sexuality.

More generally, over the last three decades we have witnessed shifts in understandings and acceptance of 'homosexuality'; we have seen the emergence and diversification of sexual identities such as lesbian, gay, transgender, queer and, latterly, pomosexual; and new social movements have fundamentally challenged traditional frameworks for understanding sexuality. Feminist theory, for example, has problematised heterosexuality and redefined lesbianism; while queer has challenged the insider/outsider sexual binary as inherently unstable. We have faced a global AIDS epidemic and its consequences and, largely as a result of feminist campaigning groups and research, begun to publicly acknowledge the extent of sexual violence and abuse and its impact on survivors. We have also seen a rapid commodification and commercialisation of sexuality to the point where, in many parts of the world, sexuality suffuses and saturates social, economic, political and cultural life.

It is claimed that a transformation of intimacy is underway, a new and radical democratisation of sexuality, in which the meanings and practices of sexual/intimate relations are changing rapidly (Giddens, 1992). One could also argue, following this, that we are witnessing a certain disruption and destabilisation of heterosexuality. In addition to the social trends in marriage and cohabitation described above, there are other indications that the normalised and naturalised status of heterosexuality is being challenged. The passing of the 1996 Defense of Marriage Act in the USA, for example, represented an attempt to confine the definition of marriage to heterosexual couples only. While this clearly re-enforces the privileged status of heterosexuality, it is nonetheless significant that marriage needs defending as a heterosexual concept. It is unthinkable that such a defence would have been deemed necessary in the 1960s. Similarly, Section 28 of the Local Government Act, which became law in Britain in 1988, stated that a local authority shall not 'promote the teaching in any maintained school of homosexuality as a pretended family relationship'. Despite the law's hostile and discriminatory treatment of lesbian and gay relationships, what is interesting is how much it reveals about social change and the hegemony of heterosexuality, in terms of the felt necessity to legally reinscribe 'family' as heterosexual.

We are, then, well poised at the turn of the century to rethink sexuality in light of the sorts of transformations that I have mentioned. In this book, I hope to contribute to this process. My aim is to examine the new ways of understanding sexuality and 'sexual politics' that are emerging, through a critical awareness of some the major theoretical and political debates in the last thirty years. At the same time, I am conscious of the sheer scale and enormity of this goal and the fact that, as a consequence, no one book could ever hope to do justice to such a project. Bearing this in mind, I have decided to focus on three main areas which will allow an opportunity to consider in detail some of the major challenges in thinking about sexuality that have occurred in recent years. The areas that I have chosen are all ones that have had a significant impact on an international scale, as well as at the level of individual identities, practices and lifestyles. They are also ones that I have written about over a considerable period of time, and which have been fundamental to debates about sexuality across different social movements, from the moral right to feminism to queer. This is the rationale for structuring this exploration or rethinking of sexuality around the three themes of heterosexuality, citizenship, and AIDS.

Part 1: New Feminisms, Queer Positions and Radical Re-presentations

The first section of the book deals with some of the theoretical developments and social transformations which have contributed in significant ways to our changing understanding of sexuality and of 'sexual politics' over the last thirty years. I should state at the outset that I do not intend to attempt a review of the history of ideas about sexuality since the 1960s. Rather, what I want to attempt is to map out some of the key themes and ideas that have emerged during this period and track their development as they resurface and re-emerge in different forms and in different historical and political contexts. My aim, in what is, in part, an attempt to identify theoretical histories of sexuality, is to highlight continuities, as well as differences, in past and present theorising.

This is less obvious than it might at first seem. As the sociological study of sexuality has grown and developed from the early pioneering research of the 1960s, which paved the way for the development of social constructionist understandings (Gagnon and Simon, 1967, 1973; McIntosh, 1968/1996), to the increasingly large and diverse body of work that exists today, we find that the lineage of ideas is all too often lost. There is a common tendency, evident in both queer writing and aspects of 'new' feminism, to construct attempts to rethink sexuality as representing a distinctive break with the past. I would argue that this is far too simplistic an understanding of the developments in the theorisation of sexuality that we have witnessed in the latter part of the twentieth century.

This relationship of past to present thinking is something that is explored throughout the book. It is an issue, however, that is particularly pertinent to Part 1, where the focus is on the impact that feminist analyses have had on ways of thinking about sexuality since the 1970s, moving on to a discussion of recent developments in both feminist and queer theory. A common theme running through this period, and one that has been central to the work of feminist and queer writers, is that of theorising heterosexuality.

In Chapter 1, I offer an analysis of attempts to problematise heterosexuality, both in the past and more recently, by questioning the assumed normativity and naturalisation of hetero(sex) and relations. Not only does a focus on heterosexuality allow us to comment upon and engage with the question of the relationship of past to present thinking, it also represents one of the most important developments in the theorisation of sexuality and, potentially, of social and political theory more generally. I draw attention to this in considering the possibilities for rethinking social knowledge in ways that challenge, for example, notions of the body, desire, family relationships, as well as conceptual binaries such as the public/private divide and the idea of the sexual and the social as separate spheres.

In the 1990s a new perspective on sexuality, and sexual politics, emerged fuelled by the impact of HIV and AIDS on gay communities and the anti-homosexual feelings and responses that HIV/AIDS revitalised, especially among the 'moral right'. Its name was 'queer'. Embracing a poststructuralist approach to understanding gender and sexuality, queer theory is centrally concerned with the homo/heterosexual binary and the ways in which this operates as a fundamental organising principle in modern societies. Chapter 2 looks at the contribution of queer theory to the theorisation of sexuality. In addition, it examines the way in which queer is often contrasted with feminist and lesbian and gay politics of the 1970s and 1980s. Typically, queer is positioned as in opposition to past gay/lesbian/feminist theorising. I argue that we need to question this characterisation through an analysis of the relationship between queer and previous research and theorising about sexuality, in order to establish where there are possible interconnections, as well as differences in approaches. In this way it will be possible to more accurately map social changes and shifts in thinking about sexuality.

Of particular significance for the development of our understanding of the relationship between queer and feminism is a rethinking of the distinction between sexuality and gender. In some theories such as, for example, in Catharine MacKinnon's (1982) work, sexuality is understood to be constitutive of gender; in others gender is regarded as underpinning sexuality (Jackson, 1999). We may, of course, theorise gender and sexuality as two analytically separate domains as does Gayle Rubin (1984/1993) and others who have been influenced by her work, such as the doyen of queer Eve Sedgwick (1990). Alternatively, we may reject all of these approaches in favour of developing the notion that sexuality and gender are inherently codependent. Tamsin Wilton (1996: 137) exemplifies this position when she states that:

> The interlocutions between discourses of gender and the erotic manifest a complexity that I suggest indicates that they may not usefully be distinguished one from the other.

While I would agree with Wilton that our contemporary understandings of sexuality and gender are such that there can be no simple, causal model that will suffice to explain the interconnections between them, I believe, as does Butler (1997b), that we do need to develop a way of thinking about sexuality and gender that does not collapse the two. The articulation of new ways of thinking about sexuality and gender in a dynamic, historically and socially specific, relationship is one of the main tasks facing both feminist and queer theory.

In Britain in the late 1990s another important trend in 'sexual politics' emerged, as a number of writers claimed to offer a 'new' feminism for a new generation of women. This is a feminism that has been characterised as more popularist, more inclusive, more willing to embrace power, more tolerant in crossing political boundaries, a feminism that belongs to men as well as women, conservatives as well as socialists, and seeks a 'new

separation' of the personal and the political. Natasha Walter's book entitled *The New Feminism* offers up just such a picture. Although Walter's
work can be critiqued on many levels, the widespread publicity accompa-
nying the book and her follow-up collection a year later, plus the fact that
she appears to have 'claimed the ground' as a voice for a new generation
of feminists, make it a useful case study. At a fundamental level, she
regards the 'new' feminism as a mainstream, majority movement:

> If feminism in the nineteenth century was defined by its outsider status, in that
> feminists then were forced to speak from the edges of society; and feminism in
> the seventies and eighties was defined by its sense of difference, in that feminists
> then wanted to mark out a separate space for themselves; so feminism at the
> beginning of the twenty-first century is defined by its insider status. (Walter,
> 1998: 177)

The 'new' feminism also differs from earlier feminist movements in that
it is not associated with 'sexual politics'. Walter (1998: 251) declares: 'The
new feminism does not want to follow women into the bedroom or examine their private sexual lives.' Her argument is that feminism has
overpoliticised our personal lives and overpersonalised the political
sphere. Walter rejects, or at least ignores, the vast body of feminist work
that now exists which critiques the public/private dichotomy, highlighting
how this is frequently employed to 'construct, control, discipline, confine,
exclude and suppress gender and sexual difference preserving traditional
patriarchal and heterosexist power structures' (Duncan, 1996b: 128). Walter
is not buying into this, she wants the distinction between the public and
private reinstated: 'So the new feminism must unpick the tight link that
feminism in the seventies made between our personal and political lives'
(Walter, 1998: 4).

This could imply that the 'new' feminism has little to say about sexuality, beyond seeking to ensure that women who experience sexual violence
or abuse find redress and support. However, sexuality infuses Walter's
book and ideas, in so far as heterosexuality permeates the concept of the
'new' feminist. (The index has no reference to homosexuality, lesbian, gay
or queer; and only one to 'lesbian sexuality'.) Moreover, it is a particular,
albeit institutionalised, form of 'new' heterosexuality that feminists will
apparently be expecting:

> The new feminist will probably still have her eyes on marriage, although she
> takes for granted that it will be a partnership of equals rather than a relationship
> with a dominant and subordinate partner . . . Such a young woman also takes
> contraceptive and abortion rights absolutely for granted, in order to control her
> fertility as far as possible. (Walter, 1998: 186)

It is, of course, precisely because many women in both developed and
developing worlds still *cannot* take such things for granted that feminists continue to highlight sexual and reproductive issues as central to

understanding gender inequality and the social control of women. In many parts of South America, for example, deaths from illegal abortions are one of the main causes of death in women of childbearing age. In countries such as Britain, where abortion is legal, it remains a major issue for the many women who find it difficult to obtain an abortion on the National Health Service, either as a result of the attitude of their doctors or cuts in health funding, and who do not have the funds to have an abortion carried out privately.

The aim of 'new' feminism, we are told, is the pursuit of political, social and economic equality, rather than liberation: 'Feminism is about equality for women, nothing more nothing less' (Walter, 1998: 41). More specifically, the 'concrete goals' that are emphasised include the reorganisation of work, with a national network of childcare and the encouragement of men to share equally in the responsibilities in the home, a reduction in poverty and a legislative and welfare system that supports rather than discriminates against women, especially those facing sexual and domestic violence. In this sense, 'new' feminism appears to be saying many of the same things that 'old' feminists of the 1970s were. A major difference, however, is in the political analysis – or rather the lack of it. 'New' feminism, I would argue, is feminism without the politics: feminism-lite. It asserts the need for a more equal society, but is without a theoretical foundation by which it is possible to identify strategies for achieving social change. As Lynne Segal (1999: 228) also notes:

> But quite how [new] 'feminism' will manage to deliver, once it remedies its ways and adopts 'a new, less embattled ideal', remains mysterious. Walter's analysis promotes no particular, collective political formations or affiliations. We are simply told: 'We must understand that feminism can give us these things now, if we really want them.' Fingers crossed!

One might, of course, want to argue that we could understand this shift in feminist thinking as part of a broader trend within western democracies towards 'third way' politics. This can be seen in the British context of 'New' Labour, for example, where it might be argued that the politics has been taken out of Politics: Blairite government is Politics as governance.

In Chapter 3 I examine how the characterisation of different strands of feminism is important in rethinking feminist theory over the last thirty years and in developing feminisms of the future. In the context of this book, it is important to look at this issue given the important contribution that feminist theorising and activism have made to the transformations of sexuality that have taken place since the 1960s. Because it is radical feminist theories, especially of sexuality, that are frequently critiqued by contemporary writers, I have used this strand as a case study in order to explore the implications of stereotyping traditions of feminist thinking as 'old' and 'new'. I focus more specifically on the attribution of essentialism,

⌐efined, and puritanism, as well as the claim that radical femi-
⌐es 'victims of women'.

⌐a⌐ ⌐exual Citizenship

The second section of the book is concerned with rethinking sexuality in a
different way. Rather than trying to tease out the interconnections between
past and present social movements and theoretical approaches, these chapters describe the rapid growth of 'a politics of sexual citizenship' that has
occurred in recent years in most western countries. These developments
represent a shift in the meaning and focus of 'sexual politics'. The prioriti-
sation in research and collective activism that took place in the 1960s and
1970s was around identity. We are now witnessing the expansion of political campaigns and literature concerned with issues of family and intimate
relationships (Donovan et al., 1999). Debates about, and campaigns to
secure, various rights of citizenship on the same basis as those of heterosexuals are increasingly the 'main story'. The AIDS epidemic has been
significant in this shift in gay politics, bringing into sharp relief the lack of
legal recognition for non-heterosexual relationships, with consequences
for access to pensions, housing, inheritance and other rights, as well as the
need for health and social care services that are accepting of, and appropriate to, lesbian and gay relationships. Other specific concerns have also
fuelled this rethinking of lesbian and gay struggles such as, for example,
Section 28 which, Weeks (1991) argues, mobilised and politicised many
non-heterosexual communities, especially in its attempts to exclude lesbians and gay men from what is thought to constitute 'a family'. As I argue
below, there are, however, broader social trends that we need to consider,
which have also had an important impact on this move towards a 'politics
of sexual citizenship'.

   The concept of citizenship, along with questions of social exclusion and
membership, has (re)emerged as one of the key areas of debate within
both political discourse and the social sciences. A central theme of these
developments is that citizenship is a contested concept: it can be used in a
variety of ways with different implications for understanding the context
in which various forms of social exclusion occur. This expansion of the idea
of citizenship is evidenced in the diversity of arenas in which citizenship is
being claimed and contested. Despite an almost exclusive focus on the
public sphere in traditional interpretations of citizenship, it would seem
that people's everyday practices are increasingly becoming the bases for
discussing citizenship. Consider, for example, the concept of healthier citizenship. As 'good citizens' we are enjoined to take care of and assume
responsibility for our own health and, especially in the case of women, any
future children that we may have. In addition to patterns of eating and
drinking, the 'private' and intimate practices of sexuality are also part of
the realms in which healthy citizenship is constituted. Thus, for example,

sexual health promotion, whether understood in the context of concerns about the spread of sexually transmitted diseases such as AIDS or the prevalence of unplanned pregnancies in certain sectors of the community, emphasises the importance of practising safer sex. That is to say, safer sex is now one of the responsibilities incumbent upon responsible and self-governing citizens.

At the same time that citizenship has (re)emerged as a dominant theme within social and political theory, social movements concerned with the organisation of sexuality and gender have increasingly drawn on the language of citizenship. We live in an age when the politics of citizenship increasingly define 'sexual politics'. Globally, we are witnessing gay and lesbian movements (and sometimes bi /sometimes transgender) which demand 'equal rights' with heterosexuals in relation to age of consent laws, to healthcare, rights associated with social and legal recognition of domestic partnerships, including the right to marry, immigration rights, parenting rights and so on. In a similar vein, there are groups campaigning for 'transsexual rights' including the right to 'sex change' treatment on the National Health Service, the legal right for birth certificate status to be changed and, related to this, the right to marry legally. Recently, there have been attempts to place 'sexual rights' on the agenda of disability movements, especially in relation to disabled people's rights to sexual expression (Shakespeare et al., 1996). We can even see some evidence of the language of citizenship being used in movements or campaigns whose politics are definitely not about seeking formal equality with heterosexuals. An example of this is the focus on prostitution as a human rights issue by some radical and revolutionary feminists (Jeffreys, 1997). As I suggested above, what these examples highlight is a shift in recent considerations of citizenship from what was previously an almost exclusive focus on the public towards an inclusion of issues that have long been associated and conflated with the 'private'.

Despite the current presence and past history of social movements campaigning for 'sexual rights', little theoretical attention has been given to sexuality and its relationship to citizenship. Recently, however, a new body of work on sexuality and citizenship has emerged. This includes work in legal theory (e.g. Robson, 1992; Herman, 1994; Stychin, 1998), political theory (e.g. Phelan, 1994, 1995; Wilson, 1995), geography (e.g. Bell, 1995; Binnie, 1995), education (e.g. Lees, 2000), literary criticism and cultural studies (Berlant, 1997; Isin and Wood, 1999) and sociology (e.g. Giddens, 1992; Plummer, 1995, 2000; Richardson, 1998; Weeks, 1998), as well as work which has raised the question of sexuality in a social policy context (Cooper, 1995; Carabine, 1996a, b; Donovan et al., 1999).

It might be claimed, given its relative newness as a field of inquiry, that it is too soon to map the shifts in understanding of citizenship that we are witnessing as a result of the inclusion of debates around sexuality. However, I would argue that it is possible to begin to identify a number of broad themes or strands within this emergent literature, which although interrelated draw upon different epistemological concerns. Over the next three chapters I will deal with each of these concerns in turn. The first relates to those analyses which are primarily concerned with the question of whether, in addition to being informed by ideas about gender, class and race, notions of citizenship are grounded in normative assumptions about sexuality.

Chapter 4 addresses this question, through an examination of definitions of citizenship as a set of civil, political and social rights in the tradition of the British sociologist T.H. Marshall (1950), as social membership, both of a nation-state and social membership conceptualised more broadly (Turner, 1993a), as cultural rights (Stevenson, 2000), and in terms of consumerism (Evans, 1993). In each case, I aim to demonstrate how claims to citizenship status are closely associated with the institutionalisation of heterosexual, as well as male, privilege. In response to my argument, Bryan Turner (1999: 32) has stressed the link with parenthood and citizenship as being more significant than that with heterosexuality. He claims that:

> The liberal regime of modern citizenship privileges parenthood, rather than heterosexuality as such, as the defining characteristic of the normal citizen and as the basis of social entitlement. That is, it recognises reproductive parenting as a foundation of modern citizenship and therefore homosexuality has been traditionally condemned because it fails to support citizenship as a buttress of the nation state . . . It is the absence of successful parenting in reproduction, not homosexuality, which challenges the Marshallian model.

I agree with Turner that in extending our theoretical frameworks in this new field of study we need to address in more detail the relationship *between* parenthood and heterosexuality, and the significance of this for understanding the construction of citizenship. However, and following on from this, unlike Turner who seems to want to attach a privileged position to parenthood as determining of citizenship status, I believe it is important to retain a theoretical apparatus that allows, indeed requires, us to think about how heterosexuality and parenthood are in a dynamic relationship with one another. Consider, for example, the extent of social resistance to lesbian and gay marriages and, more especially, of lesbian and gay parenting. What does this tell us? Indeed, where domestic partnerships between lesbians or between gay men have been legally recognised, it is frequently the case that one of the limits to gaining access to such forms of citizenship status is parenthood. In Scandinavia, for example, registration of partnership legislation specifically denies same-sex couples the right to adopt children. (This theme is taken up in Chapter 6.) Alternatively, if we reflect on the increasing diversification of forms of family and parenthood, we might also begin to identify where heterosexuality is a primary determinant of citizenship as distinct from parenthood *per se*. For example, contrast the married heterosexual couple with no children, with the single, heterosexual, never married mother of a family of four or the British gay male couple who in 1999 paid a 'surrogate mother' in the USA to donate her egg and another to give birth to twins via artificial insemination using a mixture of their sperm. Who, among these, is the more valued citizen with social, legal and economic rights attached to their family relationships?

The welfare state was predicated on the married heterosexual couple and the traditional nuclear family, and it continues to be the case that such a relationship is a factor in determining eligibility for benefit. Thus, in the case of single mothers we see a questioning of eligibility for welfare rights and entitlements, both in the USA and Britain, which is informed by their 'inappropriate' sexuality (Millar, 1994; Carabine, 1996a). In the example of the gay male couple mentioned above, the immediate response under British law was to deny them parenting rights. The social and legal rights of parenthood were conferred on the birth mother and her husband, neither of whom is genetically related to the child nor had any desire to raise the children. The question we need to ask is whether we have been 'good citizens' in fulfilling our obligations to society in being (re)productive and shouldering the burden of raising children, or whether it is how we have reproduced and in what relational context that counts? In this sense, we can analytically separate parenthood from the significance of a married, *heterosexual* context as the norm for 'good citizenship'. I would suggest, therefore, that at present the evidence is somewhat lacking in support of Turner (1999: 34) when he claims that:

> Homosexuality is only an indirect threat to the state because the real issue has been the basis of reproductive citizenship entitlements. What is clear is that we live in societies with powerful familial and reproductive ideologies that encourage marriage and fertility. Such a society will be prepared to tolerate homosexual and lesbian marriages, especially where they too may be legitimised through a system of adoptions.

The second main strand that we can identify in the increasing interest in sexuality and its connection to citizenship has as its focus a concern with developing a specific notion of sexual or intimate citizenship. Discussion of sexual citizenship often tends to focus on access to rights, although what is meant by the term 'sexual citizenship' is still in the process of being defined. Some writers use the term to refer specifically to the sexual 'rights' granted or denied to various social groups, others conceptualise sexual citizenship in much broader terms. In this regard, we need to consider the question not just of access to citizenship, but also the basis upon which such access is granted or denied. This prompts an examination of the underlying assumptions embedded in frameworks or models of citizenship, and the practice of policy, which I argue in Chapter 4 are both (hetero)sexualised and gendered. In Chapter 5, I explore the ways in which 'sexual citizenship' is currently being constructed, in order that we may begin to think about some of the theoretical and political issues raised by extending citizenship into this arena.

Work relevant to the third strand that is evident within the literature on sexuality and citizenship, has examined the question of what rights and obligations are the concerns of sexual or intimate citizenship. What do we actually mean by 'sexual rights' or, indeed, 'sexual obligations'? Furthermore, what are the principles and models of citizenship underlying such claims, as well as those in opposition to them? Chapter 6 explores these issues by focusing on the question of theorising 'sexual rights', demonstrating how this is a highly contested concept, both in terms of its meaning, given competing claims over what are defined as 'sexual rights', and in terms of differing views over its political utility.

Part 3: Sexuality, Gender and HIV/AIDS

Part 3 shifts the focus from social movements arguing for rights claims to another major influence on rethinking sexuality in the latter part of the twentieth century: the emergence in 1981 of a disease that would rapidly become a global epidemic and would later be named AIDS. Since the epidemic began it is estimated that 50 million people have been infected with HIV, of whom over 16 million have died of AIDS (UNAIDS, 1999). In recent years, however, although there is still no vaccine available, there have been a number of developments that have encouraged the view that HIV and AIDS are 'controllable'. In particular, there have been improvements in survival and quality of life due to treatment with antiretroviral therapies such as AZT. Studies have also identified interventions that reduce the risk of mother-to-child transmission of HIV. Despite these developments, many people will continue to die from diseases related to HIV and AIDS, especially in countries where poverty and poorly developed health and education systems mean there are limited resources for prevention and care. AIDS now kills more people worldwide than any other infectious disease and, in 1999, there was a record 2.6 million AIDS deaths, with an estimated 5.6 million adults and children becoming infected in the same year (UNAIDS, 1999).

Of particular global concern is the fact that the HIV positive population is still expanding. A report from the Joint United Nations Programme on HIV/AIDS in 1999 estimated that more than 33 million adults and 1.2 million children were infected with HIV, with over two thirds of this global total living in Sub-Saharan Africa. In North America the estimated figure was just under a million, whereas in western Europe it was around half a million. The report also highlighted the rapidly rising numbers of HIV positive people in the newly formed states of the former Soviet Union. In the larger region comprising these nations and the remainder of central and eastern Europe, the number of people who became infected rose by more than a third in 1999, to reach an estimated 360,000 (UNAIDS, 1999).

Fifteen or even ten years ago it was difficult to convince people that AIDS was not just a man's disease. Since then, as it has become increasingly clear that women do get AIDS, public concern about the impact of HIV/AIDS on women has grown. This is reflected in the number of books and articles now published on the subject, in papers presented at conferences, in the development of new research initiatives, as well as in the establishment of organisations specifically concerned with women and HIV/AIDS in various parts of the world.

One of the main reasons for this shift in concern is evidence from official reports, which suggests that the risk of infection is increasing for women – and therefore potentially and significantly for any children they might have – both in developed and developing countries. Studies have shown that in parts of Africa more than half of those infected with HIV are women. Male to female sexual transmission of the virus is assumed to be the main route of infection. HIV infection is also increasing among women living in the west. In the UK, for example, the number of cases of AIDS in women has been rising steadily. Elsewhere in Europe a similar pattern can be observed. In France, of the total number of cases of AIDS reported in 1985 only 12% were female. The figure ten years later was 20%. In Spain, the proportion rose from 7% to 19% of all AIDS cases during the same period (UNAIDS, 1999). Heterosexual contact accounts for an increasing proportion of AIDS cases in Europe, and has become the predominant transmission route among new AIDS cases in several countries, including France, Norway and Sweden.

There are over 14 million women throughout the world who are HIV positive, of whom 2 million were infected in 1998 alone (UNAIDS, 1999). In Europe and the USA about a fifth of all those who are currently known to be HIV positive are women. What these figures represent beyond the level of individual tragedy and suffering, is a massive impact on families, communities, households, health systems, labour markets and political economies. They also represent a significant challenge to our sexual values and practices. As a sexually transmitted disease, AIDS has thrown into sharp relief the significance of what you do, and how you do it, rather than what you call yourself. AIDS has also revitalised and been a focal point for many of the controversies in contemporary debates about sexuality such as, for example, sex education, contraception, homosexuality and prostitution. It has also given rise to new social movements concerned with the politics of AIDS and sexuality such as ACT UP and Queer Nation, which have not only demanded various rights, but have also sought to establish new definitions of sexual identity and politics.

In the final part of the book I explore how understandings of gender and sexuality have been challenged by AIDS, focusing on the ways in which HIV/AIDS has been represented since the beginning of the epidemic and moving on to a discussion of notions of risk. In Chapter 7, I begin by considering feminist responses to AIDS and discuss some of the possible reasons why the links between feminist analysis and HIV/AIDS work have been slow to develop, at least in the UK. The implications of a lack of feminist input into how we understand and respond to HIV/AIDS are also analysed.

Equally, it is important to ask how HIV/AIDS informs feminist theorising, especially of sexuality. Chapter 8 offers some examples of this, in analysing various discursive responses to AIDS in terms of the ways in which the categories 'woman' and 'man', as well as 'homosexual' and 'heterosexual', are deployed. What this highlights is how understandings of HIV/AIDS are grounded in existing ways of thinking about gender and sexual relationships. In addition to looking at how accounts of HIV/AIDS are gendered and sexualised, I argue that responses to AIDS are part of the struggles over the meaning of gender and sexuality. My aim is to show how HIV/AIDS constitutes, as well as invokes, contemporary understandings of sexuality and gender.

The final chapter continues with this theme, while also considering notions of 'risk' in the context of HIV/AIDS. The question of the relationship between sexual identity and sexual practice, often assumed to be interconnected, is central to this and affects how we think about and enact sexuality. I examine this issue by focusing on the ways in which lesbians have been represented in AIDS discourses. The focus on lesbians is extremely useful, as they have been represented as both 'high-risk', in the early years of the epidemic, and then subsequently as 'low or no risk'. These shifts highlight how interpretations of AIDS have changed over the last two decades and, as a consequence, our understandings of 'risk' in sexual relationships.

Conclusion

In this introduction to the aims and themes of the book, I have outlined some of my reasons for writing it, why I believe it is important that we think about the transformations of sexuality that are occurring, and how these relate to the past and the future. In thinking about how sexuality is undergoing transformation, this book will help to demonstrate how understandings of sexuality are crucial to the wider social, political and economic world of today.

Sexuality is a central feature of modern societies. It is the focus of major social and political issues that are global concerns ranging from sexual violence, sex education, prostitution, trafficking in women, abortion and contraception, single parenthood, AIDS, divorce, the rights of lesbians and gay men, through to the organisation of social life through the institutionalisation of hetero(norms). In the last thirty years it has become a central aspect of global capitalism. From the use of sexual imagery in advertising and marketing, to billion dollar sex industries selling pornography and sexual services, to weddings, to mail-order brides, to international sex tourism, and so on: this is the political economy of sexuality. Sexuality is also a mechanism of social control and regulation. As a consequence, it is a focus of political struggle via the efforts of social movements concerned with sexual and reproductive issues.

At an individual level sexuality is central to our understanding of contemporary identities and relationships. It is directly connected to how we feel about ourselves and others and, often, our motives for forming relationships and achieving intimacy. It is a mode for experiencing love and pleasure, as well as assessing and demonstrating personal worth.

It is for all these reasons that we need to understand the continuing transformations of sexuality and their social, personal and political implications.

PART 1

NEW FEMINISMS, QUEER POSITIONS AND RADICAL RE-PRESENTATIONS

1

THEORISING HETEROSEXUALITY

Introduction

Within social and political theory little attention has traditionally been given to theorising heterosexuality. Although it is deeply embedded in accounts of social and political participation, and our understandings of ourselves and the worlds we inhabit, heterosexuality is rarely acknowledged or, even less likely, problematised. Instead, most of the conceptual frameworks we use to theorise human relations rely implicitly upon a naturalised heterosexuality – where (hetero)sexuality tends either to be ignored in the analysis or is hidden from view, being treated as an unquestioned paradigm. Where sexuality is acknowledged as a significant category for social analysis, it has been primarily in the context of theorising the 'sexual other', defined in relation to a normative heterosexuality. Perhaps more surprisingly is the failure of a great deal of feminist work, even when writing about the family, to question a naturalised heterosexuality. Monique Wittig (1992) and Susan Cavin (1985), for example, have criticised feminist theories that attempt to explain the origins of women's oppression, for assuming the universality and normality of heterosexuality.

More recently there have been significant attempts by both feminists and proponents of queer theory to interrogate the way that heterosexuality encodes and structures everyday life, and to recognise the impact that ignoring or excluding heterosexuality has had on the development of social theory. In this chapter, I shall be examining and, I hope, furthering these debates. Ultimately, this requires not only a commitment to theorising heterosexuality, but also a recognition of the challenge posed by the theorisation of heterosexuality in so far as it invites a radical rethinking of many of the concepts we use to theorise social relations.

Heteronormativity

> 'The purpose of a man is to love a woman
> and the purpose of a woman is to love a man.'
> (*The Game of Love*)

uality is institutionalised as a particular form of practice and
s, of family structure, and identity. It is constructed as a coher-
fixed and stable category; as universal and monolithic. Despite
only represented in this way, there actually exists a diversity of
............gs and social arrangements within the category 'heterosexuality',
rather than a unitary heterosexual subject and a unified, distinct heterosexual community. However, whereas there is a growing albeit largely
North American literature documenting how race, class and ethnicity
interact with sexuality in the case of lesbians and gay men (Moraga and
Anzaldua, 1981; Torton Beck, 1982; Beam, 1986; Ramos, 1987; Roscoe, 1992;
Penelope, 1994), there is, so far, relatively little in the case of heterosexuality. Where there is a substantial literature is on the interaction of
heterosexuality and gender.

Heterosexuality and feminist theory

Heterosexuality is a category divided by gender and which also depends
for its meaning on gender divisions. For women it is an identity defined
primarily in relation to desire for men and/or the social and economic
privileges associated with being the partner of a man, in particular the
traditional roles of wife and mother. How the construction of heterosexuality both privileges and disempowers women, and the relationship
between heterosexuality and feminism, are important themes of especially
radical feminist theory (see Richardson, 1996a; Jackson, 1999). The meanings of heterosexuality for men, and its interconnections with masculinity,
are also explored in some feminist work (see, for example, Segal, 1990;
Robinson, 1996; Holland et al., 1998).

The view that heterosexuality is a key site of male power is widely
accepted within feminism (Walby, 1990, 1997; Delphy and Leonard, 1992).
Within most feminist accounts, heterosexuality is seen not as an individual
preference, something we are born like or gradually develop into, but as a
socially constructed institution which structures and maintains male domination, in particular through the way it channels women into marriage
and motherhood. Similarly, lesbianism has been defined not just as a particular sexual practice, but as a form of political struggle – a challenge to
the institution of heterosexuality and a form of resistance to patriarchal
relations.

Having said this, the critique of heterosexuality, and its role in the control and exploitation of women, has been one of the major areas of
disagreement/debate between feminists. This was particularly evident
during the 1970s with the emergence of critiques that highlighted heterosexuality as an oppressive institution. This represented a far more
fundamental critique of heterosexuality than the previous focus on
(hetero)sexual practice. Indeed, some feminists argued that, if heterosexuality is key to male dominance, feminists should reject sexual relationships

with men. In the USA, the classic 'Woman-identified woman' paper by Radicalesbians, written in 1970, asserted that 'woman-identified lesbianism' was the political strategy necessary for women's liberation and the end to male supremacy. The implication for heterosexual feminists was that they should give up relationships with men and put their commitment, love and emotional support into relationships with women (Radicalesbians, 1970). In Britain, similar ideas were put forward in a paper, first published in 1979, by the Leeds Revolutionary Feminist Group (Onlywomen Press, 1981). The paper, entitled 'Political lesbianism: the case against heterosexuality', proposed 'political lesbianism' as a strategy to resist patriarchy. It stated that all feminists can and should be political lesbians because 'the heterosexual couple is the basic unit of the political structure of male supremacy . . . Any woman who takes part in a heterosexual couple helps to shore up male supremacy by making its foundations stronger' (Onlywomen Press, 1981: 6). A political lesbian was defined as 'a woman-identified woman who does not fuck men', it did not necessarily mean having sexual relationships with other women. A similar debate occurred in France at this time, focused around the publication of Monique Wittig's *The Straight Mind* (see Wittig, 1992 and Dhavernas, 1996). Although there are important differences in their analyses and challenges to heterosexuality, one can, nevertheless, draw some comparisons to the strategy of those nineteenth-century feminists who advocated voluntary celibacy and spinsterhood as a form of resistance to the sexual subjection of women (Jeffreys, 1985).

Within hegemonic heterosexual relationships women have been expected to service men emotionally and sexually. Men have also gained from material servicing: it is women who traditionally have been primarily responsible for housework and for the work of caring for family members, including male partners (VanEvery, 1995, 1996). This has implications for women's economic independence, in terms of the relationship between women's unpaid domestic labour and their position in the labour market (Witz, 1997). Clearly for women to withdraw *en masse* from such relationships *would* be revolutionary, even if some men could afford to pay for such services. However, as many feminists pointed out at the time, 'political lesbianism' is not a choice that is equally open to all women.

In addition to the charge of ignoring differences and divisions between women, many heterosexual feminists were extremely angry and critical of such analyses of heterosexuality, arguing that they contravened the women's liberation movement's demand for the right to a self-defined sexuality. Some lesbian feminists also reacted angrily to the arguments for political lesbianism (see Onlywomen Press, 1981). Part of their concern was that lesbianism was becoming associated with a critique of heterosexuality, a rejection of men and feelings of sisterhood with other women, rather than a 'specific sexual practice between women, with it's own history and culture' (Campbell, 1980: 1). Nevertheless, the suggestion that 'Any woman can be a lesbian' did represent an important challenge to traditional assumptions about lesbianism as an immature or pathological condition of a minority group of women. By providing a political analysis of sexual relationships between women, feminism not only helped to destigmatise lesbianism, it also broadened its meaning. In other words, the women's movement not only helped lesbians to feel more positive about themselves and to 'come out', it also 'opened up the possibility for lesbian relationships for many women who had previously considered their heterosexuality a permanent feature' (Stacey, 1991).

In focusing on the 'political lesbianism' debates, we should not ignore the fact that in the early 1970s many heterosexual feminists as well as lesbians voiced criticisms of heterosexuality; however this was largely as a form of sexual practice. In particular, they challenged the centrality of sexual intercourse in heterosexual relations, pointing out that very often this is not the major or only source of sexual arousal for women. Anne Koedt, for example, in a now-famous article, criticised 'the myth of the vaginal orgasm' and stressed the importance of the clitoris for female pleasure (Koedt, 1974/1996). However, despite Koedt's acknowledgement of the implications for lesbianism, such discussions were often focused on how to get men to be better lovers through improving their sexual technique, rather than on any fundamental criticism of heterosexuality. The important concern was establishing women's right to sexual pleasure, primarily within a heterosexual context.

In a radical and highly influential article first published in 1980, Adrienne Rich examined the institutionalisation of heterosexuality, suggesting that heterosexuality may not be a 'preference' at all but something that 'has had to be imposed, managed, organised, propagandised, and maintained by force' (Rich, 1980: 20). She went on to describe some of the factors which 'force' women into sexual relationships with men rather than women: for example, a sexual ideology which presents heterosexuality as 'normal' and lesbianism as 'deviant'; the unequal position of women in the labour market; the idealisation of heterosexual romance and marriage; the threat of male violence which encourages women to seek the 'protection' of a man; and men's legitimising of motherhood.

The 1990s witnessed a re-emergence of feminist writing on theorising heterosexuality (see, for example, Wilkinson and Kitzinger, 1993; Segal, 1994; Richardson, 1996a; Smart, 1996a, b; Jackson, 1999). In addition to re-examining 'old' questions such as, for example, whether being a feminist and heterosexual is tenable, this recent output of work has tended to focus on sexual experience and practice, particularly on desire and pleasure, both in terms of a critique (Kitzinger and Wilkinson, 1994; Jeffreys, 1996) and a defence (Segal, 1994; Hollway, 1993, 1996), as well as on subjectivity. Some writers, however, have been more concerned with theorising the ways in which heterosexuality is institutionalised in society, how this is implicated in women's subordination and how heterosexuality as social practice constitutes gender (Carabine, 1996b; Richardson, 1996b; VanEvery, 1996).

The attempts by both feminists and proponents of queer theory to problematise heterosexuality have helped to deconstruct heterosexuality as a monolithic category. (Queer theory is discussed in the next chapter.) Although, within feminism, the focus has primarily been on the interaction of heterosexuality and gender, the experience of institutionalised heterosexuality is also informed by, and informs, constructions of race and class. Yet, as bell hooks (1989) has pointed out, there has been relatively little public discussion of the connections between race and sexuality. This is despite the fact that dominant discourses of sexuality refer primarily to a white, as well as male and heterosexual subject. That is, we tend to assume that '. . . "whiteness" figures the normative center of political and theoretical discussions about sexuality and identity' (Goldsby, 1993: 116). When black sexuality is represented in debates about sexuality, it has historically been as a form of hypersexuality. Most commonly, black women and men are portrayed as oversexed – as oversexed heterosexuals, that is. It is, moreover, a black especially male heterosexuality that has been perceived as posing a threat to especially white womanhood (Harper, 1993). By implication the concepts lesbian and gay are also racialised, as race is (hetero)sexualised. The image of a gay man and, perhaps to a lesser extent, a lesbian is characteristically white and, increasingly, middle class.

There is also a need to examine further the ways in which class position intersects with sexuality (see, for example, earlier work by D'Emilio, 1984/1993; Weeks 1986, 1990). This is true not only in terms of asking how might a person's class position affect the formation of sexual identities and practices, but also in terms of how notions of class are informed by the assumption of heterosexuality and how, consequently, our analysis of class may be changed by a questioning of this. Very often, in the past, within traditional left discourse, the working class was not only a masculinised but also, implicitly, a heterosexualised concept. As a consequence, lesbian and gay political struggles have often been dismissed as bourgeois.

Bodies, identities, desires, doing 'Sex'

The privileging of heterosexual relations as the assumed bedrock of social relations without which, it is posited, society would no longer function nor exist, reinforces the idea that heterosexuality is the original blueprint for interpersonal relations. According to Michael Warner, following Wittig (1992): '. . . Western political thought has taken the heterosexual couple to represent the principle of social union itself' (Warner, 1993a: xxi). This serves to delimit interpretations of both heterosexuality (as stable, necessary, universal) and the social (as naturalised heterosexuality). It also structures and organises understandings of individuals, as well as sexual and familial relationships, that are not included within the construction of the category 'heterosexual'.

In what is often described as the first major study of female homosexuality Frank Caprio (1954: 18) claims that: 'Many lesbian relationships between two women become the equivalent of a husband-wife relationship. The mannish or overt lesbian likes to take on the role of the "husband" and generally attaches herself to a female partner who is feminine in physique and personality. She regards her mate as her "wife".'

The point is not that butch/femme relationships did not exist among lesbians in the 1950s, clearly they did (Nestle, 1988), nor that lesbians did not incorporate into their lives meanings drawn from the model of the heterosexual married couple; rather, that this view is constituted as scientific truth. Of course a great deal has changed since Caprio wrote this, both in terms of lesbian and heterosexual lifestyles, and such crude characterisations of lesbian relationships as copycat 'marriages' are nowadays relatively rare. However, this is not to say that heterosexuality has relinquished its hold on conceptualisations of both the sexual and the intimate. For example, recent debates about gay marriages and the right of lesbians and gay men to have legally recognised 'domestic partnerships' have overwhelmingly been framed in a political language of inclusion (Kaplan, 1997). In assimilating lesbians and gay men, the dominant discourse of understanding familial forms is hardly undermined (Richardson, 2000b). Another example of this is the linking of parenting to gendered difference constituted through a heterosexual relationship. Hence, the tendency to see lesbian and gay parenting as confusing: 'I can't help but wonder what a child would do whose parents are two males; are they both referred to as "Daddy?" Or does the child learn to refer to one of the men as "Mom?"' (Grover, quoted in Weston, 1993: 164). Behind such questions is the belief that if one man is the father, the only identity available to his partner is mother. Similarly, to ask of lesbian parents 'What will a child call the mother's lover?' seems to invoke the idea that there must be two distinct and differentiated parental roles rather than two mothers.

Related to this analysis of how heterosexuality encodes and structures everyday life, is the question of identity. As I have already indicated, historically lesbians have traditionally been portrayed as virtual men trapped in the space of women's bodies: 'mannish' in appearance and masculine in their thoughts, feelings and desires, rendering their existence compatible with the logic of gender and heteronormativity. Although she is necessary to this logic, the complementary femme 'type' of lesbian is mentioned much less frequently in representations of lesbians in scientific discourses and popular culture – perhaps not unsurprisingly as she is more problematic.

In the 1970s, both lesbian feminist and gay liberation movements challenged dominant scientific constructions of homosexuals and women. Lesbian feminists also critiqued heterosexuality as both an institution oppressive to women, and as practice. In doing so they rejected definitions of lesbian identity, desire and practice that were seen as derived from a patriarchal and heterosexual model of society. The establishment of new lesbian identities, such as lesbian feminist, radicalesbian, political lesbian and woman-identified woman, represented something new, an attempt at

the establishment of a definition of lesbianism as a political
rather than derivative of, heterosexuality.

Judith Butler's work (1990, 1993, 1997b) represents a sop
modern attempt to theorise heterosexuality and its relationsuip
identity. Butler argues, as does Foucault, that we can never escape hege
monic discourses, so that even a lesbian/feminist identity is produced
within hegemonic heterosexual norms. However, she goes on to argue
that this is also true of heterosexuality. That is to say, far from being a natural expression of gender and sexuality, heterosexuality is always in the
process of being produced. There is, in other words, no original of which
homosexuality is an (inferior) copy. Heterosexuality is itself always in the
process of being constructed, according to Butler, through repeated performances that imitate its own idealisations and norms and thereby
produce the effect of being natural.

If our understandings of the structure of intimate relations are typically
mediated through dominant heterosexual and gender norms, it is also the
case that conceptualisations of desire and of 'sex' as a specific set of practices are similarly encoded. Central to the theorisation of desire in sexual
relationships has been the notion of desire as desire for 'the other'.
Typically, desire is conceptualised in terms of attraction to difference,
where gender is the key marker of difference. Female sexuality has traditionally been defined as different from, yet complementary to, male
sexuality. Similarly, women and men are commonly referred to as 'opposite
sex' partners in contrast to lesbian and gay relationships that are defined in
terms of 'sameness' not difference. It is this 'difference', constructed as
gendered power difference, which has often been assumed to be both natural and necessary to sexual arousal and pleasure. This approach suggests
that desire is the 'province and the privilege of heterosexuals' (Fuss, 1993:
63) or at least that to achieve desire one must identify with and mimic this
reading of (heterosexual) desire.

Historically, this is evident in theoretical constructions of sex between
women as either involving role-playing, with one woman playing the part
of the 'man' and the other the part of the 'woman', or as primarily acts of
affection and not really sex at all (Richardson, 1992). Even within the feminist literature, where theorists might have been expected to take a different
view, some writers have echoed this model in claiming that unless some
kind of tension, difference, power discrepancy is introduced into women's
relationships with each other, they are unlikely to experience sexual desire.
For example, lesbian feminist writer Margaret Nichols (1987: 103) suggests
that: 'Two women together, each primed to respond sexually only to a
request from another, may rarely even experience desire, much less engage
in sexual activity.'

In this sense, 'homosexual desire' – what Jeffreys (1994, 1996) has termed
'eroticised equality' – is not properly desire at all. The eroticisation of
'sameness' is, in short, written out of the picture, as is the possibility of
understanding difference, and its relation to desire, in terms other than

primarily gender. In this sense heterosexuality inscribes difference; it is a construction of 'otherness' in gendered terms. Clearly, as I have indicated, this has implications for our understanding of the desires of lesbians and gay men; but equally significant it also shapes the ways in which hetero-sexual desires are constructed as relations between 'others' or, even, 'opposites'.

Ideas about what is normal and acceptable sexual behaviour, indeed what is regarded as sexual practice, also reflect dominant constructions of sexuality as heterosexuality, but more especially (vaginal) intercourse. If we do not engage in such activity we are not recognised as fully sexual, we are still virgins even after a lifetime of 'foreplay'. Not only does this affect how forms of sexual activity are evaluated, as sexually satisfying or arous-ing or even as counting as 'sex' at all, it also serves to 'discipline' the body (Bartky, 1988), marking out the boundaries which represent our private and public zones, and distinguishing the potentially sexual from the non-sexual bodily surfaces and actions. (The use of the term 'privates' to refer to the genitalia is a useful example of such bodily zoning.)

For instance, both men and women have an anus. Yet the anus as a part of the sexualised body is predominantly encoded in terms of a gay male body. This has led some to ask: 'is the anus a homologue of the vagina?' (Bersani, 1987), allowing a heterosexualised understanding of penetrative sex between men which, at the same time, denies visibility to female anal-ity and anal intercourse as a heterosexual practice. Indeed, the very use of the terms heterosexual – meaning vaginal – intercourse and homosexual – meaning anal – intercourse are revealing in this respect. Similarly, our understanding of bodies has been bounded within what Butler (1993) refers to as a 'heterosexual matrix', which operates through naturalising a heterosexual morphology. That is, heterosexuality depends on a view of differently gendered individuals who complement each other, right down to their bodies and body parts fitting together: like 'a lock and key' the penis and vagina are assumed to be a natural fit. What happens, then, when the lock or the key is missing?

As I have already indicated – historically, lesbian and gay relationships have frequently been portrayed as a union of masculine and feminine 'types' who complement each other. In many accounts the lesbian body too is heterosexualised: for instance through the production of lesbian bodies with spectacular clitorises which can penetrate vaginas or in the charac-terisation of lesbians as 'boyish' with narrow hips and flat chests (Terry, 1995). The marking of lesbian bodies as non-procreative is another exam-ple of the lesbian body as only rudimentarily female. The conceptualisation of male homosexuals as feminised men with a particular body build and chemistry was also characteristic of early investigations of homosexuality (Terry, 1995). More recent work has focused on the idea that gay men have 'feminised brains' (see Byne, 1995 for a critical review of studies). Another common assumption, which has not altogether disappeared (for a review of studies see Banks and Gartrell, 1995), was that male homosexuals had reduced levels of testosterone compared with heterosexual men, resulting in the appearance of 'cross-sexed' physical characteristics such as wider hips, reduced hairiness and small-sized genitalia. By contrast, the hyper-(hetero)sexualisation of black male bodies underlies the stereotypic assumption that black men have larger than average penises. In this sense, dominant discourses of heterosexuality organise the physical and social space of our bodies.

At an individual level, this may have a significant influence on the way we experience our own bodies and those of others, discouraging us from engaging in certain kinds of bodily activities, whilst at the same time encouraging others. For instance, if a lesbian says 'If I do that I might as well go with a man', what might she mean? Her remark could be interpreted as an example of the depth to which certain conceptions of both the body and the sexual are heterosexualised (and the extent to which heterosexual and lesbian identities are bounded). Thus, certain activities may be seen by some as an imitation of heterosexuality rather than as authentically 'lesbian'. Related to this, an alternative interpretation would be that this statement represents a rejection of heterosexual norms and/or a politicisation of certain activities. Sheila Jeffreys, for instance, critiques the emergence of a developing lesbian sex industry, with porn videos, sex phone lines, and the marketing of 'sex toys', because she regards such developments as 'patriarchal practices' (Jeffreys, 1994).

Such inscriptions of the (sexual) body are highly contested. One form this has taken is in relation to the phallus. Traditionally the phallus is understood to symbolise masculine authority, and through its assumed absence or lack it is argued that women are constituted as a subjugated class. In accepting this, various writers have argued that instead of rejecting phallic signifiers, as does Jeffreys (1996) and others, we should recognise that there is no escape from the phallus because in western culture it is central to the culturally constructed meanings of gender and sexuality. Thus, it is suggested that 'reclaiming the phallus' is an important strategy for challenging ('displacing') current sexual and gender relations – a way of challenging male authority and thereby empowering women.

What does this mean in practice? Recent cultural productions of lesbian bodies by lesbians themselves have emphasised the postmodern lesbian body as phallic. It is claimed that the effect of appropriating the phallus, through 'packing'/wearing dildos (or 'phallic body prostheses' as some would have it) is to expose the assumed linkage between the phallus and the penis as artificial (Griggers, 1993). Also, as Judith Butler (1993) has argued, if the penis is only one phallus and not *the* phallus then it does not 'belong' to men: women can have it too and in their own right, not as copycats. This denaturalisation of the penis as a phallus, it is claimed, also undermines heterosexual as well as male power and privilege. Since the phallus as penis symbolises desire – hence lesbians get asked 'What do you do?' as when there is no penis it is assumed there can be no 'real' sex – the lesbian phallus, it is argued, is potentially disruptive of this and can show how the naturalisation of heterosexuality is imaginary (Butler, 1993: 91).

Whilst I can follow the above argument, I would question its political significance. I am extremely sceptical of the extent to which 'parodic replication' of heterosexual constructs such as, for instance, understanding the 'lesbian cock', or chicks with dicks, as a parody of the phallus/penis, will challenge heterosexuality as a social institution. For, as Davina Cooper (1995) points out: 'not only does hegemony operate through exclusion, but also by making visible failed attempts to attain the status of the real'. (Although I would prefer to use 'real'.) In other words, to suggest that we can effect social change through (queer) performances, however transgressive, provocative or challenging, would seem to assume, amongst other things, that such performances will have a revolutionary effect on (straight) audiences, rather than being interpreted as imitating and reproducing heterosexuality. Paradoxically, the latter would suggest that heterosexual norms are being constituted through such performances, thus confirming the effect of heterosexuality as natural. As Colleen Lamos (1994: 95) remarks: 'Alas, the dildo-bedecked lesbian may be disappointed that her parody of the phallus is interpreted differently by others, especially by heterosexuals who take the dildo or butch/femme straight, so to speak.'

Indeed, the possibilities of a queer reading would seem to be significantly constrained by the fact that historically the dominant (hetero)sexual discourse has positioned lesbians as butch or, to a much lesser extent, femme types who are, albeit in different ways, suffering from penile deprivation, thereby needing to use dildos as a 'penis-substitute'.

There are, in any case, other considerations that go beyond the currently fashionable concern with subversive performance as political strategy and social method. Whilst this may indeed be valuable in highlighting some of the contradictory meanings embedded in discourses of gender and sexuality, and the socially constructed and potentially unstable nature of identities and practices, I would argue that we also need to ground this in the context of the material conditions of people's lives at local, national and global levels. If we are to develop social theory which can adequately theorise and challenge the ways in which our everyday lives are structured by heterosexual beliefs, values and practices, within a variety of institutional domains such as families, religion, the economy and so forth, we require more than a queering of the sexual. Much more significantly, we need to rethink the social.

Sexual/social worlds

Having made the above comment, I immediately want to disown it. How can the sexual be separate from the social? What does it mean to attempt, as some have done, to theorise these as separate if related spheres? How, within social theory, are conceptual categories such as, for example, the private/public distinction, mediated through distin~ from the social?

Part of the difficulty in discussing concepts such as not to mention 'public' and 'private', is the tendenc each know what these concepts represent. Indeed, w concepts in a taken-for-granted way, as if their m tested. Yet, as we shall see, it is clear that such concepts *are* ᴄᴏ... there are different discourses which produce different understandings of 'the social' and 'the sexual' and their presumed relationship to each other.

According to some writers, the social realm is a relatively new phenomenon, 'whose origin coincided with the emergence of the modern age and which found its political form in the nation-state' (Arendt, 1958: 28, quoted in Warner, 1993a). Similarly, the emergence of the sexual as a new theoretical object, as a distinct field of knowledge and experience, is also claimed to be a relatively recent historical and cultural production (Foucault, 1979; Weeks, 1998). As a result, the sexual and the social have been conceptualised as bounded, though interconnected, realms. Thus, writers can theorise heterosexuality as sexual practices and as social practices (VanEvery, 1996); work on human identity can treat sexual and social identities as distinct (Jenkins, 1996) and theories of social and political change can explore questions of sexuality impacting on social relations or of the possibility of transforming sexual relations through social change as if these were different fields (Cooper, 1995).

The problem of separating the sexual and the social, it seems to me, is how can we have a distinct sexual experience that is not interpreted and constructed through social meanings and interactions? The conventional (essentialist) approach side-steps this by inventing the 'sexual' as something individuals possess more or less independently of their involvement in the social. Nor am I satisfied by the view that, as Connell (1995) suggests, the social is already a part of the sexual domain, and vice versa, as this still seems to imply separate, if dynamically interconnected domains. Much as Butler and others (for example, Nicholson, 1994) have argued in relation to the concepts sex and gender, I would argue for the need for a much more sophisticated analysis which examines how the production of the sexual/social is achieved. If we accept that 'the sexual' is always seen through social interpretation, then the sexual is not something that can be separated from the social but is rather that which is produced by it; it is the social organisation of knowledge that establishes meanings for the sexual. However, even this is not enough, for it almost suggests a determinacy of the social as productive of the sexual, when the notion of the social is itself a complex construction.

Most commonly, the relationship between the sexual and the social has been theorised in terms of a distinction between 'the public' and 'the private'. The 'social' realm, at least in western contexts, is usually equated with 'issues affecting daily life . . . issues like equitable distribution of resources ("poverty"), the environment, and "lifestyle"' (Patton, 1993: 172).

has the effect of disassociating sexuality, conceptually at least, from any aspects of everyday life and relationships – a belief that it lies outside the sphere of political and economic, and therefore state, influence. The sexual, by contrast, is generally associated with the individual, personal aspects of our lives, as well as with the idea of nature, more especially that sexuality is grounded in the body, in our individual, essential natures. Related to this, is the belief in sexuality as the basis for human identity, prior to other cultural or social affiliations (Kotz, 1993). In this sense, to examine the relationship between the sexual and the social is to raise questions about the relationship between human beings and nature; between the body and social membership; between the social and the natural.

What is often presupposed in this connection of the sexual with the natural is that the social sphere acts upon the sexual as a mediating or modifying influence, social institutions having the effect of both liberating and repressing different sexualities in different contexts and at different times. At the same time, the sexual is also conceptualised as outside of the social. It is, in this respect, constitutive of the social, rather than produced by it. Thus, as Diana Fuss (1990: 3) comments, 'the natural provides the raw material and determinative starting point for the practices and laws of the social'. In so far as this naturalised sexuality is interpreted as heterosexuality, albeit in particular forms of practice, it becomes a central and determining feature of our understanding of social life. The heterosexual couple is the raw material through which society may interpret and imagine itself.

To give a concrete example, in countries such as China, where due to the government's policies on population control there has been a one child per family policy operating in many parts of the country, there has been growing concern that reproductive technologies such as ultrasound and amniocentesis, followed by selective abortion, are being used to ensure that the only child is a son. As a result, new laws have been proposed to ban the use of such techniques to determine the sex of the foetus. The main concerns that have prompted this situation are the real and imagined social consequences of demographic change, as more males are being born than females. In particular, there is concern over the state of marriage, with fears that the growing number of single unmarried men within Chinese society will threaten the stability of marriages and lead to rising divorce figures. What this example and most other population control measures elsewhere demonstrate is the assumed natural, heterosexual basis of society. Society must reproduce itself as male and female in more or less equal amounts because heterosexuality, in its institutionalised form as monogamous marriage, requires one man for each woman, and vice versa. If we abandon that principle, and the assumption that social stability depends upon it, then there would be no obvious gender basis of society which needs to be regulated in this way by public policy.

If the social is interpreted through heterosexuality, it is also the case that understandings of heterosexuality are informed by definitions of the

relationship between the sexual and the social. For example,
ralised) split between the social and the sexual means that v
divorce analyses of sexual practices and relations from those a
relations: such as, for instance, analyses of the 'family', the workplace, and
domestic living arrangements (VanEvery, 1996).

The construction of the sexual as relatively autonomous, occupying its
own terrain, is also relevant to debates about heterosexuality and social
change. One interpretation of this is that the sexual (here, heterosexuality)
will not necessarily be transformed by changes in wider social relations. A
less essentialist reading of the sexual/social split assumes a sexual which
is to a greater or lesser extent modified by the social, thus allowing for the
possibility that if society changed then so might (hetero)sexualities.
Campaigner's on the 'moral right', for example, have argued for stronger
controls over sexuality, such as restrictions on sex education and a ban on
access to contraception for young people, as part of an attempt to restore
and constrain heterosexuality to married monogamous relationships.

For some, including many on the 'moral right', the sexual/social relationship is also understood to be a two way process, with the social
mediated through the sexual. The latter would seem to assume a direct link
between the social and the sexual, with sexual practices presumed capable
of generating social change. In the case of the 'moral right' this might be
envisaged in terms of sexual 'immorality' such as, for example, 'promiscuity', adultery and prostitution leading to moral and social decay. The
discourse of sexual liberation, on the other hand, has traditionally seen
sexual freedom as a force for social change, as a means for achieving social
and individual freedom. More recently, albeit with a different, postmodern
conceptualisation of sexuality, some associated with queer politics and,
also, with sex radicalism have also sought to disrupt the dominance of heterosexuality and the hegemony of particular desires and practices through
'transgressive' sexual practices such as butch/femme, S/M, and the
(queer) use of dildos. (For a discussion see Cooper, 1995; Jeffreys, 1996
and the following chapter in this volume.)

In the early 1970s, many feminists also made a connection between the
'repression' of female sexuality and social powerlessness, believing that
'discovering' one's sexuality, largely conceptualised in heterosexual terms,
would empower women. This association has subsequently been critiqued
and there has been considerable debate and argument between feminists
over the relationship between sexuality and social change. In the context of
heterosexuality the tension has primarily been around the extent to which
sexual relations are determined by, or are determining of, other social relations (Richardson, 1997). For some, especially radical feminists, the main
concern is not so much how women's sex lives are affected by gender
inequalities but, more generally, how heterosexuality as it is currently institutionalised constrains women in various aspects of their lives. Here, then,
the emphasis is primarily upon how gendered power inequalities in the
social realm are constructed and maintained through sexuality as a key

mechanism of patriarchal relations, itself a construction, of course. For others, there is a much greater emphasis on how gender inequalities in sexual relations are determined through inequalities in the social sphere, delimiting personal pleasures and desires. Thus, for example, Lynne Segal, in her book *Straight Sex: Rethinking the Politics of Pleasure* concludes by saying: 'Straight feminists, like gay men and lesbians, have everything to gain from asserting our non-coercive desire to fuck if, when, how and as we choose' (Segal, 1994: 318).

The sexual/social distinction is also significant in the construction of boundaries between heterosexual/lesbian/gay. Or, to put it another way, the sexual/social split is also part of the means by which divisions between heterosexuals and sexual 'others' are produced. As I have suggested above, heterosexuality infuses the social realm; it represents the idea of normal behaviour that is central to the concept of the social and the process of socialisation into the social realm. Consequently, heterosexuality is defined primarily in terms of social identification; for instance, identities such as 'wife'/'husband', 'girlfriend'/'boyfriend', 'mother'/'father' are rooted in heterosexuality. Although, as feminist writers have pointed out, this is gendered: heterosexuality is more of a principle site of identity construction for women than it is for men; which is not to say that heterosexuality is unimportant in the production of conventional masculinities (see Holland et al., 1996).

Indeed, heterosexuality's naturalisation means that it is rarely acknowledged as a sexuality; as a sexual category or identification. By contrast, historically lesbians and gay men have been defined primarily as sexual beings, placed outside (the underworld) or at the margins (the twilight zone) of the normative boundaries of the social realm. As a result, homosexuality is defined primarily in terms of sexual identification, and very rarely are the social relations within which lesbians and gay men are embedded acknowledged. Once named as lesbians and gays we are at risk of the vast complexity of our lives – even our claim to a certain race, religion, ethnicity, nationality, or even in some cases humanity itself – disappearing under the dominant sexual marker: non-heterosexual. In this sense, the notion of the social/sexual split is a sexualised notion, establishing heterosexuals as a socially inscribed class and lesbians and gay men as a sexually inscribed grouping. It is also a gendered and racialised concept. Thus, for instance, the category 'gay man' is a more sexualised concept than 'lesbian'; as is black heterosexuality compared to white heterosexuality.

Defining public and private boundaries

As I mentioned above, the relationship between the social and the sexual has often been understood in terms of the public/private distinction, itself a cultural construction, with the social associated with the public and the sexual with the private. Yet, this division can immediately be questioned: social relations occur in the domestic, increasingly private sphere; and there is public expression of sexual relations – what many refer to as a sexualisation of modern western societies. Similarly, feminist theory has critiqued this separation of the public and the private in ways that have illuminated understandings of, for example, women's position in the labour market, the sexual division of labour, as well as violence against women (Walby, 1997). The claim that 'the personal is the political', a feminist catchphrase of the 1970s and 1980s, also reflects the emphasis placed within feminism on disrupting the public/private binary. In this context, however, I wish to draw attention to the ways in which the private/public distinction serves to influence the process of the production of sexualities.

The association of sexuality with the private as distinct from the public sphere is institutionalised. In the UK, for example, it is part of the current legal constitution and the definition of the role of the state in individuals' lives. The Wolfenden Report (1957), which led to the liberalisation of laws on prostitution in 1959 and male homosexuality in 1967, concluded that it was not the role of the law to interfere in the private lives of citizens, but rather it was the law's duty to preserve public order and decency. Issues like homosexuality and prostitution (and later abortion and pornography) were thus defined as matters of individual conscience, acceptable as private actions of the individual, as long as they did not encroach into the public arena. Thus, whilst homosexuality may have been defined as a matter for individual conscience, the 1967 changes to the law pertaining to sexual acts between men nevertheless maintained legal limitations that did not apply to heterosexuality, on the grounds that 'homosexual' acts in public might cause offence to others. By implication, public decency and public order – indeed the public sphere as it is defined in legal terms – is identified with heterosexuality.

More recently, there has been a shift towards understanding the construction of public space in terms of modes of cultural production, as well as through social institutions such as the law. Once again there is an identification of the public sphere (as cultural space) with heterosexuality (see Richardson, 2000a and Chapter 4 in this volume).

These examples serve to highlight how heterosexuality, more especially within a married relationship, has normally been granted both more privacy and more public recognition than other sexualities. In other words, not only can the public be understood as characterised by heterosexual norms, but so too can the private in so far as it is traditionally associated with domestic and (heterosexual) family life. Some have related this to the notion of a 'homosexual diaspora' (Mort, 1995), crossing nation-states and linking lesbian and gay communities. However I wonder whether this term is appropriate for the sense of cultural and spatial exclusion lesbians and gay men frequently experience. Rather than an original 'homeland' from which homosexuals were dispersed, I would argue that any sense of loss/exclusion is largely connected with the heterosexualisation of the private and the public, rather than a loss of country or nation-state. It is from the domestic 'homeland' that lesbians and gay men are often estranged: 'Citizens who inhabit the same country may live worlds apart. Queer youth often feel homeless in their own homes even before some of them are thrown out onto the streets' (Tucker, 1995: 25). Similarly, to become homosexual is to be *en route* from the public as well as from the private. It may be that lesbians and gay men do not get told to 'get back from where you came from' on the grounds of their sexuality (although they may in so far as it intersects with their racial and ethnic identifications) but they can be told to get back to the private if they are seen as challenging the boundaries of public 'tolerance'.

The private/public distinction is, then, a sexualised notion: it has a different meaning depending on whether one is applying it to a heterosexual or homosexual context. For lesbians and gays the private has been institutionalised as the border of social tolerance, as the place where you are 'allowed' to live relatively safely as long as one does not attempt to occupy the public. In some instances that might even mean feeling uncomfortable about talking about lesbian or gay issues in one's own garden or backyard. For heterosexuals not only is the construction of private space likely to be very different, but the public is also likely to be a far less contested or constrained space than for most homosexuals. Although, once again, we need to relate this to race and gender; various forms of oppressive practice, most notably racialised and/or sexual violence, also render the public a contested space and the private/public distinction a gendered and racialised construction (Richardson and May, 1999).

Much of feminist theory, as I have already mentioned, has focused on how the separation of the public and the private is a patriarchal construction (Duncan, 1996b; Walby, 1997). Queer theory has also challenged the public/private distinction within its more general critique of the heterosexual/homosexual binary and its resistance to a normalised and naturalised heterosexuality. In the following chapter I will explore the challenges which queer theory offers to theorising sexuality and, in addition, consider the way in which such developments relate to past and present feminist theorising.

2

FROM LESBIAN NATION TO QUEER NATION: SEXUAL POLITICS AND SOCIAL CHANGE

In this chapter I want to consider certain aspects of the development of sexual politics over the last thirty years: a particularly active period with interesting shifts in notions of both identity and political practice. I also want to examine how far the emergence of queer theory and activism represents a break with earlier social movements concerned with sexuality as is often claimed.

The late 1960s and 1970s was undoubtedly one of the most important periods in the history of sexual politics this century. This was a time which saw the revival of feminism and the emergence of lesbian and gay liberation movements, at the same time as morality campaigners redoubled their efforts to resist social changes associated with 'sexual liberalism' and, as a perceived consequence, 'moral decay', leading to the establishment of new campaigns. For example, in Britain, the National Viewers and Listener's Association (NVALA) spearheaded by Mary Whitehouse (see Morrison and Tracey, 1979; Durham, 1991) and, in the USA, Anita Bryant's 'Save Our Children' campaign which in its literature referred to tolerance based on: '. . . the understanding that homosexuals will keep their deviate activity to themselves, will not flaunt their lifestyles, will not be allowed to preach their sexual standards to, or otherwise influence, impressionable young people' (Hart, 1981: 45).

A major concern for lesbian/feminist and gay liberation movements in the 1960s and 1970s was to fundamentally question assumptions about sexuality and gender that were common to both liberalism and moral traditionalism. In particular, they challenged dominant 'scientific' constructions of women and the category 'homosexual', which were seen as responsible for the production of oppressive identities. One might characterise this as a time of the politics of self-discovery and of personal authenticity, a politics of the reformulation of the (positive) self and an attempt at a new construction of both the female body and the homosexual body. The female body was constituted as no longer sexually 'passive' and 'disciplined'/ordered, the (male and female) homosexual body as no longer diseased and sexually dis-ordered, the lesbian body as no longer non-reproductive.

In this sense, resistance was not only about achieving political recognition in the public sphere, through legal and economic reforms, but personal goals which included for both feminists and gay liberationists a (re)claiming of a sexuality that had previously been denied them. Whilst feminists were claiming the right to better sex – albeit, initially, primarily in heterosexual relationships – and a recognition of autonomous female sexuality that named the clitoris as a woman's best friend (Jeffreys 1990, 1994; Segal, 1994; Koedt, 1974/1996), lesbians and gay men were also claiming the 'power to name' for themselves (Weeks, 1977/1990). The emphasis was on the establishment of positive lesbian and gay identities in the political process of coming out, and through the contestation of medical and psychological concepts of 'homosexuality'.

Many writers now regard such struggles over the meaning of lesbian and gay identities as an example of 'identity politics', referring to the strategic implications of mobilising around identity formations (as women, lesbian, gay) supposedly united by common interests. (This is a continuing debate as is evidenced, for example, in work on sexual citizenship; see p. 96.) A major criticism of 'identity politics' is that it has allegedly reinforced an essentialism which does little to threaten the sexual status quo (Wiegman, 1994). A new understanding of the concept of identity, emphasising fragmentation and fluidity, flourished in the 1990s out of and alongside new social movements associated with 'sexual politics', many fuelled by AIDS activism, such as, for example, ACT UP, OutRage!, Lesbian Avengers and, in the USA, Queer Nation.

The emergence of a new 'politics of identity' owes something to the shift in the 1980s towards analysing difference. Over the last fifteen to twenty years many of the major debates within feminism have been concerned, in one way or another, with the question of difference between women and, related to this, the meaning and political utility of the category 'woman'. In part, this reflects the influence of poststructural and postmodern perspectives on feminist theory, as well as social/political theory more generally, which challenge the idea of 'woman' as a fixed natural category, regarding it instead as a 'constantly shifting signifier of multiple meanings' (Stacey, 1997: 55). Another important reason for this problematisation of the category 'woman' (and to a lesser extent 'man') has been the response of women who had felt excluded from such a 'unitary' category. Black, working-class and lesbian feminists in particular have critiqued the way in which use of the category 'woman' within feminism has often served to conceal racial, class and sexual difference (see Bhavnani, 1997).

This new focus within 'sexual politics' also grew out of political divisions between lesbian/feminists that erupted in the 1980s which, in combination with increased attention to difference, exposed how categories like lesbian and feminist were not unified political communities. Debates over

butch/femme, AIDS, lesbian pornography and S/M in particula
lighted this. Indeed, such was the extent of political divisions ove.
issues that some writers have referred to this as the 'feminist sex
(Duggan and Hunter, 1995). In this context, as awareness of diversity ...ia
difference increased and the theoretical project of deconstruction of sexual
and gender categories gained prominence, the 'lesbian subject' and 'the gay
subject', like 'woman' and 'man', were increasingly problematised.

The emergence of queer

The term that is often used to encapsulate this shift in sexual politics is
'queer'. Queer theory represents a diverse body of work and there are different interpretations of what this term might encompass. It is often
identified, especially in its initial emergence, with the work of writers who
are associated with literary criticism and cultural studies, and generally
denotes a poststructuralist and postmodernist approach to understanding categories of sexuality and gender. The work of Eve Sedgwick (1990),
Judith Butler (1990, 1993), and Teresa de Lauretis (1991), for example,
might be taken as key to the development of queer theory. Others still
might point to the edited collection by Michael Warner (1993b) and, offering a more sociological perspective on queer studies, that edited by Steven
Seidman (1996), as illustrative of the range of queer writing.

As an example of the latter, Amber Ault (1996: 322) offers the following
broad definition: 'In its latest incarnation, and as it is deployed by "queer
activists" and "queer theorists", the term "queer" signifies not only those
who mark themselves as gay or lesbian, but anyone whose proclivities,
practices, or sympathies defy the strictures of the dominant
sex/gender/sexual identity system.' More narrowly, queer represents an
appropriation, a 'reverse affirmation', of a pejorative word, in a similar
way to the use of 'nigger' by certain black groups. As Judith Butler (1997a:
12) writes:

> The term 'queer' has operated as one linguistic practice whose purpose has
> been the shaming of the subject it names or, rather, the producing of a subject
> through that shaming interpellation. 'Queer' derives its force precisely through
> the repeated invocation by which it has become linked to accusation, pathologi-
> sation, insult.

This is clearly welcomed by many as a new way of describing themselves in the social/sexual order, although it has come to mean different
things to different people. For some, especially a younger generation of
'lesbians' and 'gays', calling themselves queer represents a newer version
of a term signifying sexual 'difference' or 'deviance'. Others use the term
queer critically, to indicate a position which questions and rejects the very
notion of 'sexual difference/deviance', where 'difference' and 'deviance'
are dependent for their meaning on an assumed (hetero)sexual norm.

With its multiple meanings, queer also suggests wider political possibilities in so far as queer politics has sought to construct a broad political base across multiple social constituencies. Proponents of queer claim that it is about seeking a system of political values that can validate both diversity and solidarity. Thus, for example: 'I use [queer] externally to describe a political inclusivity – a new move towards a celebration of difference across sexualities, across genders, across sexual preference and across object choice' (Semple, quoted in Smyth, 1992: 21).

In this sense the meaning of queer is as an inclusive label incorporating gay/lesbian/bisexual/transgender and other (queer) sexualities rather like, as Gamson (1996: 403) suggests, the phrase 'people of colour' acts as an inclusive shorthand for different ethnic and racial groups. However, it is precisely the issue of 'inclusivity' which prevents some from using the term queer. One concern is that it is a false 'queer nationalism' and that, in fact, queer reinforces a spurious idea of lesbian and gay sexual homogeneity. The perceived risk is that in embracing 'unity in difference' certain social inequalities will be marginalised within the 'queer nation', in particular issues of race and gender.

This questioning of queer as a 'catch all' term is a view expressed by a number of those interviewed in the *Lesbians Talk Queer Notions* collection edited by Smyth (1992). For example: 'I'm more inclined to use the words 'black lesbian', because when I hear the word queer I think of white, gay men' (Mack-Nataf, 1992: 21). This is echoed by Butler (1997a) who claims that, in some contexts, queer 'has marked a predominantly white movement', as well as 'a false unity of women and men'. At a theoretical level, the question this raises is whether queer makes interconnections between different forms of social divisions and power inequalities or is erasing/ignoring the specificities of important material differences.

In addition to acting as a form of sexual shorthand, queer also articulates a particular theoretical sensibility that is expressed in political terms as transgression or 'permanent rebellion' (Seidman, 1997). A principle characteristic of queer theory and politics in so far as they are interrelated, (see de Lauretis, 1991) is that it problematises sexual and gender categories in seeking the deconstruction of the binary divides underpinning and reinforcing them: conceptual dualisms such as, for instance, woman/man; feminine/masculine; heterosexual/homosexual; essentialist/constructionist (McIntosh, 1993; Wilton, 1996). The notion of identity is also problematised. Identities are seen not as authentic properties of individual subjects, but as: 'fluid and shifting, to be adopted and discarded, played with and subverted, strategically deployed in differing contexts' (Jackson and Scott, 1996: 15). The argument is that there is no fixed, stable category of, say, gays or heterosexuals, rather such categories are 'fictions', an illusionary unity which masks difference within those categorisations. Queer theory here converges with queer politics in the strategic refusal to label oneself as X or Y or Z, with a call for dissolution of sexualised gender systems. We are, it is suggested, post such identities: post woman, post man we are transgender; post lesbian, post gay, post heterosexual (perhaps?) we are queer.

Queer aims to destabilise identity as a ground for politics, and a primary arena of political struggle are multiple sites of cultural production. In trying to achieve this, writers such as, for example, Doan (1994) have emphasised strategies which include the use of subversive performance as disruptive of conventional sexual and gender binaries and through exposing contradictions in discourse. The notion of gender as performative is associated with the work of Judith Butler (1990), whose work I have already referred to in the previous chapter. Gender, Butler argues, is performatively enacted through a continual citation and reiteration of social norms. Subversive performance is possible through the deployment of transgressive practices such as, for example, 'parodic replications' – as distinct from imitation – of heterosexuality in, say, butch/femme, or of gender in, say, drag kings.

One can, of course make links with postmodernists' use of 'playfulness' and irony as political strategies and those of earlier lesbian and gay struggles: 'In much the same way, lesbian/gay culture has often made use of camp, drag and other cultural strategies' (Stein and Plummer, 1996: 136). However, in assessing such strategies, I think it important to question the possibility of doing subversion, of queering the subject. That is to say, what are the possibilities as well as the *constraints* on our ability to use speech, and to enact non-normative performances, in ways that reinscribe our understanding of the world in terms of sexual and gender norms? Although she has begun to address these issues in some of her later work (Butler, 1997b), I would argue that an important gap in Butler's conception of gender as performativity is the question of how symbolic norms are related to wider social, political and economic structures. What is important here is the relationship between the power to speak and the power to be heard. Who, in other words, is capable of symbolic resignification; of 'being queer'; of 'the improper use of the performative'? And, related to this, who has the ability to be listened to, to be heard and read as queer? To put this a slightly different way, in embracing the conceptualisation of gender and sexuality as performative and the power of subversive performativity to bring about social change, I would argue that there is a danger of losing sight of the ways in which gender and heterosexuality are structurally deeply embedded in the social order, with important material consequences for our lives. (For further discussion and critique of such developments see, for example, Wilson, 1993; Lamos, 1994; Jackson, 1996a, 1996b, 1999; Jeffreys, 1996 and, also, Chapter 1 in this volume).

From the margins to the centre: queering heterosexuality

The aim of queer theory is to reframe sexuality within a postmodern framework; in particular to disrupt the hetero/homo binary and denaturalise heterosexuality. Queer theory insists on the centrality of homosexuality to heterosexual culture; in claiming that the hetero/homo-sexual binary serves to define heterosexuality at the centre, with homosexuality positioned as the marginalised 'other'. Homosexuality is constructed as 'different' (or 'deviant') in contrast to a normalised, natu-ralised sexuality, which is institutionalised as a specific form of married, reproductive heterosexuality. Heterosexuality is nothing without homo-sexuality: it depends on homosexuality as its 'opposite' for its meaning and its coherence. It *appears* to be 'natural' and 'normal' because it constructs homosexuality as un-natural, as not the norm, as a poor imitation or copy of the 'real thing'.

Queer therefore seeks to disrupt the (hetero) centre and, in so doing, the notion of sexual difference; for with no centre who or what can one be defined as different to? In this framework, as with feminist perspectives, heterosexuality itself is problematised. Moreover, following Butler (1990, 1993), it is argued that far from being fixed and naturally occurring, het-erosexuality is 'unstable', dependent on ongoing, continuous and repeated performances by individuals 'doing heterosexuality', which produce the illusion of stability. There is no 'real thing' to be copied or imitated: het-erosexuality is itself continually in the process of being re-produced.

While queer theory aims to develop existing notions of sexuality and gender, it is important to recognise the broader implications of such inter-ventions. Writers such as, for example, Michael Warner (1993a) have argued that the main project is the queering of existing theory rather than the production of theory about queers. This is the point Eve Sedgwick (1990: 1) famously makes in the introduction to her book *Epistemology of the Closet* which, in many ways, has come to be seen as initiating queer into lit-erary studies. She proposes:

> . . . that many of the major modes of thought and knowledge in twentieth cen-tury western culture as a whole are structured by a chronic now endemic crisis of homo/heterosexual definition. This book will argue that an understanding of virtually any aspect of modern western culture must be not merely incomplete but damaged in its central substance to the degree that it does not incorporate a critical analysis of modern homo/heterosexual definition.

In this sense, queer claims it represents a radical critique of categories of identity associated with gender and sexuality, though as I will go on to argue it is perhaps less of a break with previous traditions than it suggests (see also McIntosh, 1993; Stein and Plummer, 1996; Stacey, 1997). Within queer theory, sexuality is the primary lens through which to analyse – in particular the hetero/homo binary – and, whilst acknowledging the importance of gender, it suggests that sexuality and gender can be sepa-rated analytically. The focus is on how the construction of heterosexuality privileges some women *and* men and disempowers others. (Gayle Rubin (1984/1993) raised similar questions in the context of earlier feminist debates about sexuality.) Feminist perspectives, on the other hand, have tended to privilege gender – the 'woman'/'man' binary – and, in the main, are concerned with sexuality in so far as it is seen as constitutive of, as well as determined by, gendered power relations (see Richardson, 1997). The main focus is on how constructions of (hetero)sexuality both privilege and disempower women.

Clearly there are significant areas of overlap here. In both cases sexuality is seen as a mechanism of power, in the former for promoting the interests of heterosexuals over non-heterosexuals, and in the latter recognising that the privileging of heterosexuality relates to women's unequal position in social, political and economic worlds. In both cases, sexuality – especially the hetero/homosexual binary – is conceptualised as something that is encoded in a wide range of social institutions and practices not normally thought of as connected with sexuality such as, for example: housing, urban planning, health services and care of the elderly (Warner, 1993b); labour markets, educational opportunities, leisure pursuits and travel (Richardson, 1997).

Queer is not only concerned with theorising the hetero/homosexual binary, it is also about resisting regimes of the normal, all those desires and interests that are marginalised and excluded in the straight and main stream. Queers are united through opposition to disciplining normalising forces, not by an assumed identity based on sexual desire or practice. Queer, it is argued, displaces previous sexual categories such as 'lesbian', 'gay', 'bisexual' *and* 'heterosexual'. As I stated earlier, the claim is for a politics that can break with and overcome pre-existing identities with their associated political differences and divisions.

In this and in certain other respects it has been suggested that queer marks a discontinuity with many assumptions of the past. Thus, for example, *Sisters, Sexperts Queers* (Stein, 1993), a collection of essays on lesbian politics, has as its subtitle *'Beyond the Lesbian Nation'*, a reference to Jill Johnson's (1973) book of the same name, which I will discuss later, implying that queer represents a moving on from earlier lesbian feminism. This distinction from previous theoretical traditions like feminism is, ironically given queer's postmodern lineage, frequently couched in modernist narratives, where queer is positioned as progressive relative to previous attempts at theorising sexuality. As Stacey (1997: 63) argues:

> This kind of characterisation of queer theory in relation to feminist theory constructs a linear progress narrative in which Theory (capital T) has rescued feminism from its early naivety. It represents developments in feminist theory as a journey from essentialism to fluidity, from ignorance to enlightenment.

According to some writers such as, for example, Woods (1995: 31) queer also represents a form of sexual politics that sees 'the labels gay and lesbian as proscriptive; as having become as oppressive as heterosexuality in restrictiveness'. In this sense, queer is positioned not only as a theoretical advancement on previous accounts of sexuality, but also as politically opposed, in this case, to certain kinds of lesbian and gay movements. Discussing this point Steven Seidman (1997: 92) writes:

> I take as central to queer theory its challenge to what has been the dominant foundational concept of both homophobic and affirmative homosexual theory: the assumption of a unified homosexual identity. I interpret queer theory as contesting this foundation and therefore the very telos of Western homosexual politics.

Queer theory and politics are also often expressed in terms 'explicitly oppositional to feminism, especially radical feminism' (Kitzinger and Wilkinson, 1994; Wilkinson and Kitzinger, 1996) which, as I shall discuss in the next chapter, is often characterised as moralistic feminist separatism. In this sense, queer is frequently set up as opposed to feminism, and lesbian and gay politics of the 1970s and 1980s, despite sharing many of the same concerns.

Generally speaking, queers have distanced themselves from earlier social and political movements in a number of key areas. In the remainder of this chapter I want to explore three of these in particular, which seem to me to be central to the claims for a shift to a new position in social theory and sexual politics: (1) assimilation versus transgression; (2) essentialism versus fluidity; and (3) a focus on 'space', especially as it is encoded by the private/public binary.

Assimilation versus transgression

A common claim is that queer is anti-assimilationist (Stein and Plummer, 1996). Typically, in this respect, it is contrasted with lesbian and gay 'identity politics' characterised as a politics of inclusion; as primarily about political struggles for minority civil rights. 'Equal rights' approaches have been most obvious in the USA, although they are increasingly becoming the dominantspeak of social movements concerned with sexual politics in Europe (see Richardson, 2000b and Chapter 6 in this volume). At the same time, we are witnessing a rapidly expanding commercialisation and commodification of gay and, to a lesser extent, lesbian 'communities'. Such developments centre on the idea of a (quasi) ethnically based interest group with a particular urban lifestyle, seeking lesbian and gay marriages (and honeymoons!), insurance and legal services, therapists, fashion, perfume, hairstyles, jewellery, holiday resorts, music, bookstores, magazines, TV programmes, restaurants, cruises and so on.

Queer politics is highly critical of what is often referred to as 'lifestyle politics'. Hence the slogan: We're Here, We're Queer And We are *Not* Going Shopping. Queer politics is characterised by confrontational, direct action strategies and aims to be transgressive of social norms. It is not about

seeking social integration, but then neither is it de
the margins. What queer seeks to do is to contest the
eronormative order by claiming this space. For soi
dawning of a 'new gay radicalism', which has the pc
significant changes in 'the way that we think about
selves and society' (Seidman, 1997: 197). Others su
Elizabeth Wilson (1993) and Davina Cooper (1995
whether such strategies are likely to result in the kind
mations that queer hopes for.

It is clear that some lesbian and gay movements can be characterised as
assimilationist, particularly in the USA where, as I have suggested, there
exists a strong tradition both of liberal feminism and 'equal rights' lesbian
and gay politics. In Britain also, organisations such as, for example, the
Homosexual Law Reform Society during the 1960s, the Campaign for
Homosexual Equality in the 1970s and early 1980s and, more recently, the
cross-party campaigning and lobby group Stonewall can all be seen, to
greater or lesser extent, as following integrationist strategies to achieve
social change. It is far more difficult, however, to see how social movements such as, in the USA, National Gay Liberation and, in the UK, The
Gay Liberation Front, which flourished in the late 1960s and early 1970s,
could be interpreted as assimilationist.

This same thing could be said about lesbian/feminist movements. In
the first place, as adumbrated in the previous chapter, lesbian/feminist
activism and scholarship has developed critical perspectives on the social
construction of gender and (hetero)sexuality. In particular, lesbian and
radical feminist theory directly challenges the structures and ideologies
which maintain the distinction between heterosexuality and homosexuality, and which confirm the former as the norm (Jackson, 1996: 37).
Hence, the aim is not to assimilate into, or even seek to reform, the current
sexual system, but rather to challenge and transform it in such a way that
heterosexuality is displaced from its status as privileged, institutionalised
norm.

Interestingly, where there is some acknowledgement of this, a different
argument is sometimes employed and lesbian/feminists are criticised for
their attempts at *non*-assimilation. Heads you win, tails you loose (yet
another binary!). More generally, the form this queer critique takes is of les-
bian/feminism as a form of 'separatist politics' that, it is suggested, leads
to an isolationist position that undermines the possibilities of social transformation.

Essentialisms

It has also been claimed that queer is a reaction to an overreliance on essentialised notions of fixed sexual and gender identities and on conceptual
dualisms, more especially the hetero/homo binary (Warner, 1993a). A

conviction is that sexual and gender identities are self-construc-
, and emphasis is placed upon the fluidity of identity, identity as
rformance, as style. Often lesbian/feminist work is contrasted with
queer theory in ways which position the former as essentialist, not in the
sense of biological determinism, but in relation to an attributed understanding of identity which assumes universal and unified meanings to the
category lesbian/woman. Lesbian/feminist perspectives may also be
regarded as essentialist if, like for example Monique Wittig (1992), they
position lesbianism as outside of, and opposed to, patriarchal (heterosexual)
relations (see Fuss, 1990).

This construction of feminist theories of sexuality as essentialist and
universalistic is overly simplistic. The theoretical emphasis within gay
liberation and feminism in the 1970s and 1980s was on understanding
sexuality and gender as 'mediated by society, rather than biologically
given' (Segal, 1994: 178). Although it is possible to identify forms of essentialism in feminist thinking about sexuality in the early years of the
women's liberation movement, in particular an emphasis on 'discovering'
or 'reclaiming' an authentic female sexuality, in many other respects feminist accounts represented a massive shift away from essentialist accounts
of sexuality. The notion of 'choice' featured strongly, especially in feminist
accounts of sexuality, so much so that a common charge was voluntarism.
Also, long before queer theory was ever heard of, concepts such as political lesbianism (Leeds Revolutionary Feminist Group, 1981), the
woman-identified woman (Radicalesbians, 1970) and the lesbian continuum (Rich, 1980) posed a radical challenge to the heterosexual/
homosexual binary, blurring the boundaries between straight and lesbian. Similarly, Adrienne Rich's (1980) groundbreaking work on
'compulsory heterosexuality', in highlighting the socially and economically constructed nature of heterosexuality, represented an early attempt
to denaturalise heterosexual society, an aim which queer theory has more
recently claimed.

In a similar vein, the appearance of militant lesbians and gay men in the
1970s also disrupted expectations of the natural order of heterosexuality
(Weeks, 1995). One way they did this was by challenging the, then, dominant medical and psychiatric accounts of sexuality. Within such accounts,
heterosexuality was understood to be the outcome of normal development and, as such, was unproblematic and, as a consequence,
undertheorised. Homosexuality, on the other hand, defined in relation to
this social/biological (hetero) norm of sexual development, was widely
regarded as pathological: as immature or abnormal development (see
Richardson, 1981). Indeed, it is important to remember that it was not until
1973 that the American Psychiatric Association removed homosexuality *per
se* from its list of diagnostic categories of mental ill health, and even then it
was not completely depathologised, as a new classification termed 'ego-
dystonic homosexuality' was still included (Burns, 1992).

Paradoxically, however, by challenging the medicalisation of 'homosex-

uality' and stressing the importance of coming out as a 'new
bians and gays, lesbian and gay liberation movements ra
seemingly emphasising the importance of identity as an esse
self and the idea of a shared common identity and 'commun
ular, in demanding a public visibility and a voice, as well a
public expression of same-sex 'love and affection' (Jeffery-Poulter, 1991),
such movements contributed to furthering the consolidation of the categories 'lesbian' and 'gay' – albeit with different and more positive
meanings attached to them – that had been taking place in Europe over the
previous two hundred or so years (McIntosh 1968/1996; Weeks, 1990).
This process, in turn, reaffirms the hetero/homo binary and the idea of
fixed, discrete sexual categories.

This is not in dispute. What is important to recognise, however, is the
extent to which this was problematised at the time. For example, the
British sociologist Kenneth Plummer, who from the 1970s onwards has
had an enormous and continuing influence on the development of social
constructionist theories of sexuality (1981: 108), referred to this as 'the
paradox of categorisation'. The recognition that however much we may
seek to eliminate sexual labels politically, the categories or labels we are
ascribed also act as a way of establishing and maintaining a sense of our
existence.

> On the one hand, labels are useful devices – they give order to chaos, structure
> to openness, security to confusion. Knowing that one is gay is much more com-
> forting than living with the precariousness of confused sexual identities. On the
> other hand, labels are destructive devices – they restrict where other choices are
> possible, they control and limit possible variety, they narrow human experi-
> mentation. In the short run, labels are comforting; in the long run, they are
> destructive. (Plummer, 1981: 108)

Echoing some of the concerns that Plummer and others were grappling
with almost twenty years earlier Judith Butler (1997a: 26) has also asked
why we 'sometimes cling to the terms that pain us?'. It is, she suggests,
'because, at a minimum, they offer us some form of social and discursive
existence'.

I am arguing that queer theory overestimates the extent to which earlier
generations of lesbians and gays and feminists believed in essential identities, rather than viewing sexual and gender identities as 'necessary
fictions' for the purposes of protest and political recognition. Judith Butler
(1997a: 15) again:

> We no more create out of nothing the political terms that come to represent our
> 'freedom' than we are responsible for the terms that carry the pain of social
> injury. And yet, neither of those terms are as a result any less necessary to work
> and rework within political discourse . . . In this sense, it remains politically nec-
> essary to lay claim to 'women', 'queer', 'gay', and 'lesbian', precisely because of
> the way these terms, as it were, lay their claim on us prior to our full knowing.

Resignifying space

The concept of space (and place) has emerged as one of the key areas of debate within the social sciences in recent years, especially in geography. Feminist analyses in particular have examined the relationship between ideas about the social nature of 'space' and the construction of gender and gender relations (Massey, 1994; Duncan, 1996a; Women and Geography Study Group, 1997), as well as – along with queer and gay writers – the interconnections between sexuality and space (Colomina, 1992; Bell and Valentine, 1995; Duncan, 1996a; Ingram et al., 1997).

As I have indicated in the previous chapter, a major contribution of feminist thought to conceptualisations of space, has been the theorising of the public and the private, their interrelationship and the politicisation of areas of life normally construed as belonging to the private (Duncan, 1996b; Walby, 1997). A specific concern has been the establishment of safe public and private space for women in relation to the risk of violence to the person. This is, perhaps, hardly surprising when one considers how, in one way and another, the concept of space has been interwoven in earlier feminist thinking and concerns. To take a concrete example, which affords interesting contrasts with queer, *Lesbian Nation: The Feminist Solution*, first published in the early 1970s, is the title of a book, referred to earlier, by the American lesbian feminist Jill Johnson. The proposed feminist solution that she alludes to is the formation of a separate social and cultural space for lesbians to exist, a 'lesbian nation', formed from tribal groupings of 'fugitive' women. This political goal of establishing a separate, independent, lesbian and/or women only 'space' is necessary because:

> Radical lesbians know that men will not soon 'get better' through the efforts of women to re-educate them. They envision the process of gay feminist revolution as an extended struggle. Tribal groupings of such women, the fugitive Lesbian Nation, have begun and will continue to serve as sustaining support and psychic power bases within the movement. (Johnson, 1973: 181–2)

The idea of creating a separate 'women's space' led to the establishment of women-only and women-owned geographical regions or lands, with names like 'herland' and 'wimminsland', in various parts of the world, including Australia and parts of the United States. More recently the idea of a 'Woman's Nation' has resurfaced with Andrea Dworkin (2000) arguing for the establishment of a separate (home)land for women. In a much broader sense, and without sharing Johnson's ideas or even reading or knowing about her book, during the 1970s and 1980s many women did come to believe that establishing women's space was a major issue. Women-only events, women-only 'consciousness raising' groups, discos and clubs, Women's Studies courses with women-only space in the classroom, were all fought for and established.

This linking of notions of independent space with women's autonomy and freedom was not a new concern. Earlier generations of feminists had also recognised the importance of having 'separate space'. In 1928, for example, the British writer Virginia Woolf published *A Room of One's Own*. In an era when women were only admitted to college libraries if suitably escorted or provided with letters of introduction, she declared 'Lock up your libraries if you like but there is no gate, no lock, no bolt that you can set upon the freedom of my mind.' But still she wrote: 'A woman must have money and a room of her own if she is to write.'

Paralleling this, one can also see a concern with space within lesbian and gay rights movements. Indeed, an important form of social control of lesbians and gay men this century has been their institutionalised exclusion from social and cultural spaces (Russo, 1981; Sanderson, 1995; Sibley, 1995; Pakulski, 1997; Richardson, 2000a), in particular the limitations on safe spaces and places where lesbians and gay men might meet. To paraphrase Joan Nestle (1988), lesbians and gay men have been 'citizens of a restricted country'. This issue of access to space is examined in a global context by Neil Miller (1993: 361), who concludes that one of the social conditions necessary for a modern gay and lesbian identity and community to emerge in any given society is, borrowing from Woolf, the ability to have 'a room of one's own':

> Argentina was a country where it was difficult for gays and lesbians to live by themselves. To lead an openly gay life, one needed the financial means to live away from one's family, to have, at the very least, 'a room of one's own'. A flat was freedom. In places where this was a problem – Argentina, Egypt and Hong Kong, for example – gay movements were weak. Where it was increasingly possible, such as Japan, the gay and lesbian community was becoming stronger.

In addition to safe social and cultural space, other conditions for the emergence of specific sexual/social movements with their attendant identities include a decline in the power of the family and religious institutions in defining and determining many aspects of an individual's life, the emergence of a community which supports this sense of self, which in turn depends on a certain level of economic development that allows some degree of independence and social mobility, and a certain level of social tolerance of difference and of pluralism.

A concern with space is also a feature of newer forms of sexual politics. This is exemplified by Queer Nation, which emerged in April 1990 in New York, in part out of the AIDS-related politics of ACT UP and, also, as a response to the 'queerbashings' of lesbians and gay men that were happening in parts of the city. Queer Nation is regarded by some writers as representing a major turning point in sexual politics. To quote Seidman (1997: 192): 'Perhaps no event announces a new era of politics as dramatically as the appearance of Queer Nation.' As a new and distinctive movement, queer soon attracted attention. A few months after Queer Nation was established, during the 1990 New York City Pride Parade in

June, a broadsheet was distributed entitled *Queers Read This*, an anonymously authored series of short essays which culminated in what was to become a highly controversial piece entitled 'I Hate Straights' (Reyes, 1990). A concern with 'space' was evident: 'Being queer is not about a right to privacy; it is about the freedom to be public.'

There are echoes here of Johnson, not only in the use of a language of nation and talk of tribes, but also in the linking of freedom with the establishment of territory. However, where the Lesbian Nation was symbolised as a different *fugitive* space to that colonised by 'the enemy', queer nationals were seeking to claim 'straight space' as their own: 'Let's make every space a Lesbian and Gay space. Every street a part of our sexual geography. A city of yearning and then total satisfaction. A city and a country where we can be safe and free and more.'

The question of whether Queer Nation might lead to a call for a queer homeland is perhaps prompted by the suggestion on the part of some writers that there exists a well-established 'homosexual diaspora' (Mort, 1995). The spoof headline 'GAYS WANT OWN COUNTRY, UN asked to find separate country for gays and lesbians', in Amsterdam's free gay newspaper (issue 29, vol. 2, August 1994) can be read as a play on this theme. What is also interesting is that such 'joking' is intelligible precisely because the notion of the lesbian and gay community living apart from straight society is more or less what has happened in many cities. Arguably, one can observe a colonisation of and commercialisation of space by lesbians and gays in the gay-occupied spaces in urban environments such as, for example, Old Compton Street in Soho, London; the Castro district of San Francisco; parts of Amsterdam; and the Oxford Road area in Sydney.

A main goal of queer politics is to increase public visibility. To quote Geltmaker (1992: 650): 'Our refusal to live in a closet is one way of "just saying no" to a world, a nation, and a regional culture intent on closing borders to those who are "different".' Being queer is not about seeking the democratic right to privacy, the right in private to do what one wants to sexually, it is concerned with the freedom to occupy the public, establishing safe space for public sexualities that are currently bounded by straight (in)tolerance. In the United States, for example, one of the stated aims of Queer Nation was to expose the straightness of public spaces and to reterritorialise them (Berlant and Freeman, 1993). This emphasis on occupying space both culturally and socially can be observed in earlier social movements. Indeed, the politics of representation has a long history within feminism (Marshment, 1997), from the trashing of the 1968 Miss America pageant which was the first widely publicised event of the women's liberation movement, through to the present day, as it does also for lesbian and gay movements for whom visibility, and the challenging of negative stereotypes, have been crucial political issues.

Queer theory, like feminism, has also challenged the public/private binary. There is an identification of public space as heterosexualised, in a similar way to feminism's identification and critique of the public sphere as masculinised and the private sphere as feminised (Duncan, 1996b). Queer also shares with certain strands of feminism, a desire to reterritorialise public space and, in so doing, disrupt the ways in which certain issues (marriage, domestic violence, incest) as well as subjects (women, gay men, heterosexuals) are constituted as belonging in public or private spheres. For example, one might compare the feminist Take Back the Night campaigns, whose aim is to focus attention on the right of women to safety from male violence, with forms of queer activisms such as, for example, Queer Nation's shopping mall 'visibility actions' in the USA, where the aim is to challenge the heterosexualised family environment of shopping malls through public 'performances' of lesbian and gay, or Queer Nights Out in straight clubs, something that groups such as, for example, Lesbian Avengers have carried out. Indeed, in some cases there has been a direct borrowing of the slogans and organisational strategies of the 1970s, for instance appropriating Take Back the Night as a form of resistance and protest against gay bashing (Cottingham, 1996). However, such continuities are frequently ignored. To quote Cherry Smyth (1992: 28), writing as a feminist who is sympathetic to queer:

> Queer rhetoric often gives the impression that direct action politics was invented in 1987 [when ACT UP (AIDS Coalition to Unleash Power) was formed in New York], that the Black and Women's Liberation Movements haven't happened, that the campaigns for or against nuclear weapons, abortion, reproductive rights and violence against women have not occurred and have had no influence on the way queer activism manifests itself.

Conclusion

Queer claims to be a new mood in 'sexual politics' – a reaction to feminist, as well as lesbian and gay, politics of past generations. In practice, this has meant a (re)alliance of many lesbians with gay men – as queers – rather than with feminism. The divisions that raged between feminists over issues such as, for example, pornography and S/M practices during the 1980s is often cited as one of the reasons for this, as well as the emergence of AIDS and the forms of political response it generated such as, for example, ACT UP. While not wanting to deny that there have been significant shifts in theory and political practice associated with queer – for instance the positive inclusion of bisexuals marks a difference with earlier lesbian/feminist and gay activism as does the idea of being queer and heterosexual – I question the way in which such developments are frequently characterised as a break with previous theoretical traditions and politics.

In this chapter I have suggested that, in fact, queer has much in common with the ideas and thinking of earlier forms of 'sexual politics'. This is a view shared by Stein and Plummer (1996: 130). Commenting on the rapid rise and status attributed to queer theorists, they state that: 'These scholars are succeeding in placing sexual difference at the centre of intellectual inquiry in many fields . . . Their success is particularly striking and even ironic in view of the fact that they are using social constructionism as if it were a new discovery . . .'.

The idea that sexuality is socially constructed was developed by sociologists, especially symbolic interactionists such as Gagnon and Simon (1967, 1973) and Plummer (1975), and by feminist theorists (see Jackson and Scott, 1996; Richardson, 1997), at least twenty years or more before articles and books on queer theory began to appear. This is especially true of some lesbian/radical feminist work, as I have indicated, both in its concern with developing a theoretical critique of heterosexuality and political opposition to the privileging of heterosexuality. Indeed, many of the radical theories and ideas of the 1970s and 1980s (re)appear in queer theory. The work of feminists such as Monique Wittig (1992), for example, has informed a number of key queer theorists such as, for example, Judith Butler (1990, 1993) and Michael Warner (1993a). Writing in the 1970s, Wittig highlighted how in western political thought the heterosexual couple represented the principle of social union, of normativity, respectability, of being human.

Queer theory also owes much to radical feminism in terms of the development of a deconstructive model of gender and sexuality. As I have outlined, the notion that lesbian was a social construct is one that was voiced loudly in lesbian/feminist accounts of the 1970s and 1980s, along with attempts to problematise heterosexuality and challenge the categories 'men' and 'women' (see, for example, Delphy, 1984). As Stevi Jackson (1996c: 176) says in response to the claims of queer theory, '. . . treating the categories "lesbian" and "heterosexual" as problematic is by no means antithetical to radical feminism: indeed, I would argue that it is essential'. Similarly, the work of lesbian and gay sociologists and social historians has challenged taken-for-granted notions of essential sexual/gender identities. We can also see in the importance given to the queering of theory by queer theorists, parallels with the ways in which feminism has challenged many of our basic assumptions about what counts as knowledge (Harding, 1992; Stanley and Wise, 1993). If queer is to avoid the charge of misrepresentation and erasure it is important that writers acknowledge its theoretical and political ancestry.

In the next chapter I will explore some of these issues further in the context of the changing preoccupations of feminist theory and the implications of this for representing theoretical histories.

3

'NEW' FEMINISMS FOR 'OLD'?

Introduction

The term 'feminism' has many different meanings and perhaps never more so than today when feminist theory and politics are much more plural and contextualised than ever they were. Typically the three classic feminist positions are characterised as: radical, Marxist/socialist, and liberal feminism. However, since these forms of feminism established themselves in the 1970s, many different kinds of feminism have appeared. This is to be expected. New generations of feminists will develop different forms of feminism in so far as women's experience of their lives, and the issues facing them, are different to those of previous generations, as well as the intellectual tools at their disposal. These contributions to the development of feminist theory include, for example, black feminist perspectives, lesbian feminism, postmodern feminism, queer/feminism and eco-feminism. Given this fragmentation, is it the case that we have reached a point where distinctions between what Mary Maynard (1995) refers to as the 'Big Three' are no longer useful?

The practice of classifying feminist theories is problematic in a number of respects. To refer to a specific 'type' of feminism can imply a 'false unity' within that particular category. It can also mean that the categories are presented as if they are unchanging, with insufficient recognition of the historical development of feminist thought, both at the level of the individual writer and more broadly. As a consequence, labelling feminism as, say, radical, socialist, or liberal can encourage narrow stereotypes where instead there exists a rich diversity of ideas and perspectives. While I accept that too rigid a categorisation may lead to an oversimplification of feminist thinking, I am, nevertheless, interested in examining how the continued use of these categories can lead to strands of feminist thought being (mis)represented in particular ways. In particular, I want to consider the possible consequences this may have for the historical development of feminist theory and how feminist knowledge is constructed. The development of contemporary feminist theory is informed by versions of earlier feminist theories which, in a modernist tradition, have often been taken as a knowledge position from which to move forward. It is therefore important to examine how different forms of feminism are represented – as well as *whether* they are, for erasure can also have a significant influence on the development of social theory (Bhavnani, 1997). This also impacts on the kinds of issues that are seen to be socially and politically relevant for feminism.

The example I shall use is the representation of radical feminism. There are a number of important reasons for wanting to examine radical feminism as a category to which certain beliefs and practices are often imputed. Historically, radical feminism has often been perceived within popular culture as the extreme wing of feminism. This arises, in part, from its 'radicalism' in its attitude to men and to heterosexuality, and in its political goals. Radical feminism is 'radical' in focusing on why and how men oppress women – as distinct from capitalist economic systems *per se* – and in its desire to revolutionise, rather than reform, social, economic, legal and political systems and practices which currently privilege and benefit men. Its depiction as 'extreme' also reflects the concerns and issues that have been prioritised by radical feminists, in particular violence, reproduction and (hetero) sexuality.

Another reason for choosing radical feminism is that it is frequently constructed as an oppositional category within feminism, as well as outside it. Typically, in the past, Marxist/socialist feminism has been polarised against radical feminism. Stanley and Wise (1993), for example, point to the amount of 'energy devoted by Marxist feminists to criticising and discrediting radical feminist work' (in Maynard, 1995: 266). In recent years it would seem that radical feminism has been identified as 'a position' against which a new generation of feminists and, as I detailed in the previous chapter, queers have rebelled. For example, a number of books which purport to represent 'new feminism' have attacked radical feminism (Roiphe, 1994; Denfeld, 1995; Walter, 1998, 1999) or, alternatively, have largely ignored its contribution (Findlen, 1995).

As new trends in the politics of sexuality and gender emerge and become established, it is important to consider what this means for those positioned as opposed to them. One of the consequences of the development of such polarities is that it encourages the presentation of feminist theories in terms of narrow stereotypes that I referred to above. Another result of this oppositional type of classification is that it implies an either/or understanding of different categories. For example, during the 1970s and 1980s, in polarising socialist against radical feminists it might be assumed that the latter were not interested in class issues and did not perceive the need for socialism, which was clearly not the case. In the more recent example of 'new feminism' and queer theory the danger is that radical feminism is assumed to have relatively little in common with contemporary movements. Thus, both in its depiction as 'extreme' and as a position against which a new generation of theorists distance themselves, and which is hence at risk of being seen as outdated or irrelevant, radical feminism is extremely useful in highlighting some of the difficulties associated with the ways in which feminist thought has been classified. In the remainder of this chapter I will, therefore, critically examine some of the stereotypes of radical feminism and consider the wider implications for feminist theory and practice.

Essentialism

One of the most common criticisms of radical feminist thinking is that it is essentialist. Although this can usually be interpreted as implying a reductive or deterministic theoretical approach, the term essentialist is not unproblematic. As Diana Fuss (1990) and others have pointed out, essentialism and social constructionism, with which it is usually contrasted, are not two distinct and opposing positions. These are relative and not absolute terms (though I would suggest it might make more sense to talk of theories being more or less essentialist than more or less constructionist), and it may be more helpful to think of a social constructionist/essentialist continuum along which theorists may be placed.

This is reflected in the different meanings attached to the 'essentialism' imputed to radical feminism. In some accounts radical feminist theory is identified as locating women's subordination in biological differences between women and men which are relatively 'fixed'. For example, although they state that not all radical feminists accept 'biological theories', British sociologists Pamela Abbot and Claire Wallace (1996: 12) nonetheless feed this caricature of radical feminism as biologically determinist when they claim that: 'Women's oppression is seen as rooted in women's biological capacity for motherhood or in the innate, biologically determined aggression of the male, as manifested in rape'.

In some cases the emphasis is on how radical feminists have supposedly appealed to a concept of women's biological superiority and 'special nature' in their theoretical accounts of gender relations. The term 'cultural feminism', which I discuss in more detail later, is often used to characterise this form of feminist essentialism. To quote Tamsin Wilton (1995: 106):

> An alternative strategy, that of cultural feminism, has been . . . to reverse the values inherent in the patriarchal regime of gender. Woman has been constructed within/by patriarchal discourse as gentle, caring, nurturing, emotional, spiritual, etc., and biological difference has been held up as evidence of her natural inferiority to man. Cultural feminism simply reverses the values assigned to these sets of characteristics, asserting that women's gentleness, spirituality, capacity to give birth, etc. are signs of her natural *superiority* to men, whose lack of these attributes has got us and the planet into the mess we are in now. (Original emphasis)

It is thus suggested that through a positive affirmation of roles and attributes typically associated with women, those roles and attributes are essentialised as female.

The portrayal of radical feminist analyses as biologically determinist/essentialist is surprising, especially in relation to sexuality. Although a few writers such as, for example, Mary Daly (1978) have alluded to an essential female selfhood, they are not typical of radical feminist theories. Within most radical feminist writing it is abundantly clear that sexuality and gender difference are understood to be socially constructed, not biologically determined, and that the emphasis is on challenging essentialist notions of male and female sexuality. As Denise Thompson (1991: 116, 165) states:

> To insist, as radical feminists do, that there are differences between the sexes, and that those 'differences' are the stuff of male domination, is not to appeal to 'biology', nor to be pessimistic about the possibility of revolutionary change. In fact, it is to insist on that very possibility, else why would we bother? . . . Why is it not possible to argue *both that* female and male sexualities are different, or rather (to put it less essentialistically) that women and men have different interests, purposes, desires and needs in relation to sexuality, *and* that those differences are engendered by specific historical conditions, without positing any essential genesis or causality at all? (Original emphasis)

In fact, the essentialist/social constructionist debates during the 1980s were significantly influenced by contributions from radical and other feminists arguing a social constructionist position. Where this is recognised, radical feminists are sometimes criticised for employing a different form of essentialism from biological determinism. The term essentialism is used to imply that radical feminism is based upon a form of cultural determinism which relies upon an essentialised notion of 'woman' as an oppressed category (Weedon, 1987) and/or a view of the role of culture as one where it interacts with male biology in some inevitable and immutable way (Segal, 1987a). Such classification usually takes the form of claiming that radical feminists conceptualise women's subordination as universal and unchanging, failing to acknowledge historical and cultural difference. Thus, for example, Ann Ferguson (1989: 54) states that: 'Though these [radical feminist] social constructionist theories may not technically be biologically essentialist, they are still a form of social essentialism: that is, they assume a social divide between male and female sexual natures which is unconvincingly universal, static and ahistorical.'

As Sylvia Walby (1990) and others have pointed out, typically radical feminist analyses are historically and socially sensitive, concerned with the ways in which patriarchy or – as Walby (1997) refers to in her later work to signify a more dynamic and contextualised understanding of gendered power relationships – patriarchal 'gender regimes' impact on women in particular socio-historical contexts. They do not assume female and male sexuality to be universal and unchanging. On the contrary, central to radical feminist perspectives is the belief that if sexuality is socially constructed, then it can be reconstructed in new and different ways; sexuality need not be coercive or oppressive, it can be challenged and changed.

Despite this, the construction of radical feminism as essentialist has prevailed. During the 1970s and 1980s it was a significant aspect of Marxist/socialist feminist critiques of radical feminist work (see, for example, Segal, 1987a; Rowbotham, 1990). More recently, the increasing influence of postmodernist ideas within feminism has revitalised this perception. Feminist postmodernists regard the use of the notion of 'patriarchy', as well as the categories 'woman' and 'man', as problematically essentialist. Such critiques stem from an emphasis within postmodernism on deconstructing such categories in order to demonstrate that they are 'regulatory fictions', rather than naturally occurring categories, which have no fixed, consistent, unitary meaning. In this respect Stevi Jackson is right to ask, 'So what's new?' Most radical feminists assume the category woman is socially constructed and recognise its diverse meanings, being 'just as concerned as any post-modernist to challenge essentialist conceptions of women' (Jackson, 1992: 28). Indeed, although it is rarely acknowledged, many of the ideas associated with postmodernism are also products of radical feminist thinking: the idea of knowledge as contextual and situated; the recognition of the importance of language in constructing difference; the questioning of notions of 'truth' and 'the self' as unitary and consistent. The important difference is that radical feminists along with others, including some socialist and 'new' feminists (e.g. Walby, 1997; Walter, 1998; Segal, 1999), purposively seek to retain the possibility of some kind of collective use of the term 'woman' – and, related to this, the concept of 'women's oppression' – however varied and uneven the relations of power may be in different contexts. In other words, it is argued that, however diverse and varied our experiences may be, women exist as a political and as a socially constructed category whose lives are materially shaped by belonging to that category. That is to say, 'woman' can be used as a unifying, if not unified, concept.

There are a number of possible consequences arising from this classification of radical feminist theory as feminist essentialism. For instance, such stereotyping may, in part, explain the perception of radical feminism as overly simplistic and lacking in theoretical analysis especially of differences between women (Eisenstein, 1984). Implicit in what I am saying is that the use of the term 'essentialist' is value laden, and can be used in such a way as to discredit writers despite the fact that their work may have stressed the socially constructed nature of gender and sexuality. To quote Teresa de Lauretis (1994: 11):

Doesn't the insistence on the 'essentialism' of cultural feminists reproduce and keep in the foreground an image of 'dominant' feminism that is at least reductive, at best tautological or superseded, and at worst not in our interests? Doesn't it feed the pernicious opposition of low versus high theory, a low-grade type of critical thinking (feminism) that is contrasted with the high-test theoretical grade of a poststructuralism from which some feminists would have been smart enough to learn?

The imputation of essentialism can therefore serve as a mechanism of social control within feminist discourse, a means of undermining the legitimacy of, in this case, radical feminist theory. If this is the case it suggests that the determination to single out radical feminists as essentialist and the unwillingness to recognise their rejection of essentialist conceptions of gender, serve as more than a theoretical critique. Indeed, it is worth asking why other feminisms have not been 'accused' of essentialism when there is clearly a possibility of doing so. There was, for example, a tradition within Marxist and socialist feminist thought which regarded sexuality as repressed by capitalism, implying that women have an authentic sexuality that can be liberated from such repressive forces. However, relatively speaking, socialist feminists are rarely criticised for being essentialist, at least not in this sense.

If some critics have misread radical feminism as essentially essentialist, conceptualising sexuality as universal and unchanging, others have accused radical feminism of over-emphasising the possibilities for change and the potential for transforming our sexual practices and ideas about sexuality. For example, the political lesbian debate in the 1970s and early 1980s led to accusations of voluntarism, that radical feminists simply assumed that sexual practices and desires can be changed through individual efforts, ignoring the social and economic constraints to 'choice'. This is despite the fact that the work of Adrienne Rich (1980) and that of many other writers associated with radical feminism since (see, for example, Jeffreys, 1990, 1994; Wilkinson and Kitzinger, 1993; Richardson, 1996b; Jackson, 1999) has highlighted ways in which (hetero)sexuality is socially instituted and maintained, creating the prescriptions and the conditions in which women experience (hetero)sexual relations. Similarly, although lesbianism has been written about as a political choice, the possibility of women living independently of men has also been acknowledged to be socially and economically determined (Jeffreys, 1990; Jackson and Scott, 1996; Richardson, 1997).

Past its sell-by date?

There has been a tendency to reduce the diverse strands of radical feminist thought to a relatively few sources. Typically, it is the work of a number of North American writers, whose cited works are usually books published in the 1970s and 1980s, that has come to represent the category of radical feminist thought. For instance, Shulamith Firestone's forward looking and influential work *The Dialectic of Sex*, first published in 1970, is still frequently cited thirty years later as if it were representative of radical feminism. Although issues of sexuality and reproduction remain central to radical feminist theorising, few nowadays would agree with Firestone's argument that in order to achieve liberation women must be freed from their biological capacity for motherhood through technologies of artificial reproduction. Other works frequently used to illustrate radical feminism include Kate Millett (1970), Susan Brownmiller (1976), Mary Daly (1978), Adrienne Rich (1977, 1980), Monique Wittig (1979, 1981), Susan Griffin (1981), Andrea Dworkin (1981, 1987), Catharine MacKinnon (1982) and Christine Delphy (1984).

This limited representation of radical feminist thought is problematic in a number of respects. One important consequence of this tacit stereotyping of radical feminists is that it suggests a far narrower range of radical feminist views than actually exists (see, for example, Douglas, 1990; Bell and Klein, 1996; Adkins and Leonard, 1997). In addition to encouraging a view of radical feminism as unitary and monolithic, it also encourages the individualisation of radical feminist thinking through its association with the work of a handful of writers. A further major concern is that it seriously undermines the perceived relevance of radical feminism to contemporary debates. Indeed, one could be forgiven for thinking that, with a few exceptions, radical feminist writers are a thing of the past. I am not suggesting that feminist texts from the 1970s and early 1980s have no relevance for feminist theory and practice today, rather I am pointing out that one mechanism by which contemporary feminists can discredit and dismiss radical feminism is through claiming it is outdated and old-fashioned.

Another example of erasure is the fact that radical feminism is often ignored in published accounts of feminist theory and feminism's history. The omission of radical feminist thinking in British feminist accounts is evident in, for instance, Terry Lovell's (1990) *British Feminist Thought* and Maggie Humm's *Feminisms: a Reader* (1992). A somewhat different form of erasure is evidenced in Alice Echols' (1989) book *Daring To Be Bad: Radical Feminism in America 1967–1975*, in which it is suggested that radical feminism ceased to exist as a movement in the United States after the mid-1970s, evolving into what Echols labels 'cultural feminism'. Cultural feminism is a controversial term that some writers use interchangeably with radical feminism. For others, however, it has a more specific meaning, as I indicated earlier, referring to a form of feminism rooted in feminist essentialism and the celebration of the 'essential female'. Lynne Segal, for example, writing in the mid-1980s, defines cultural feminism as a new form of radical feminism which '. . . celebrates women's superior virtue and spirituality and decries "male" violence and technology' (Segal, 1987a: 3).

Cultural feminism is not a term that is largely chosen by radical feminists themselves, but rather one which has been applied by others to their writings (see Cameron (1993) for a more detailed discussion of this). Echols does herself acknowledge that others would use the term 'contemporary radical feminism' rather than 'cultural feminism', and that those she labels as cultural feminists would most likely call themselves radical feminists. For Echols, however, cultural feminism is seen as an aberrant form of radical feminism that is unworthy of the name, hence the need to apply a different label. Echols (1989: 6–7) distinguishes the two in the following way:

> In the terminology of today, radical feminists were typically social construc-
> tionists who wanted to render gender irrelevant, while cultural feminists were
> generally essentialists who sought to celebrate femaleness . . . whereas radical
> feminists were anti-capitalist – if often only implicitly – cultural feminists dis-
> missed economic class struggle as 'male' and, therefore, irrelevant to women.

Thus we have radical feminism, post-1975, identified once again as essentialist and, also, unconcerned with class issues.

Differences

Another common criticism of radical feminism is that it is theoretically underdeveloped compared with other forms of feminist analyses, especially in relationship to an 'oversimplified conception of power and of gender . . .' (Hollway, 1993: 412) and attention to the question of difference. Writing on radical feminist critiques of new reproductive technologies, for example, Elaine Denny (1994: 75) comments that:

> The radical feminist tendency to treat women as a homogeneous group, univer-
> sally oppressed and passive, and to treat all relationships with men as
> exploitative, leads to an oversimplification of the issues. One way this is mani-
> fested is in the widely held feminist assumption that the experience of women as
> an oppressed group has led to similarities in all women that outweigh differ-
> ences of class, colour, ability, etc.

I would not want to claim that radical feminism has, in the past, dealt adequately with class, ethnicity and racism, because I do not believe it has. Where I take issue with Denny and others who voice similar criticisms is in the suggestion that radical feminism is inherently more likely than other forms of feminism to result in a denial of the different interests between women. For example, in a paper which raises critical questions about the racism embedded within contemporary feminist thought, Kum-Kum Bhavnani (1997: 35) argues that: '. . . it is a radical feminist, and related, analysis that is most likely to lead to a denial of differing and contradictory interests between women of colour and white women'.

The argument seems to be that in using the concept of patriarchal gender relations to theorise the common and specific oppression of women, differences between women and the existence of other forms of oppression (and their interconnection with gender) are likely to be ignored or marginalised. However, at a theoretical level, it is important to disentangle the issue of the universalism of women's oppression from the theorisation of difference between women, rather than, as is often the case, eliding from one to the other. It is possible to offer generalised theories of oppression *and* theorise how and why the social practices that are identified as key to women's subordination affect women differently according to, for instance, class, race, ethnicity and sexuality. Equally, we may develop theories that do not claim the universality of women's oppression and still ignore important differences between women. A good deal of feminist work on women's role as carers within the family, for example, has implicitly accepted a heterosexual framework. Attention has also been drawn to this issue by Stacey (1993: 63) who makes the point that 'plenty of feminist theory that is not claiming the universality of women's oppression can be challenged for its racist assumptions, and likewise generalised theories of oppression are by no means the prerogative of white feminists'.

To put it another way, it is important to distinguish accounts of women's subordination in terms of patriarchal gender regimes and the claim for the universal validity of theoretical models developed from an under-standing of white, and here one could also add heterosexual and middle-class women. The question surely is whether sufficient attention is given within radical feminist writing to the interconnections of patriarchal gender relations with class and racism, as well as the ways in which eth-nicity and gender relations interact historically. This is an important criticism and one which radical feminists continue to need to address in their work. However, such a criticism can be made of most (white) feminist accounts, including liberal and socialist feminist writing; it is not specific to radical feminism.

New purity feminists?

In addition to the claims that it is outdated and conceptually weak, radical feminism has also been branded in some accounts as 'oppressive' and 'anti-woman'. This takes a number of forms. In many cases it is linked with the construction of radical feminism as narrow and judgmental. The flavour of this is captured in the following quote from Jane Ussher (1991: 224–6):

> Much of the radical feminist theorising is potentially very anti-woman in its implications and very divisive, setting up criteria for how 'good' women, 'good' feminists should behave, and dismissing those who do not comply . . . This arrogant dictating of appropriate 'feminist' behaviour is no different from the elitism and oppression practised by the patriarchs for centuries. Such feminists may have rejected the phallocentric discourse, but they have in its stead created new discursive practices that are as oppressive and misogynistic as those of the men.

The view of radical feminism as 'prescriptive feminism' which dictates to women what they shall or shall not do has been expressed in the main by Marxist/socialist feminists, sexual libertarians, and, more recently, by some advocates of 'new feminism' and queer theory. I say 'new' because a great deal of the work popularised under this label bears a striking resemblance to a liberal feminist agenda of the 1970s. In Britain, Natasha Walter, who has promoted herself as a mouthpiece for *the* new feminism via a mainstream book of this title, exemplifies this trend. Walter (1998: 76) identifies the need to get away from what she describes as the 'tendency towards puritanism and political correctness' of previous feminisms, but more especially of those for whom issues of sexuality have been central:

> The links that feminists have drawn between the personal and the political mean that they believe they can tell other women how to behave with impunity. Yet this distracts us from the real battles and arguments that these women may be fighting for, and it alienates other women from joining in feminist debates. This is one primary question that the new feminism must pose: isn't it time for us to free ourselves from the weight of personal guilt that even feminists have tried to put upon women . . . .

In the United States, writers who formerly identified with radical feminism but who now reject its political agenda have also been prominent in the trashing of radical feminism as conservative and moralistic (see, for example, Echols, 1989). It is a view that is particularly apparent in critiques of radical feminist accounts of sexuality and, more especially, of pornography, some of which suggest that radical feminism can be understood as a new form of fundamentalism that was consolidated in the 1980s (Segal, 1999). In a similar vein, others have suggested that radical feminists are moralistic adherents to a kind of new social purity movement. For example, Margaret Hunt (1990: 38) refers to revolutionary and radical feminists as 'new purity feminists', claiming that: 'Most of us – some of us to our great personal distress – are familiar with the attempts revolutionary and radical feminists have made to purify sexual practices within the British and North American women's movements.'

The construction of radical feminists as the 'new moralists' is also evident in the claims that radical feminism has aided the oppression of women through being useful to the Right in their conservative agenda (Rodgerson and Wilson, 1991; Segal, 1994, 1999). For example, Judith Halberstam (1997: 326) states:

> Instead of the anti-pornography position developing into a call for sex education or for the fostering of sexual diversity . . . it actually fed into moralist fears about perversity and a religious right-wing effort to legislate against certain forms of sexual expression . . . As had happened at the beginning of the century in relation to first-wave feminism, sexual purity and moralism became a feature of lesbian feminism.

Speaking more broadly about the impact of radical feminism on social and cultural practices in the USA in the 1980s, Sara Dunn (1995: 46) echoes this view, claiming that 'mainstream educational institutions, the judiciary, government and the media in Reagan's US all found radical feminism relatively easy to accommodate and marginalised other feminist voices'. This portrayal of radical feminism as the 'acceptable' face of feminism I find both surprising and unconvincing, especially when one considers that it is radical feminism that is most often defined as extreme by those on the Right *and* the Left. It is even more ironic in the context of the USA, where the strong tradition of liberal feminism and its concern with civil rights is surely that which has been most acceptable to the mainstream (see Chapter 6 in this volume).

Even where radical feminist arguments have been adopted by the Right, leading to charges of collusion and alliance between radical feminists and the moral lobby, this does not mean that this is necessarily sought or desired by feminists. In Britain, for example, radical feminists have strongly denied any willingness to work with the religious right-wing on the grounds of differing theoretical positions and political aims (Kelly, 1992), some claiming that the suggestions of alliances represent a strategic misrepresentation by feminists who hold different positions to radical and revolutionary feminists on issues such as pornography (Jeffreys, 1990, 1994). As a recent study of women on the 'moral right' in the UK demonstrates, the 'acceptability' of the idea of working together with feminists reflects important power imbalances which: 'favour the position of the morally conservative women, and therefore make it less dangerous, indeed in some ways advantageous, for them to consider such alliances in a way that is not true for radical feminists they propose to support' (Luff, 1996: 136). Moreover, where feminist arguments are appropriated by the Right it is very often the ideas of nineteenth-century feminists, and the involvement of some of these feminists in social purity movements, which are drawn on. This is not so surprising when we consider the contradictions involved for the moral right, ardently pro-family, in supporting modern-day radical feminist thought in which a critical analysis of the heterosexual nuclear family as a key site of patriarchal relations is central.

In contrast to this, the emphasis on sexuality within radical feminist theory has sometimes led to the charge that radical feminists attribute tremendous power to sexual activity as a political strategy and a means to social change (see, for example, Hunt, 1990), drawing parallels with a sexual libertarian rather than a conservative agenda. In fact, the notion that we can change the world through what we do – or do not do – sexually is often critiqued by radical feminists as part of the discourse of sexual liberation (Jeffreys, 1990, 1994). Having said this, within radical feminism it is recognised as centrally important not to depoliticise sexual interactions; not only is it understood that these reflect wider social relations, but also that they can shape social practices and meanings. Sexual practices within the home, for instance, 'help shape the character and meaning of home-life' (Cooper, 1995). The important theoretical distinction to be made here is between a radical feminist approach to changing sexual practice and desire through challenging patriarchal practices and structures in the wider social

order, and the libertarian assumption that one can transform gender relations through 'liberating' sexualities.

Anti-sex

Related to this characterisation of radical feminism as reactionary and/or
'moralistic', it is not uncommon for radical feminists to be described as
'anti-sex' or 'sex-negative', usually in contrast to other 'pro-sex' feminists
and some queers. (Though I am not here equating all those who embrace
the label queer necessarily with a non radical/feminist stance; see Wilton
(1995) for example.) For example, David Evans (1993: 266), following Gayle
Rubin (1984/1993), identifies the perspective of radical feminism, which he
labels 'cultural feminism', as that which 'condemns almost all forms of
sexual expression as anti-feminist'. Underlying this division, there is often
a binary view of sexuality as danger versus sexuality as pleasure. Thus, for
example, Ken Plummer (1995: 59), who refers to writers such as Sheila
Jeffreys, Andrea Dworkin and Catharine MacKinnon as 'radical anti-sex
feminists', remarks that there were factions within feminism from the early
1970s which '. . . gave rise to the "sex" war debates (notably around
pornography) which polarised "purity, revolutionary feminists" telling
tales of sexual danger, and "pro-sex, socialist feminists" telling tales of
sexual pleasure'.

This kind of stereotyping has given rise to another version of radical
feminism as oppressive to women: in this case the charge is that it has
silenced some women and made others feel guilty and ashamed in respect
of their sexual feelings and desires. For example, a commonly expressed
view is that heterosexual feminists have been silenced as a result of radical
feminists making them feel guilty about their sexuality and, more especially, (hetero)sexual pleasures. This was a central theme in debates about
heterosexual feminism and political lesbianism that occurred in the late
1970s (Onlywomen Press, 1981), which I discussed in Chapter 1. It is also
evident in more recent work on theorising heterosexuality (Wilkinson and
Kitzinger, 1993). For example, Wendy Hollway (1993: 413) claims that:

> Of course heterosexual feminists have good reasons for dwelling on the contra-
> dictions [of heterosexuality], since they are trying to engage in intimate
> relationships based on mutuality and reciprocity in the wider context of
> women's subordination. Not to find any would smack of denial and defensive-
> ness. But dwelling on the difficulties is also motivated by guilt; a guilt which
> reproduces and is reproduced by the dominant radical feminist discourse on het-
> erosexuality.

Others such as, for example, Robyn Rowland (1996) question this, arguing that it will not do to blame radical feminism for the reluctance on the
part of heterosexual feminists to discuss their sexual relationships with

men. As Victoria Robinson (1993) points out, this cannot 'adequately explain the continued silence (mainly) from heterosexual women on their sexuality'. One suggestion is that such guilt may, in part, be a product of the awareness of the history of anti-lesbianism within feminist movements which, especially in the early days of the women's liberation movement, resulted in pressures on lesbians to downplay their sexuality to avoid 'giving feminism a bad name' or scaring off heterosexual women (Tsoulis, 1987). A hangover from the times when writers such as Betty Friedan (1965), a key figure in the emergence of second-wave feminism in the USA, famously referred to lesbians in the movement as the 'lavender menace', who by their very presence might endanger the acceptability of the feminist cause.

This perception of radical feminism as a pressure on women to keep silent about their sexual pursuits and pleasures has also been evident in debates about S/M and butch/femme (Segal, 1994). Indeed, some writers have suggested that the popularisation of these forms of practice, rather than an outcome of the commercialisation and cultural dominance of certain sections of gay male and lesbian culture, is a consequence of radical feminism itself! More specifically, it is suggested that it is the result of the desire to transgress radical feminist 'norms'(Faderman, 1993). Chris Woods (1995: 54) exemplifies this when he says that: 'For some women in the 1980s, the adoption of SM was not from an actual desire to practice it, but as a statement of political opposition to a particular radical feminist proscriptive line.'

Implicit in suggestions such as these is that radical feminist discourses have had more 'disciplinary power' to influence women's lives than other feminist perspectives. Beatrix Campbell makes this point when, speaking of British feminism in the 1970s and 1980s she claims that a 'feminist sexual politics was defeated indirectly by the hegemony of radical feminism' (Campbell, 1987). Her view is shared by other writers such as, for example, Segal (1987a) and Evans (1993) who imply that radical feminism has served to police sexual practice, heterosexual, gay and lesbian, through the enforcement of hegemonic cultural norms which define what is 'politically correct' and 'politically incorrect' sex. Along with Caroline Ramazanoglu (1993), I think we need to question this assumption. For example, in terms of the earlier question of whether radical feminism has had the power to constrain heterosexual women's authority to speak, in particular about their sexual satisfactions and pleasures, I have suggested that we need a much more careful delineation of what this may represent. Ramazanoglu (1993: 320) adds to this by suggesting that: '. . . if heterosexual women persistently report negative sexual experiences in their relationships with men, it seems more obvious to look at their relationships with men, than at the failures of feminism, in order to explain this'.

To interpret critiques of certain forms of sexuality as 'anti-sex' is fundamentally flawed. It is the case that radical feminists have problematised concepts of desire and pleasure, as well as being critical of current constructions of sexuality. However, to be legitimately described as 'anti-sex' one would surely have to declare oneself opposed to all forms of sexual experience. In the early days of the women's liberation movement a few radical feminist writers did argue against any involvement in sexual relationships. In her early writings, the American writer Ti-Grace Atkinson, for instance, argued that any sexual expression perpetuated women's domination by men, and she emphasised celibacy (Atkinson, 1974). Similarly, feminist arguments in favour of celibacy were a feature of nineteenth-century feminism, both in Britain and the USA (Jeffreys, 1985). Yet it is not these earlier feminists who, as Thompson (1991) suggests, might well be described as 'anti-sex', that are being singled out. The accusations of being 'anti-sex' are directed at feminists who have critiqued certain expressions of sexuality, in particular where sex is coercive, violent or abusive and where it involves practices that eroticise dominance and submission (see Jeffreys, 1990, 1994).

The use of the terms 'pro-sex' and 'anti-sex' by critics of radical feminism are interesting in themselves. To claim that certain feminists are not 'pro-sex' is to construct sex (and good sex) in certain kinds of ways. It is to suggest that the kinds of 'sex' that so-called 'anti-sex' feminists defend, or at least do not critique, is not sex and that 'sex' is best equated with those activities which 'pro-sex' writers celebrate/defend in their work. It is also important to recognise that radical feminists are not alone in criticising certain forms of sexual practice and desire; so have some so-called sex radicals, queers and socialist feminists (Rubin, 1984/1993; Nichols, 1987; Smyth, 1992; Segal, 1994, 1999). A good example of this is the derogatory use of terms like 'vanilla' and 'politically correct' sex. For example, Nichols (1987) uses the term 'politically correct sex' to imply a curtailment of sexual desires and practices, which provides a context for critiques of 'vanilla sex' as dull and unexploratory.

Victims

The view of radical feminism as oppressive – hence 'powerful' – is also reflected in the view advocated by certain writers that radical feminism is a discourse which constructs women as victims, with potentially negative and far reaching effects on women's attitudes and behaviour. Denny (1994), for example, states that 'the experiences of individual women have been lacking from most radical feminist literature, women have been portrayed as powerless victims'. A further very graphic example of the view that radical feminism portrays women as weak and helpless victims, and thereby encourages women to position themselves as vulnerable and at risk, can be found in the following characterisation of Catharine MacKinnon's work, which refers to her '. . . fatalistic depiction of women as so many little bunny rabbits hopping around in the middle of the road, waiting for the next juggernaut to come thundering round the corner' (Bennett, 1994: 27).

This type of criticism is particularly linked to an emphasis within radical feminist accounts on men's control of women through forms of violence and, also, on sexuality. Lynne Segal (1987a: 70), for example, claims that: 'The identification of sexuality as "the primary social sphere of male power" was . . . disastrous in my view, because it encouraged "all women" to identify themselves as the victims of "all men"'. Similarly, in relation to analysing violence, Hester Eisenstein (1984: xix), also writing of feminism in the 1970s and 1980s, adopts a similar tone when she criticises cultural feminism's '. . . pessimistic depiction of women as the innocent, passive and powerless victims of male violence'. More recently, attempts to articulate a 'new' feminism of the future also appear to contain elements of this notion of feminism as encouraging a 'victim mentality' in women. Identifying herself with a new generation of 'new' feminists, Katie Roiphe (1994: 44), for instance, uses the example of marches against rape to illustrate the idea that 'old' feminism has positioned women as victims: 'The marchers seem to accept, even embrace, the mantle of victim status. As the speakers describe every fear, every possible horror suffered at the hands of men, the image they project is one of helplessness and passivity.'

Some writers have gone on to further argue that an emphasis by radical feminists on 'female victimisation', in particular through highlighting men's violence towards women, has led to younger women's rejection of feminism (Segal, 1994). The blaming of radical feminism for the alleged decline of feminism is not new, others have pointed to divisions between radical and socialist feminists as leading to the break up of the British women's liberation movement in the 1970s and early 1980s. In the present context of writers claiming to represent a 'new feminism' it would appear that it is still primarily radical feminism that is blamed for the 'failures of feminism'. However, implicitly, so too is postmodern feminism, albeit to a lesser extent, associated with a shift away from 'concrete' and material issues such as, for example, the sexual division of labour and women's position in the labour market, toward an emphasis on cultural practices as constitutive of gender. Natasha Walter (1998: 4–5), for example, appears to believe that, to a large extent, feminism itself is to blame for the failure of various social changes in women's lives to happen:

> Feminism has recently been associated more with a movement to change women's attitudes and society's culture than with . . . material inequalities. If feminism is to mean anything to women in this generation, this is an emphasis that must shift. In the seventies, feminism did win concrete battles, especially over equal pay and abortion rights. But it gradually became primarily associated with sexual politics and culture . . . the new feminism must unpick the tight link that feminism in the seventies made between our personal and our private lives . . . identifying the personal and political in too absolute and unyielding a way has led feminism to a dead end.

The association of radical feminism with social/biological determinism may, in part, explain the conceptualisation of radical feminism as overemphasising the role of coercive forces and underestimating women's agency. However, as I have argued earlier, to claim that there exist patriarchal gender relations is not to suggest that such relations may not be successfully challenged. On the contrary, as with other strands of feminist thought, radical feminism regards women as active agents in the processes of social change. Nevertheless, this question of depicting women as victims is one that needs addressing and is relevant to the development of feminist theory in general. How do we draw attention to the 'atrocities committed against women, while at the same time asserting women's strength' (Thompson, 1991: 123)? Bearing this in mind, it is interesting to ask why it is the case that if, for instance, we draw attention to conditions of high unemployment, poverty and economic 'harsh truths' facing women, both locally and globally, we are unlikely to be seen as rendering women powerless and of portraying certain groups of women as victims of institutional realities. And how often when we are concerned with identifying the injustices that men have suffered is it suggested that this will turn men into victims? Related to this, it seems clear that the term 'victim' rather than being carefully defined and used as a critical concept is more often imputed to certain feminist perspectives and issues in a simplistic manner which serves to undermine their legitimacy and relevance. To quote Scott Tucker (1995: 36): '*Victims* has become the favourite swear-word of the far right, but it echoes from other political quarters with varying degrees of contempt' (original emphasis).

It is also important to recognise that for some the word 'victim' can, in certain contexts, be construed in a positive sense, as an acknowledgement that they were victims and in no way responsible for what happened to them. A clearer delineation of the term 'victim' also queries the equation of victim with passivity or lack of agency. To see oneself as not to blame for something is also to begin to be able to see oneself as someone who does not have to feel guilty or ashamed. It potentially allows us to make sense of our experience in an active and much more positive way. In this sense victim narratives can be transformative and part of a politicisation process. Plummer (1995: 76), for example, discussing feminist narratives of rape, points out that this process of identifying as a victim can be a crucial and necessary step in a woman seeing herself as a person with control over her responses to the victimisation, as a survivor, a woman who is 'more determining than determined'. It is this kind of distinction that radical feminist accounts of especially sexual violence towards women have articulated and which allow for an acknowledgement of a felt sense of victimisation alongside the possibility of this generating personal and political change.

Conclusion

In this chapter I have highlighted some of the main ways in which radical feminism is (mis)represented and often misunderstood, one of the

consequences of which is to often discredit or even dismiss radical feminism as a strand of contemporary feminist thought. There are, of course,
criticisms that can be made of radical feminism, serious gaps in understanding, and areas that are under-theorised. At the same time, many of the
criticisms that are levelled at radical feminism are inaccurate and without
foundation.

As feminism develops and undergoes transformation we need to continue to ask what these practices mean for how we interpret feminisms,
both past and present. Are we, for example, in danger of losing a complex
history of feminism in the representation of certain strands of feminist
thought in the sorts of ways that I have described? Are we at risk of paying
insufficient attention to the continuities in past and present feminist theorising, even if similar themes and issues resurface in different forms? If we
fail to accurately represent some strands of feminist thought in feminist
discourse, does this serve to seriously diminish our understanding of
women's lives, as well as their experience of and resistance to varying
forms of oppression? What issues may lose their political significance and
what issues may gain in perceived relevance? For example, one possible
outcome of radical feminist work being discredited as a 'spent force', or
ignored, is that matters of continuing importance to women's lives that are
associated with radical feminism, such as, for example, violence and sexuality, may also be minimised. With the establishment of feminist theory
within the academy, we might also ask what does this mean for the teaching of gender and women's studies? Arguably, the misrepresentation of
radical feminism and the erasure of its influence in certain historical
accounts of feminist theory and practice has resulted in radical feminism
being very poorly understood by students, who frequently paraphrase the
stereotypic assumptions contained in numerous texts.

This process of (mis)representation also raises the question of how our
political identity and chosen theoretical perspective can interact with how
we are positioned as 'other'. As I stated at the beginning of this chapter,
radical feminism has often been perceived within popular culture as the
extreme wing of feminism, with the conflation of radical feminism and lesbian feminism serving to strengthen the view of radical feminism as both
unacceptable and 'other'. Is it also the case, as Teresa de Lauretis (1994: 33)
suggests, that what motivates the (mis)representation of radical feminism
on the part of some feminists, in particular the imputation of essentialism,
is the challenge it poses to the institution of heterosexuality?

> . . . the challenge (to the social-symbolic institution of heterosexuality) has been
> posed, and most articulately by precisely those feminists who are then accused
> of separatism in their political stance and of essentialism with regard to their
> epistemological claims. I do not think it is a coincidence.

PART 2

SEXUAL CITIZENSHIP

4

CITIZENSHIP AND SEXUALITY

What do we mean by 'citizenship'?

Discussion of citizenship has been dominated by a model based on the work of T.H. Marshall (1950), a British sociologist who shaped post-war thinking about citizenship. Marshall defined citizenship in terms of three sets of rights: civil or legal rights, political rights and social rights. Civil or legal rights are institutionalised through the law and include things such as the right to own property; freedom of speech, thought and faith; liberty of the person; and the right to justice. Political rights are institutionalised in the parliamentary political system and councils of local government and include the right to vote and participate in the exercise of political power. Social rights include the right to a certain level of economic welfare and security as well as the right 'to share to the full in the social heritage and to live the life of a civilised being according to the standards prevailing in the society' (Marshall, 1950: 10). These are rights that are institutionalised in the welfare state, for example unemployment benefits, and provision for health and education. According to Marshall, these rights evolved historically in a certain order, civil rights emerging first in the eighteenth century, political rights in the nineteenth century and social rights in the twentieth century.

In this and in subsequent analyses, the primary focus has been on the relationship of social class and citizenship (Marshall, 1977), with some discussion of nation/ethnicity. The question of the relationship of citizenship to gender, until recently, has been largely absent from much of the debate within the social sciences, and in the case of sexuality almost non-existent. For example, in *Citizenship and Social Theory*, although passing reference is made to the fact that many of the new issues of citizenship 'appear to centre around gender politics' and that 'interesting and radical developments appear to be centred around . . . the struggle for homosexual rights' (Turner, 1993a: 13), none of the contributors elucidates how the study of such social movements might change notions of citizenship and, more significantly, its presumed relation to social theory. Ken Plummer (1995) makes a similar point in discussing the way in which social theorists have ignored and/or marginalised sociological work on lesbian and gay lives, highlighting the study of social movements and the study of identities as classic examples.

What has been termed a 'gender-blind' understanding of citizenship has been challenged by, in particular, feminist analyses (Lister, 1990, 1996, 1997a; Ellis, 1991; Phillips, 1991; Walby, 1994, 1997; Voet, 1998). Thus, for example, Sylvia Walby criticises, along with other aspects of his analysis, Marshall's conception of three stages of the attainment of citizenship on the grounds that it is contradicted by the history of the development of women's rights. That is, 'for first world women political citizenship is typically achieved before civil citizenship, the reverse of the order for men' (Walby, 1997: 171). Underlying this body of work is the assumption that access to citizenship is a highly gendered process and that, despite claims to universality, a particular version of the normal citizen/subject is encoded in dominant discourses of citizenship. Historically, citizenship has been constructed in the 'male image'. Indeed, in ancient Greece, where concepts of civil and political citizenship have their origins, women, along with children and slaves, were excluded from the status of citizenship and, it is argued, have continued to be marginalised in contemporary accounts where the paradigmatic citizen is male (Wilton, 1995). Traditional accounts of citizenship have also been much criticised, again often by feminist writers, for neglecting to consider the relationship of concepts of citizenship with race. This too has become an important area of debate as various writers have outlined how ideas of citizenship are racialised, as well as gendered (Anthias and Yuval-Davis, 1992; Alexander, 1994; Taylor, 1996).

In part reflecting these critiques, the Marshallian notion of citizenship as a set of civil, political and social rights has been more broadly criticised in recent years as much too simplistic. Other definitions have emerged in response to social changes in the family and the economy, in particular the idea of citizenship as social membership, as common membership of a shared community. Bryan Turner (1993a: 2), for example, suggests that citizenship may be defined as 'that set of practices (juridical, political, economic and cultural) which define a person as a competent member of society, and which as consequence shape the flow of resources to persons and social groups'. Within this framework citizenship has been traditionally defined in terms of national identity: citizenship as a set of practices which define social membership in a particular society or nation-state. A citizen is someone who belongs, who is a member of a given nation or a member of a given city or particular region within a nation-state. By implication those who are perceived as not belonging to the city-state or the nation-state can be excluded from the rights of citizenship. They are non-citizens, denied the right of membership of, or belonging to, a particular community with a shared identity.

Such an analysis of citizenship raises the question of how 'nationhood' is defined. Rather than understanding 'nation' as an unproblematic, timeless, given, it is argued that most modern nations are of recent invention.

For example, Benedict Anderson (1991) has argued that nations are 'imagined communities', systems of cultural representation whereby we come to imagine a shared experience of belonging to a particular community. Although the idea of nation as an invention has received wide theoretical attention, there has been relatively little discussion about how assumptions about gender or sexuality are implicated in the representation and creation of such 'imagined communities'. Joanne Sharp (1996: 99), for example, argues that gender difference is in-built into Anderson's notion of nations as imagined communities: 'Anderson's thesis of imagined communities assumes an imagined citizen, and this imagined citizen is gendered . . . Women are scripted into the national imaginary in a different manner. Women are not equal to the nation but symbolic of it.'

Anne McClintock (1995: 353) similarly argues that the concept of nationhood tends to emphasise unity, while manifesting itself as masculine and sanctioning institutionalised gender differences and inequalities:

> All nations depend on powerful constructions of gender . . . No nation in the world gives women and men the same access to the rights and resources of the nation-state. Rather than expressing the flowering into time of the organic essence of a timeless people, nations are contested systems of cultural representation that limit and legitimise peoples' access to the resources of the nation-state.

This idea that nations are (gendered) 'fictions', reproduced across space and time through shared representations and practices, is therefore important to understanding how citizenship status is dependent on practices through which social difference is invented/produced.

Definitions of citizenship as national identity have increasingly been brought into question as a result of social and political changes which have challenged traditional boundaries of nation-states, in particular the process of 'globalisation' as well as changes in eastern and central Europe (Turner, 1993b). New modes of electronic communication also have the potential to encourage the development of shared communities that go beyond regional or national identities. It is changes such as these that have encouraged discussion of whether we might need to think about citizenship developing within the context of larger forms of social membership than nation-states. In a 'post-national' context what becomes the basis for unity or belonging? What is the basis for common membership of a shared community? We might, for instance, consider citizenship at a more global level as grounded in a notion of a union across various nation states, as exists in the 'European Union', or alternatively in terms of religious unity, for example in speaking of the Islamic or Christian 'world'. We may even consider citizenship as social membership in a more fundamental sense, in terms of belonging to the human race – of being a part of 'humanity'. There are already signs of 'rights being linked to the status of human beings (human rights), rather than citizens of the state' (Pakulski, 1997: 84).

In this respect it is important to recognise that 'human being' is a concept which, whilst seemingly abstract and universal, would appear to be, along with 'citizenship' and 'nation', both gendered (Phillips, 1991) and – as will be discussed later – sexualised.

The concept of cultural citizenship has also been part of recent debates on citizenship. Along with civil, political and social aspects of citizenship, it has been suggested that a cultural dimension to citizenship should be included (Turner, 1994; Pakulski, 1997; Stevenson, 2000). Although the concept of cultural rights is not new, it has tended to be understood within broader debates on social rights rather than as a separate dimension of citizenship. Indeed, as Turner (2000) points out, sociologists generally have not addressed the issue of cultural rights and cultural citizenship, despite the fact that these are issues that are intimately connected to the processes of multiculturalism, globalisation and the development of mass education and communication systems. The emergent debates in cultural citizenship seek to establish cultural rights and obligations as a new set of citizenship claims, in particular in the spheres of education and mass communication. Within these debates it is clear that cultural citizenship is still in the process of being defined. It can be conceptualised broadly in terms of 'the capacity to participate effectively, creatively and successfully within a national culture' (Turner, 2000: 12). Cultural rights, institutionalised through the 'cultural industries' such as the mass media, would include the right to participate in the culture of a particular society and to representation in the media and popular culture. In these terms social exclusion can be understood partly in terms of the denial or relative lack of cultural space accorded to certain groups in society. This is recognised by Pakulski (1997), who analyses cultural citizenship in terms of the right to symbolic presence and visibility (vs marginalisation); the right to endignifying representation (vs stigmatisation); and the right to propagation of identity and maintenance of lifestyles (vs assimilation).

In addition to these aspects, a consideration of cultural citizenship also raises questions about the role of the media and popular culture in constructing concepts like 'nation' and 'citizen'. Thus, for instance, writers have pointed to the significance of watching television and reading daily newspapers in the construction of such imagined communities and collective identities (Anderson, 1991).

Finally, it is important to acknowledge a shift in recent years to defining citizenship in terms of consumerism (Evans, 1993). This representation of the citizen as a consumer is related to the emphasis on individual choice and commercialism associated with the free market economy that has dominated government policies in Britain as well as elsewhere. Increasingly, the focus is on the rights of citizens as consumers of goods, commodities and services in the public and private sector. The publication in Britain of the Citizen's Charter (1991) reflected this shift of emphasis, explicitly defining citizenship status in terms of the twin responsibilities of consumer and taxpayer.

This use of citizenship as a concept is about membership based on the consumption of certain lifestyles – consumer communities: 'As consumers we are unique individuals with needs, identities and lifestyles which we express through our purchase of appropriate commodities' (Evans, 1993: 45). However, the ability to exercise the right to consume depends on money or other resources to trade with as a prerequisite for citizen membership. Thus, as with the other forms of citizenship that have been considered, behind the appeal to universal rights lies a 'citizenship machinery' which excludes some from full citizenship For example, as Lister (1990, 1997a) has pointed out in relation to social and political citizenship, women's position in the labour market and the disproportionate role women play in caring work places them at a disadvantage in access to income, limiting their effective participation in consumer citizenship.

These are some of the key ideas about citizenship. In the following section I want to examine these different definitions of citizenship in relation to current debates about sexuality.

Sexuality and citizenship

My starting point is the argument that claims to citizenship status, at least in the west, are closely associated with the institutionalisation of heterosexual as well as male privilege. As I have outlined, within discourses of citizen's rights and the principle of universal citizenship the normal citizen has largely been constructed as male and, albeit much less discussed or acknowledged in the literature, as heterosexual (Warner, 1993a; Phelan, 1995). This latter point is evidenced when the association of heterosexuality with citizenship status, as national identity say, is challenged or threatened. To illustrate this interconnection I will give an example under each of the different definitions of citizenship that I have previously described.

Within the traditional and dominant model of *citizenship as a set of civil, political and social rights* it can be argued that lesbians and gay men are only partial citizens, in so far as they are excluded from certain of these rights. This is evidenced by attempts by lesbian and gay movements and campaigning groups to get equal rights – such as, for example, formal marriages and similar legal status within the armed forces – with heterosexuals. A further aspect of civil citizenship, which relates to Marshall's conception of the right to justice, is the lack of protection in law from discrimination or harassment on the grounds of sexual difference/orientation.

Turning to political citizenship, although lesbians and gay men are not denied the vote and are a part of the electorate, their ability to exercise political power is delimited. The knowledge that someone is lesbian or gay has long been seen as a positive disadvantage, if not a disqualifier, for political office (see Hemmings, 1980), although the fact that a number of 'out' politicians successfully fought seats in the 1997 British general election, and that some of these are now cabinet ministers, does suggest that this may be beginning to change. Although the question of the acceptability of an 'out' Prime Minister or party leader may still be some way off, as the ruminations on Michael Portillo's chances of becoming the next leader of the Conservative party, in the light of his coming out as having previously had gay relationships, helped to demonstrate.

More significantly, the incorporation of lesbian and gay concerns within mainstream politics occurs very rarely at both local and national levels. (For a discussion of some of the factors which influence the reluctance to include such issues at local governmental level see Carabine, 1995.) On the contrary, political parties are often at pains to distance themselves from being seen to be connected with lesbian and gay causes. For example, speaking on the financial support given to lesbian and gay organisations by the National Lottery Charities Board the then British Prime Minster, John Major, commented: 'A small number (of grant awards) do not in my judgement reflect the way Parliament and the public expected lottery money to be spent' (*The Guardian*, 12 June 1996). Similarly the Labour party has at times sought to rid itself of the 'loony left' image which, fuelled by the association of certain Labour councils with lesbian and gay rights, was used by the Conservatives to discredit them (Stacey, 1991; Reinhold, 1994). In a political context when mention of advocacy for lesbians and gay men is perceived as an 'electoral liability', it is far from clear that lesbians and gay men 'can ever expect British parliamentarianism to recognise our demands for civil rights across a wide range of institutions' (Watney, 1991: 175). It is this kind of denial of social constituency that has led some writers to claim that one of the main issues for lesbian and gay politics is to seek public recognition as members of the political community (Phelan, 1995).

Social citizenship tends to be interpreted in terms of the social rights of welfare, and once again lesbians and gay men have highlighted their disadvantaged position. For example, in Britain, as in many other parts of the world, same-sex relationships are not officially recognised or sanctioned; this affects pension rights and inheritance rights, and denies lesbian and gay couples the tax perks to which married couples are often entitled. Other areas where access to full social citizenship is (hetero)sexualised include education, parenting, employment, and housing (Rosenbloom, 1996a).

In most countries, the law and social policy deny lesbians and gay men full citizenship, what Anya Palmer refers to as the 'sexual equivalent of apartheid' (Palmer, 1995: 33). Nevertheless, it is important to recognise that the dominant ideology of liberal citizenship in the west has been receptive to certain lesbian and gay rights claims. This has been primarily through the construction of lesbians and gay men as a minority group, different and less than the norm, but who can't help 'being that way' and therefore should not be discriminated against on that basis. A classic example of this rationale is the 1967 Sexual Offences Act, which decriminalised consensual sexual acts between men over the age of twenty-one in 'private'. The 1967 law reform applied only to England and Wales; such practices remained illegal in Scotland until 1981 and in Northern Ireland until 1982. At the time of writing the current (unequal) legal age of consent for sexual relations between two men stands at eighteen years of age. Having being reduced to 18 from 21 in 1994 under the Criminal Justice Act, it was further decreased to 16 years of age in 1998 as part of the Crime and Disorder Act. However, this was overthrown in the same year by the House of Lords.

Legitimate claims to citizenship are here grounded in essentialist understandings of sexuality and a liberal framework for understanding 'rights'. Indeed, the term commonly used in anti-discrimination laws and equal opportunity policies is 'sexual orientation', itself an essentialist concept. It is also a concept that erases the gendered nature of citizenship in collapsing lesbians and gay men's claim to equal rights under one category.

Lesbians and gay men are, then, seen as deserving of certain rights and protections in many western countries; however, the terms on which these 'rights and protections' are 'granted' are the terms of partial citizenship. Lesbians and gay men are entitled to certain rights of existence, but these are extremely circumscribed, being constructed largely on the condition that they remain in the private sphere and do not seek public recognition or membership in the political community. In this sense lesbians and gay men, though granted certain rights of citizenship, are not a legitimate social constituency.

This is a model of citizenship based on a politics of tolerance and assimilation. Lesbians and gay men are granted the right to be tolerated as long as they stay within the boundaries of that tolerance, whose borders are maintained through a heterosexist public/private divide. Furthermore, the expectation is that lesbians and gay men should remain minority groups. As 'responsible/good citizens', they should not increase in numbers either through, in the words of section 28 of the 1988 Local Government Act, 'promoting homosexuality' or by raising children who, it is feared, might grow up to have lesbian or gay relationships themselves (Sedgwick, 1993).

This construction of lesbian and gay relations as belonging to the private sphere does suggest a difficulty in addressing citizenship using conventional frameworks that focus almost exclusively on participation in the public. The role of the public/private structuring of social relations in the exclusion of women from full access to the rights of citizenship has been highlighted by feminist theory (Lister, 1996, 1997a; Walby, 1997). Such analyses have critiqued traditional conceptions of citizenship which use the private/public divide to draw a boundary around what can usefully be discussed in relation to claims to citizenship. For most social and political theorists, as Sylvia Walby remarks: 'The concept of citizenship depends upon the public sphere; the term has no significant meaning in the private' (Walby, 1997: 176). Taken to its logical conclusion, this would mean that social relations in the private sphere are considered to be of little or no relevance to understanding citizenship.

There is an interesting tension in the use of the term 'private' to demarcate the boundaries of (homo)sexual citizenship. Whilst lesbians and gay men are banished from the public to the private realm, they are, in many senses, simultaneously excluded from the private where this is conflated with 'the family'. As Alan Sinfield argues (1995), the state withholds various rights of citizenship, 'especially in familial and quasi-familial contexts (partnerships, childbearing, entertainment in the home)', which are facets of the private sphere where lesbians and gay men are supposedly 'licensed'. Thus, notions of privacy, as well as of public space, are exclusionary, the right to privacy being primarily a right of legally married heterosexuals. In this sense, both the public and the private need to be understood as sexualised concepts.

If we take citizenship to mean *social membership of a nation-state*, it would appear that even though lesbians and gay men are legal citizens of different 'nations', they are normally excluded from the construction of 'nation' and nationality. According to Taylor (1996: 162), citizenship carries with it:

> ... not just the formal membership of a nation state, but a whole set of socio-economic and ideological practices associated with nationalism. These amount to mechanisms of exclusion and inclusion of particular groups and categories of individual. These have included, most notably, those without property, women, racialised groups and the differently abled, children and lesbians and gay men.

In many if not most nation states, citizenship is associated with a naturalised heterosexuality. As David Sibley (1995: 108) suggests in relation to Britain, we can recognise a number of 'key sites of nationalistic sentiment, including the family, the suburb and the countryside, all of which implicitly exclude black people, gays and nomadic minorities from the nation'. That is, it is implicitly the heterosexual (as well as white and non-nomadic) citizen who symbolises an imagined national community and underlies the construction of a notion of a shared collective national identity.

This is evidenced in a variety of ways. For example, the term 'homosexual' has long been associated with the charge of treachery and treason (Edelman, 1992), usually 'justified' with the claim that homosexuals are liable to blackmail (Ellis, 1991). This image of 'the homosexual' as a potential traitor has been used to signal fear of a threat to national security. Hence, this particular historical construction of homosexuality, based upon a presumed risk of betrayal, undermines the position of 'homosexuals' as legitimate members of a particular nation-state.

In Britain, homosexuality has been perceived as a threat to the nation-state in other respects. A common version of this is the claim that the, preferably married, heterosexual nuclear family, which is frequently conceptualised as both natural and necessary for the good of the nation, is being undermined and destroyed by the emergence of different sexualities and family networks. The traditional family therefore needs defending against lesbians and gay men and other groups, such as single mothers, who supposedly pose a threat to it (Stacey, 1991; Thomson, 1994). Appealing to such arguments, some politicians and policy-makers have justified the introduction of laws that are hostile to lesbian and gay relationships. For example, David Wiltshire, the member of parliament responsible for introducing Section 28 of the 1988 Local Government Act which outlawed the 'promotion' of homosexuality in local authority schools, claimed that his actions were motivated by the principle of supporting normality: 'Homosexuality is being promoted at the ratepayers' expense, and the traditional family as we know it is under attack' (*The Guardian*, 12 December 1987).

The exclusion of lesbians and gay men from the meaning of 'family', thus reinscribing it as a heterosexualised concept, is evidenced in the government's definition of homosexuality as a 'pretended family relationship' in Section 28. The discussion around Section 28 also raised other issues of citizenship and its relationship to heterosexuality, where citizenship can be interpreted as social rights expressed through social policy. Although the linking of social rights to welfare policy has been critiqued by feminists and others, it is nevertheless important to recognise, in the arguments of David Wiltshire and others in support of Section 28, that not only is it implied that lesbians and gay men are not ratepayers, but also that they are not deserving of social services funded by local authorities (Carabine, 1996a, b).

Elsewhere, the State may also act to construct the nation as heterosexual. For example, speaking at the opening of the Zimbabwean International Book Fair in August 1995, from which the organisation Gays and Lesbians of Zimbabwe had been prevented from participating, the then President of Zimbabwe, Robert Mugabe, made an outspoken attack on lesbians and gay men. In condemning homosexuality and lesbianism, Mugabe claimed that such practices were 'un-African'. This was a view echoed in newspaper reports at the time which emphasised that homosexuality was a 'foreign idea' and that those who engaged in such practices were the victims of cultural imperialism (War on Want, 1996: 9).

Other examples of attempts to deny lesbians and gay men inclusion within national boundaries include the attempts of the United States government, in the aftermath of the second world war, to control homosexual behaviour. As Lee Edelman (1992: 269) outlines: 'those efforts responded to the widespread perception of gay sexuality as an alien infestation, an unnatural because un-American practice, resulting from the entanglement with foreign countries – and foreign nationals – during the war'. A more recent attempt to confound the categories of nationalism and (hetero)sexuality is evidenced in the resistance offered by the Romanian government to campaigns to decriminalise same-sex relations (for an account see Baciu et al., 1996). Thus, for instance, speaking at the CEPES-UNESCO Conference in Bucharest on the justification of homosexuality as a human right in 1995, a representative of the Romanian Ministry of Justice asserted that homosexuality was not Romanian: 'the nature of the Romanian does not admit this unnatural law [homosexuality], this immorality' (Report of the Conference Proceedings, 31 May 1995).

Related to this, it would seem that very often the role of sexuality in the construction of concepts of nationality is not merely linked to heterosexuality, but to a form of heterosexuality that is to varying extents anti-gay and lesbian. Speaking of nationalisms in the United States, Henry Louis Gates Jr claims that: 'national identity became sexualised in the 1960s, in such a way as to engender a curious subterranean connection between homophobia and nationalism' (Gates, 1993: 234). Similarly, as I have already discussed, in the UK homosexuality, but more especially homosexual family relationships, has been perceived as a threat to the nation-state (Reinhold, 1994). Political contestation of (American) nationality has been apparent within lesbian/feminism and, more recently, queer politics: for example, Lesbian Nation (Johnson, 1973), Bitch Nation (quoted in Berlant and Freeman, 1993) and Queer Nation (Berube and Escoffier, 1991).

This association between homophobia and nationalism, as Gates puts it, may be interpreted as politically expedient in contexts where traditional concepts of national boundaries are being challenged, with the consequent threat to the construction of national identities and national publics. That is, if we regard citizenship as a set of social practices which 'define social membership in a society which is highly differentiated both in its culture and social institutions, and where social solidarity can only be based upon general and universalistic standards' (Turner, 1993a: 5). In such contexts heterosexuality, conceptualised as universal, natural and normal, may indeed serve as an important unifying principle, a means of achieving social solidarity among different and differentiated groups.

In so far as the nation-state is constructed as heterosexual, this does not mean that all forms of heterosexuality are necessarily regarded equally. It is heterosexuality as marriage and the traditional, middle-class nuclear family that is commonly held up as a model of good citizenship, necessary for ensuring national security and a stable social order. By implication, other forms of heterosexuality, for instance young women who are single mothers, imperil the nation. Also, as I have already indicated, the association of heterosexuality and nation also intersects with concepts of race. Historically it is a white heterosexuality which has been privileged in the British context, and we can find many examples, both in the past and more recently, of the construction of black as well as working-class heterosexual relations as a supposed threat to the nation-state (Alexander, 1994; Williams, 1989).

Heterosexuality is often implicit in the 'right' to other forms of social membership, for instance based on religious or ethnic identifications. For example, in 1995 the organisers of the annual St Patrick's Day Parade in Boston successfully sought a court order banning Irish-American lesbians and gay men from marching in the parade under their own banner. In

previous years, lesbians and gays had also been denied the right to march
as a distinct contingent in the St Patrick's Day Parade in New York City.
Such controversies were essentially battles over the definition of Irishness
(and what it means to be Irish-American) and the inclusion or exclusion
from such membership. As Tim Davis (1995: 297, 301) states, those in opposition to protests by lesbians and gay men at their exclusion saw this as 'an
affront to their own identity, defined as Irish-American, Catholic and heterosexual . . . Symbolically, the very existence of alternative sexualities
was a threat to the locally prevailing notion of what it meant to be Irish'.

Similarly, writing about the (hetero)sexualisation of black identities in
the USA, Goldsby (1993: 122–3) claims that:

> This ideology [of American slavery] privileged and enforced heterosexuality as
> authentically 'black' because the regulation of black reproductive rights
> demanded this definition . . . No wonder, then, that black homophobes charac-
> teristically malign homosexuality as a 'white thing', as a relationship that, by
> definition, re-enacts slavery itself.

Examples of similar exclusionary processes can also be found in the UK,
as is illustrated below.

> Last month Brian Gordon, a member of the Board of Jewish Deputies, attacked
> a fellow member for addressing the World Congress of Gay and Lesbian Jewish
> Organisations in Brussels: 'Their [gays and lesbians] activities have no more
> legitimacy under a Jewish banner than, say, pork-eating.' (*The Guardian*, 8 July
> 1995: 7)

Finally, if we take citizenship as social membership to mean 'humanity',
belonging to what is called the human 'race', even then it can be argued
that citizenship is premised within heterosexuality. Historically, there is a
long tradition of understanding what it is to be human in essentialist
terms. The term human is commonly used to refer to group membership
based on biological criteria; the belonging to a particular species. Although
this way of thinking continues to exert influence, within social theory the
view has emerged that humanity should be thought of as socially constructed. In other words, we become human through the process of social
interaction whereby the categorisations 'person' and 'human' are attributed to individuals (Shotter, 1993).

This is significant in terms of understandings of citizenship as social
membership, for it suggests that, even at the most fundamental levels of
social inclusion, the boundaries of membership are a cultural construction. Thus, it is possible for people to be constructed as 'other' through
relegation to the borders of human existence. One example of this process
of dehumanisation is through the claiming of animal attributes for certain
groups, thereby legitimising exclusionary practices on the grounds that
they are less than human. This has been particularly evident in relation to
the representation of colonised people, especially Australian Aborigines

and African slaves, as well as other groups such as Jews and Gypsy communities (Sibley, 1995).

Such dehumanising processes of exclusion can also be observed in relation to gender and sexuality. In so far as women have often been identified as closer to 'nature', they have also been at risk of exclusion from 'civilised' society. The interaction of gender with race, ethnicity and class has been important in this respect; it is particular groups of women, for example black and working-class women, who have traditionally been represented as closest to nature and therefore lower ranking in a 'hierarchy of being' (Sibley, 1995). Interestingly, whereas in the example cited above the processes of dehumanisation operate through the exclusion of those deemed to be closest to nature and, therefore, more 'animal-like', in the case of sexuality it also operates to exclude those who are not a part of nature so defined (as heterosexual), who are constructed as un-natural (as homosexual). In other words, in this case disenfranchisement is facilitated by a complex construction of homosexuality as both 'unnatural' and as too close to a state of nature, expressed in the stereotypic representation of homosexuals as only interested in sex. The naturalisation of heterosexuality not only serves to dehumanise lesbians and gay men, it also provides the context in which the right to existence of lesbians and gay men may be questioned. Indeed, the connection between (hetero)sexuality and humanity is reflected in those who would question the right to life of lesbians and gay men (Richardson and May, 1999). In some parts of the world such views are institutionalised through laws which recommend the death penalty for homosexuality; in countries where homosexuality is legally 'tolerated' targeted violent attacks on lesbians and gay men have led to killings (see War on Want, 1996; Amnesty International, 1997).

At an institutional level, processes of de-personalisation and de-humanisation can have important implications for access to rights. For example, despite appeals to universalism in speaking of basic human rights, conventional human rights frameworks have been selective in their use of this term. The women's human rights movement has demonstrated a number of different ways in which the dominant human rights discourse fails to address human rights abuses against women (Peters and Wolper, 1995; Rosenbloom, 1996b). Despite this, there is growing acceptance of women's rights as human rights; where there has been less progress is in addressing human rights violations against lesbians and gay men (Rosenbloom, 1996a). The struggle to get lesbian and gay rights recognised as human rights reveals the way in which the concept of 'human rights' has historically developed in ways that have failed to recognise many of the abuses perpetrated against certain social groups. It also raises the question of whether such discourses serve not only to authorise which human rights claims are recognised as basic to humanity, but also to actively shape the social meaning and construction of what it means to be a 'person' who is recognised, to a greater or lesser extent, as 'human'. In this sense we can understand the demand for lesbian and gay rights as a struggle not only about rights *per se*, but also about what those rights signify; as 'a struggle for membership in the human community' (Herman, 1994: 19).

Definitions of citizenship in terms of *cultural citizenship* also raise questions about the sexualised, as well as gendered, nature of social inclusion and exclusion and access to 'rights and entitlements'. (For a more detailed discussion of the relationship between sexuality and cultural citizenship see Richardson, 2000a.) Historically, lesbian and gay relationships have been systematically denied and ignored in popular culture, existing only in covert or disguised articulations or, in the rare cases where lesbian and gay themes are made explicit, in highly negative and unidimensional representations. For example, in a comprehensive survey of images of lesbians and gays in films Vito Russo (1981) found only a handful of examples, 'all of which only figure momentarily in the films and some of which you could easily not see as representing gays or lesbians at all' (Dyer, 1990: 7). Critiques of such stereotyped and negative representations have been an important concern of both feminist and gay movements since the 1970s. Although rarely expressed in terms of rights to cultural citizenship, such resistance has led to the production of more positive images and texts in a range of cultural sites.

In recent years, there has been a gradual increase in the participation and representation of lesbians and gay men in the media and popular culture, perhaps most noticeably on television, for instance in primetime 'soaps' such as *Brookside* and *EastEnders*, in Britain, and *Friends* and *Ellen*, in the United States. The significance attached to such sociological shifts is that whereas previously the focus of lesbian and gay representation was largely subcultural, as a result of cultural efforts by and for lesbians and gay men themselves, it is now increasingly mainstream (Cottingham, 1996). At one level, it is possible to regard the inclusion of lesbian and gay images and narratives in dominant culture as constituting an important form of social recognition and access to cultural citizenship. However, such an interpretation is questioned by those who argue that the greater visibility of lesbians and gay men in mainstream cultural life is less an acknowledgement of cultural rights than evidence of a process of commodification and assimilation into dominant culture (see, for example, Clark, 1993; Torres, 1993; Cottingham, 1996). That is, cultural space is still normatively constructed as heterosexual. This is evidenced in responses to greater coverage of lesbians and gay issues in the media. For example, one newspaper editorial complained: 'Radio Five is devoting a weekly programme to homosexuals and lesbians. Why should this minority get so much special attention?' (*The Daily Star*, 15 March 1994, quoted in Sanderson, 1995: 34).

Paradoxically, it is when we come to define *citizenship as consumerism* that non-heterosexuals seem to be most acceptable as citizens, as consumers with identities and lifestyles which are expressed through purchasing goods, communities and services. This has often been referred to as the power of the 'pink pound', although this commercialisation has been predominantly western and male. However, in the last few years there have been signs of a new commercialism associated with lesbians as consumers (Woods, 1995).

What are the links between rights as consumers and other citizenship rights? Some regard this new 'commercial power' of (some) lesbians and gay men as productively linked to access to other forms of citizenship, such as the development of social rights and entitlements. As David Evans (1993: 2) states:

> Sexual minorities have progressively become distinct, formal though not neces-
> sarily formally clear, participants with the citizenship of developed capitalism,
> whilst simultaneously becoming, not surprisingly *for of course the two are closely
> connected*, legitimate consumers of sexual and sexualised commodities marketed
> specifically for their use and enjoyment. (My italics)

For others, however, the impact of the increasing commercialisation and commodification of gay and lesbian 'identities and lifestyles' is viewed much more critically (Woods, 1995). For example, Jon Johnson points out that 'you cannot "consume" yourself out of being sacked purely because of your sexuality, being demonised because you are a lesbian teacher or jailed for having sex at the age of 17' (Johnson, 1994: 14).

Also, as with the other aspects of citizenship that have been considered, access to the right to consume is both a gendered and sexualised experi-ence. Lesbians and gay men may be free to consume but only within certain spatial and cultural boundaries. The boundaries of citizenship as consumerism are the limits to where, when and how we can consume les-bian and gay 'lifestyles'. That is the boundaries of (heterosexual) tolerance and of 'public spaces' in which consumer communities can exercise their right to consume. Jon Binnie (1995) illustrates this in his discussion of the development of gay commercial districts in London and Amsterdam. It is also important to recognise, in considering the role of the market in sexual cultures, that consumer citizenship is significantly structured by access to time and money. This is a point that has been made earlier in terms of the limitations on women's effective participation in various forms of citizen-ship (Lister, 1996).

Conclusion

In this chapter I have outlined various notions of citizenship and tried to show how heterosexuality is constructed as a necessary if not sufficient basis for full citizenship. In this sense we can talk of the sexualisation of cit-izenship, rather as others have talked of the 'racialisation' of citizenship (Taylor, 1996) and of how citizenship is gendered (Lister, 1990, 1997a; Walby, 1994, 1997). More specifically, I have highlighted how certain forms of citizenship status are closely associated with the hegemonic form of heterosexuality, as 'marriage and the family' (VanEvery, 1996), which is institutionalised and dependent for its meanings on gender divisions.

The focus of this chapter has been on the issues surrounding lesbian and gay claims to citizenship. The points that it raises, however, demand that we consider more fully the implications for other sexualities, including different heterosexualities. Little attention has traditionally been given to theorising heterosexuality (Richardson, 1996a). Such examinations would extend the process of deconstructing a monolithic understanding of heterosexuality and contribute to recent debates on (hetero)sexuality, in particular within feminist and queer theory. (Some of these debates are explored in Part 1.) In addition to addressing these and related questions in developing our understanding of how concepts of citizenship are grounded in normative assumptions about sexuality, there is also a need to examine the different meanings attached to the emergence of a new idea: that of sexual or intimate citizenship. This will be the central theme of the next chapter.

5

EXTENDING CITIZENSHIP?

In this chapter I want to look at how the concept of sexual citizenship is in the process of being constructed and, associated with this, to go on to draw out the implications of these debates for the (re)framing of claims for 'sexual rights' in Chapter 6.

It is clear that the idea of sexual citizenship is work in progress, still very much in the process of being elaborated and defined. This is likely to be no easy task, given that both 'citizenship' and 'sexual' are ambiguous terms whose meanings are contested. There is a historical specificity to the question 'what is sexual citizenship?' in a rather different sense. The 'sexual citizen' who lays claim to certain rights in the name of a particular sexual constituency is itself a relatively recent historical phenomenon. It is a concept dependent on a culturally and historically specific idea of sexuality as a core characteristic of personhood, which allows the development of a certain subjectivity whereby those belonging to 'sexual minorities' are able to: 'define themselves both in terms of personal and collective identities by their sexual attributes, and to claim recognition, rights and respect as a consequence' (Weeks, 1998: 36).

Attempts to theorise the relationship between sexuality and citizenship are not only contingent on definitions of sexuality. As I suggested in Chapter 4, they have also been shaped by the history of ideas about citizenship. Until recently, there has been an almost exclusive focus on 'the public' in rights discourse, with issues of citizenship constituted as located in the public realm. In contrast to this, and despite the multiple meanings accorded to it as a concept, sexuality is commonly understood as being a personal and private matter, linked with the body, the individual and concepts of nature. Although the notion of a public/private divide has been subject to fierce criticism, especially within feminist theory, it is important nevertheless to recognise the continuing ideological and normative power of this conceptual division (Cooper, 1993). Thus, to discuss sexuality in terms of claims to citizenship may be seen as invalid on the grounds that social relations in the private sphere are considered to be of little or no relevance to understanding citizenship, which focuses on participation in the public. In this sense, the idea of sexual citizenship can be considered to be 'a contradiction in terms' (Weeks, 1998). There is, however, an interesting paradox here. I have suggested that the exclusion of sexuality as a legitimate issue for citizenship can be understood to derive in large part from its construction as private; yet it is 'the right to privacy' which has often been the basis for the recognition of citizenship claims in relation to sexuality.

Bearing these issues in mind, my aim is not to try to provide an exhaustive review of what sexual citizenship might mean. Rather, my focus here is to explore some of the questions raised by this newly emerging body of work, through an examination of the ways in which different writers have addressed the question of sexual citizenship. Viewed in this way, I will be able to avoid a narrowing of the debate around questions of definition and focus on the wider implications of the application of the concept to social institutions and practices. Also, by focusing on the kinds of debates mobilised in attempts to define sexual citizenship, I want to highlight some of the possible problems associated with such a concept.

What is meant by sexual or intimate citizenship?

Surveying the literature, it seems that a broad distinction can be made between analyses which place greater emphasis on the discussion of rights *per se* and struggles for rights acquisition, and those which are concerned with wider social and theoretical implications. These two approaches, although not exclusionary, reflect somewhat different forms of usage of the term 'sexual citizenship'. In a narrow sense, it may be used to refer specifically to the sexual rights granted or denied to individuals and social groups. A central question that is addressed is 'How are we entitled to express ourselves sexually?' In this sense we may, like Evans (1993), whose work is discussed below, conceptualise sexual citizenship in terms of varying degrees of access to a set of rights to sexual expression and consumption and, also, to assumed responsibilities and obligations. We can also think about sexual citizenship in a much broader sense, however, as: a new form of belonging (Weeks, 1998); a new transformation of democratic practice in interpersonal relationships (Giddens, 1992); a new politics of everyday life (Plummer, 1995) – to name just a few possibilities.

One of the first to claim to address citizenship and its relation to sexuality was David Evans in his book *Sexual Citizenship* (1993). However, on close inspection one finds that a great deal of this book is taken up with a review of the historical development of sexual categories and contemporary sexual politics, rather than an exposition of a notion of sexual citizenship. Indeed, surprisingly perhaps for a book with this title, nowhere does Evans offer an explicit, clear and succinct definition of the term 'sexual citizenship'. Rather, one has to go looking for such meanings. In his concern to examine what he terms the 'material construction' of sexual citizenship, the (critical) approach Evans takes is to stress the idea of citizenship as consumerism. It is here, embedded within this broad

...at one finds some clarification of a concept of sexual citizen-
...vans (1993: 64) states that: 'sexual citizenship involves partial,
...orimarily leisure and lifestyle membership'.

...vides examples of what he delineates as different *forms* of
....ship, including the experience of male homosexuals, bisexuals, transvestites, transsexuals and children. Of the latter, he asks: 'Can
children in modern societies be legitimately regarded in any sense as
sexual citizens? Do they have sexual rights? Do they consume, or are they
merely consumed sexual commodities?' (Evans, 1993: 209). In posing such
questions Evans highlights the right of consent to sexual behaviours as
basic to sexuality as citizenship status, alongside a notion of the citizen as
consumer.

Elsewhere, Evans explores the moral dimensions of sexual citizenship.
As a number of writers, such as Bryan Turner (2000), have argued, citizenship is closely associated with ideas about moral behaviour: what is and is
not considered fit and proper conduct. The continued belief among certain
individuals and social groups that engaging in particular forms of sexual
conduct is immoral if not criminal behaviour is clearly relevant here. For
example, Evans (1993: 100) describes 'male homosexual citizenship' in the
following terms:

> . . . male homosexual citizenship is predicated on the conjunction of individual
> consenting adult freedoms including, indeed particularly, those of a consuming
> market, and the reinforced stigma of immorality which bans this citizen from the
> 'moral community' and polices him into privacy.

For Evans, then, sexual citizenship is primarily constructed as membership of sexual communities, with rights and privileges determined by their
relative moral worth and status as consumers.

Evans' work is useful in developing a framework for understanding
how formalised degrees of citizenship are accorded to categories of sexual
difference and, also, what might be termed 'sexual rights'. However, a distinction can be made between his approach and that taken by other writers
whose interests are to rethink citizenship and/or sexuality more generally.
This broader focus includes the work of Anthony Giddens (1992) on the
democratisation of intimate relationships, which he takes to include sexual
relations. In exploring the values of the intimate sphere, Giddens argues
that relationships built on a sense of equal vulnerability and mutual trust,
respect and care, where there is an absence of coercion or violence, are
democratic. He uses the term 'pure relationship', defined as 'a relationship
of sexual and emotional equality' (Giddens, 1992: 2), to refer to the democratic restructuring of intimacy. Giddens suggests that it is lesbians and gay
men who are the pioneers in this respect, more likely to be living this kind
of relationship than are women and men in heterosexual relationships. In
this sense, although he does not talk about categories of sexual citizenship
in the way that Evans (1993) does, Giddens 'nevertheless implies a link

between the historical attainment of forms of sexual or intimate democracy and different sexualities' (Richardson, 2000b: 278).

Giddens claims that it is through a 'transformation of intimacy', in which so far women are deemed to have played a major part, that there exists the possibility of a radical transformation of the personal sphere. This, he argues, will have consequences for wider social and political citizenship. Indeed, Giddens (1992: 195) states that: 'The advancement of self-autonomy in the context of pure relationships is rich with implications for democratic practice in the larger community.'

Conversely, Giddens also claims that democratisation in the public domain shapes democratic practice in personal relationships – what he terms emotional democracy but others might prefer to call sexual or intimate citizenship. As an illustrative example, it is the case that women's social and legal status as citizens has been significant in seeking to establish the right to freedom from coercive and abusive relationships both within and outside of marriage. We can therefore infer from Giddens' analysis that sexuality and citizenship are seen as linked through a dynamic process, whereby citizenship status has implications for how sexual relations are ordered and vice versa.

The idea that there is a dynamic relationship between democratic norms and sexuality is not new. It can be found in the work of earlier generations of writers such as, for example, Wilhelm Reich (1962) and Herbert Marcuse (1970) who, influenced by Marxism and Freudian psychoanalytical theory, both believed that social reform and sexual liberation were interconnected. According to their interpretation, modern societies depend upon a high level of sexual repression; liberating erotic potential is a prerequisite to a more civilised, egalitarian society. Such ideas have also been apparent in early 'second wave' feminist accounts. Many feminists in the 1970s made a connection between the assertion of women's right to sexual freedom and pleasure and women's liberation, believing that (re)discovering a sexuality that had been previously suppressed and denied them would empower women and help bring about equality between the sexes (for an account see Segal, 1987a; Jackson and Scott, 1996). With hindsight, many feminists have since questioned such an assumption (see Jeffreys, 1990, 1994), although there are echoes of such beliefs still to be found in the work of a few contemporary feminists (for example, Segal, 1994, 1999).

A concern with the relationship between citizenship and intimacy can also be found in the work of other sociologists. For example, Ken Plummer proposes that a 'fourth notion of citizenship' is added to those based on the traditional Marshallian model of civic, political and social rights (Marshall, 1950): the idea of 'intimate citizenship'. By his own admission, Plummer (1995: 17) offers a very 'loose definition' of what he means by intimate citizenship. It is, he argues:

> . . . a cluster of emerging concerns over the rights to choose what we do with our

bodies, our feelings, our identities, our relationships, our genders, our eroti-cisms and our representations.

Although Plummer opts to rethink citizenship through notions of 'the intimate' rather 'the sexual', it is clear that the spheres he mentions cut across the terrain of sexual relations. Much of this new space of citizenship that he proposes is concerned with 'those matters which relate to our most intimate desires, pleasures and ways of being in the world' (Weeks, 1995: 121). Although it need not necessarily be so: in contemporary western societies notions of intimate desires, pleasures and ways of being in the world are commonly interpreted through the frame of sexuality. In this context, it is therefore all the more significant that these formulations of new spaces of citizenship emphasise intimacy and not sex.

This approach is also echoed in Jeffrey Weeks' desire to broaden the interpretation of existing notions of citizenship, based on a recognition and validation of difference. This requires, he argues, that we explore the values of the intimate sphere, the domain of 'intimate citizenship', for: 'It is here that the life experiments promoted by contemporary sexual move-ments and communities give rise to claims for the recognition of certain rights of everyday life, the necessary complement of a politics of solidarity, respect and diversity' (Weeks, 1995: 123).

A different conception of sexual citizenship can be found in the work of those who are critical both of a 'rights-based' reading of the term and of an emphasis upon intimacy. For some, there is a concern that these kinds of formulations, whilst they emphasise love, domestic partnerships and friendship, do not give adequate consideration to sex. Thus, for example, writers such as David Bell and Jon Binnie are concerned to 'bring in the erotic and embodied dimensions excluded in many discussions of citizen-ship' (Bell and Binnie, 2000).

Another important aspect of such critiques is a contestation of the locus of sexual citizenship. The issue of the relationship between intimacy and privacy is a complex one (Squires, 1994), and although some theorists insist on a necessary relationship between the two, no such simple reading can be made from Plummer's vision of intimate citizenship. Nevertheless, it can be argued that one of the effects of discussions of sexual citizenship which focus on the 'private space' of intimate relations, and of accounts of the rights and freedoms granted to particular categories of sexual citizen which are frequently based upon privacy-based rights claims, is a (re)pri-vatisation of sexual citizenship. Following this argument, and against a construction of sexual citizenship as located in the private, there has been an attempt by various writers to focus on the meaning of sexual citizenship in the *public* sphere which, in some instances, incorporates a concern to 'put back the sex in sexual citizenship'. For example, David Bell (1995) has written about public sex in the context of developing notions of sexual citizenship.

This discussion touches on a tension, referred to earlier, in bringing together the two terms sexuality and citizenship. On the one hand, we can understand the expansion of the concept of citizenship to include sexual or intimate citizenship as a radical move, since such issues have previously been excluded from discourses of citizenship on the grounds of their being private rather than public matters. Here, then, we can read the work on sexual or intimate citizenship as a radical attempt to inscribe the private as a space for a politics of citizenship. On the other hand, the recognition of citizenship claims in relation to sexuality on the basis of a 'right to privacy' represents a form of sexual politics that has a long history both in Europe and the United States. Moreover, it is primarily through utilising such discourses of citizenship that rights movements have been successful in gaining specific rights and freedoms, much more so than more radical campaigns (Cooper, 1993). This, as it is often termed, integrationist or assimilationist approach to sexual citizenship is regarded as reformist rather than radical, especially by lesbian/feminist and queer movements where the focus is upon critiquing and destabilising the public/private binary. Thus, in the context of discourses of sexuality, the linking of 'the private' to sexual citizenship can be read as problematic, leading some writers to claim that a more radical focus is to rethink citizenship through a resistance to privacy and an examination of democratic sexual citizenship enacted in public spaces (see, for example, Ingram et al., 1997).

In the following section I will go on to examine in more detail some of the ways in which feminist work on sexuality and on citizenship has, or has not, engaged with this new area of analysis: sexual or intimate citizenship.

Feminist responses

The relative lack of attention to sexuality in debates about citizenship is not restricted to 'mainstream' accounts, but is also a feature of much feminist writing in this area. For example, Ruth Lister, in her book *Citizenship: Feminist Perspectives*, asserts that historically women's exclusion from citizenship in western societies is intimately linked to an 'identification of women with the body, nature and sexuality' (Lister, 1997a: 70). Although she recognises that issues such as pornography, sexual violence and harassment, and reproductive rights have ramifications for the question of women's citizenship, and also acknowledges that the language of citizenship is increasingly shaping the theorisation of lesbian and gay politics, these aspects are not systematically explored.

A similar picture is evident in a recent collection devoted to women and citizenship, whose contributors usefully examine a range of important issues, including constructions of citizenship in relation to disability, gender, race and ethnicity (Feminist Review, 1997). The issue of sexuality, however, is barely mentioned, except in passing as an aspect of difference (see, for example, Lister, 1997b: 37) or as a specific example to illustrate a more general point (see, for example, Yuval-Davis, 1997: 17). Zillah Eisenstein hints at more when, commenting on the visions of democracy at the UN Fourth World Conference on Women at Beijing in 1995, she describes a notion of sexual rights which encompasses women's control over their bodies as a fundamental human right. She goes on to state that: 'This notion of sexual rights rewrites rights discourse. It redefines the relationship between public and private life because sexual rights break through the borders of patriarchal citizenry' (Eisenstein, 1997: 161). What Eisenstein seems to be implying is that the issue of sexuality is, or ought to be, of central concern to a feminist critique of models of citizenship. However, there is little or no analysis of what this statement might mean beyond an acknowledgement that 'issues of sexual freedom, as distinguished from sexual rights, have yet to be articulated' (Eisenstein, 1997: 163).

At one level, the relative absence of sexuality from feminist analyses of citizenship is surprising given that from the nineteenth century to the 1990s, feminists have engaged in a whole variety of debates and campaigns around specific rights connected with sexuality. The point might also be made that, beyond a focus on rights claims, debates on citizenship and sexuality cut across one another's intellectual terrain and that this would facilitate a recognition of the interconnections between the two. Commenting on the re-emergence of the notion of citizenship in political, academic and popular discourses in the 1980s, David Bell and John Binnie would appear to offer some support for this position in claiming that 'the field of sexual politics in its broadest sense seemed to embody many of the debates activated by a focus on citizenship (and vice versa), with its crossing of boundaries between the public and the private, between the collective and the individual, between entitlements and duties' (Bell and Binnie, 2000).

In the introduction to this chapter, I suggested that we might understand the failure to theorise the relationship between sexuality and citizenship more generally in terms of the public/private divide and how this maps onto the concepts of citizenship and sexuality, respectively. The question of why sexuality has not been a focus of attention in much feminist work on citizenship would seem to demand a different explanation, given that feminists have critiqued the private/public divide to demarcate what can be usefully discussed in relation to citizenship (Lister, 1990, 1996, 1997a, b; Voet, 1998; Walby, 1997).

One possible explanation for the relative lack of attention to sexuality in feminist critiques of models of citizenship is that it is gender that has been privileged. Feminists have identified the 'gender-blindness' of most theories of citizenship and, drawing on this, reconceptualised notions of the 'citizen' as well as the boundary between the public and the private. As a consequence of this focus on the gender omissions of 'mainstream' accounts, and the concern to develop new frameworks that acknowledge the gendered nature of citizenship, there is a risk that other dimensions of difference, such as sexuality, may be ignored or marginalised. (A useful parallel can be made here with explanations of the omission of sexuality in feminists' critiques of social policy; for a review, see Carabine, 1996b.) This is partly a reflection of a tendency to treat categories such as gender, race, disability and sexuality as discrete issues, *and* the lack of a sufficiently developed theoretical machinery which allows us to articulate the complex processes by which these categories are mutually constitutive of each other (see Bhavnani, 1997).

In the case of sexuality this is further complicated by the interlinking of gender with sexuality in feminist accounts, albeit in differing ways, which may result in sexuality not being identified as a distinct issue for analysis where the focus is on gender. This is compounded by the fact that, within social and political theory more generally sexuality has rarely been acknowledged or analysed as a basis of social divisions (Richardson, 1996a). Having said this, it is the case that attempts to rectify this have come primarily from feminist and, more recently, queer theory. However, whereas the vast majority of work on (hetero)sexuality as a social institution stems from radical feminist approaches, a great deal of feminist work on citizenship has developed out of a socialist feminist tradition which has tended to place less significance on sexuality in analyses of patriarchal processes or 'gender-regimes' (Walby, 1990, 1997). This may provide another possible explanation for the omission of sexuality in some feminists' critiques of citizenship.

In addition to asking to what extent feminist work on citizenship has considered sexuality, we can also ask the question in the reverse direction. How far have debates around sexual citizenship incorporated feminist concerns? One important parallel to be drawn with feminist work, it seems, is the question of whether we are encouraged to theorise sexual or intimate citizenship in terms of universalistic notions of 'the sexual citizen' or to embrace a sexually (and gender) differentiated model which would allow for a specific notion of, say, 'lesbian citizenship', 'gay citizenship' 'queer citizenship', 'transgender citizenship', 'bisexual citizenship', 'S/M citizenship' and so on. Within feminist perspectives, this issue of universality versus differentiation has been a central concern in relation to the relationship between gender and citizenship. The question is whether acknowledgement of the gendered nature of citizenship strengthens the notion of universalism through such incorporation, or whether we need a differentiated notion of citizenship. (For a full discussion, see Lister, 1997a, who discusses the problematic nature of this strategy of arguing simultaneously for equality and the recognition of difference.)

Evans (1993) and others, including some feminists (see below for a discussion of lesbian citizenship) have developed a differentiated model of sexual citizenship. In contrast to this, the 'equal rights' campaigns of some lesbian and gay movements, for example, can be seen as illustrative of a more universalistic model of sexual citizenship, based on the principle of equality with heterosexuals, rather than a particularistic claim based on their sexual difference. This sexuality-neutral rather than sexuality-differentiated model of sexual citizenship is also evident in recent work on sexual citizenship. For example, Jeffrey Weeks (1998: 35), refers to the 'sexual citizen' (or would-be sexual citizen) in the following very broad terms:

> The sexual citizen, I want to argue, could be male or female, young or old, black or white, rich or poor, straight or gay: could be anyone, in fact, but for one key characteristic. The sexual citizen exists – or, perhaps better, wants to come into being – because of the new primacy given to sexual subjectivity in the contemporary world.

Weeks does not here deal directly with the question of the tension between universality and difference. However, despite his very inclusive and, some might want to argue, universal definition of 'the sexual citizen', he clearly suggests a desire to embrace a 'differentiated universalism' rather than the either/or positions referred to above. For example, he talks of the importance of 'balancing the claims of different communities with constructing new common purposes' and of 'learning to live with diversity at the same time as building our common humanity' (Weeks, 1998: 49). Once again, this mirrors much of the feminist literature on citizenship, especially that which has been critical of binary characterisations and has attempted to 'ride the tension between the universal and the particular' (Lister, 1997a: 200).

I would not want to imply that feminists are not concerned with questions of sexual citizenship. For example, many radical and revolutionary feminists are employing rights discourse to discuss issues such as prostitution and forms of sexualised violence (see, for example, Jeffreys, 1997). Another aspect of feminist work on sexuality and citizenship, also primarily influenced by radical/lesbian/feminist accounts, is concerned with the development of legal theory and models of 'sexual justice' (Robson, 1992; Phelan, 1994, 1995; Wilson, 1995).

One of the main ways in which sexual citizenship has been addressed within feminist texts, however, is through an examination of the relationship of lesbian and gay rights to the state. In her discussion of local government initiatives for lesbian and gay rights in the UK in the 1980s Davina Cooper (1994), for example, looks at the discourses of citizenship that were utilised. Didi Herman (1994) likewise has analysed the arguments of lesbian and gay rights movements and their opponents in Canada. Cooper (1995) further develops her ideas in *Power in Struggle: Feminism, Sexuality and the State*, in which she considers strategies for 'sexing the state'. In her analysis, Cooper examines the relationship between the state and sexuality as a two-way process. It is, she suggests, 'not simply that the state affects the forms that modern sexuality and its struggles take but also that the nature of the state is influenced by sexual identities, ideologies and culture' (Cooper, 1993: 191). Employing a concept of the state as complex and varied, Cooper recognises that institutions such as the welfare state, education and the criminal justice system are 'sexualised'. This echoes the more general call to integrate sexuality into social policy analyses and critiques by writers such as, for example, Jean Carabine (1996a, b), who highlights the processes by which prevalent sexuality discourses inform and constitute social policy.

Another important theme in feminist work that has engaged with questions of sexual citizenship, and which relates to the notion of a sexualised state, is the emphasis placed upon the relationship between citizenship and institutionalised heterosexuality. This was the focus of the previous chapter, in which I argued that the hegemonic regime of heterosexuality underpins the construction of the normal citizen and that what we have conventionally understood as 'citizenship' is itself a dominant form of sexual citizenship. Similarly, a number of other writers, albeit at differing levels of specificity, have contended that citizenship is constituted through heterosexual norms and practices (see, for example, Wilson, 1993; Cooper, 1994, 1995; Herman, 1994; Phelan, 1994; Duggan, 1995).

The notion of the normative category 'citizen' as heterosexual is not limited to feminist analysis. Some queer/gay male writers have also addressed this issue (see, for example, Kaplan, 1997). In part, this reflects the centrality of the concept of 'heteronormativity' to queer theory which, in common with especially radical feminist approaches, has problematised the heterosexual/homosexual binary (Warner, 1993b). Nor is it only feminist writers who have addressed the relationship between sexual citizenship and gender. For example, David Evans (1993), in his discussion of both a specific 'female sexual citizenship' and a specific 'male homosexual citizenship', implies that sexual citizenship is gendered. As I stated earlier, Evans has a sexually differentiated as well as a gendered model of sexual citizenship in which, for example, he delineates male homosexual citizenship from the experience of bisexuals, transvestites and transsexuals. Interestingly, however, the experience of lesbian citizenship is hardly mentioned, neither under the heading of homosexual nor female sexual citizenship. This is interesting for a number of reasons, not least because it prompts the question of how useful it is to employ discrete categories of sexual citizenship in the manner that Evans does. In addition, it highlights how the question of the inter-relationship between gender and sexuality, crucial to much feminist theory, is not adequately addressed.

Whilst Evans can be criticised for ignoring lesbians, other authors have been accused of neglect of a different kind. The dominant trend in analyses which conceptualise sexual citizenship in terms of varying degrees of access to specific sets of rights has been to focus upon 'lesbian and gay' struggles for equality, rather than specifically analysing lesbian citizenship *per se*, thus failing to differentiate lesbians from other 'queers' or 'gay men'. What we then have are 'lesbian and gay' citizens or queer citizenry, which embraces lesbian, gay, bisexual and transgender citizens. This is particularly salient given that, in many countries, such rights movements are associated historically with demands, mainly by gay men, for the decriminalisation of 'male homosexual' offences, in particular age of consent and sodomy laws (Herman, 1994). Thus, in making no distinction between lesbians and gays the concern is not simply that possible differences in the experience of social inclusion/exclusion are being ignored, but that lesbians are at risk of being subsumed under the category 'gay'. As Shane Phelan (1994: xi) points out: '. . . the 1990s paradigm of "lesbian and gay" too often heralds a return to male-dominated politics'.

It is in the context of critiques that lesbians have either been ignored altogether or made invisible, to varying extents, through being subsumed under a universal notion of the 'sexual citizen' or a sexually differentiated but not gender specific category such as 'queer citizen' or 'lesbian and gay citizen', that we need to understand the development of analyses of lesbian citizenship. Ruthann Robson (1992), for example, arguing the case for lesbian legal theory, has put forward the view of the lesbian citizen as an (out)law. That is, rather than seeking rights *in* law, Robson argues that lesbians should be without and create their own approach to the law. Instead of conceptualising a universal system of citizenship which can and should be modified to include the demands of lesbians, lesbians are seen as a socially distinct group with their own specific interests who need to develop a uniquely lesbian approach to legal reasoning. In distinguishing lesbian experience from that of both gay men and heterosexual women, Robson's is both a gendered and sexually differentiated notion of sexual citizenship. Within this kind of framework we can think about lesbian citizenship not as a set of equal-rights demands, but rather in terms of the elaboration of a 'lesbian specific' system of rules of justice governing claims to citizenship.

One of the major criticisms levelled at such an approach is that it presupposes that we know who we 'lesbians' – or any other sexually categorised grouping – are, and that there are clear and identifiable shared common 'lesbian interests' which may be expressed as demands (Phelan, 1994; Herman, 1995). Since the 1980s, it has become increasingly clear that the term 'lesbian', far from defining a unitary and homogeneous category, encompasses a complex and diverse population of women who hold multiple social identities and different political positions. The contested terrain among lesbians over many 'rights claims', such as, for instance, lesbian marriage, motherhood and various forms of sexual practice, is further evidence of the difficulty of 'speaking with one voice'. Furthermore, the influence of postmodernism on lesbian/feminist thinking has brought new understandings of lesbian identities as fluid and shifting, rather than as fixed and stable (Doan, 1994). In the light of such criticisms, writers such as, for example, lesbian political theorist Shane Phelan (1994, 1995) have put forward a 'third way' of thinking about lesbians and sexual citizenship, as distinct from either an 'equal rights' or 'separatist' perspective. Phelan argues that lesbians should claim 'the space of citizenship', understood here as a claim to political participation and public recognition. However, she dismisses the idea that within this space of citizenship we can predetermine what will be a 'lesbian issue'. She still talks of specific citizenships, of which 'lesbian citizens' are an example, and of forging bonds 'between specificities'. (There are echoes here with Weeks, 1998.) What Phelan is trying to achieve is recognition that there may be concerns specific to lesbians, though not all lesbians may share in these, and that other groups may have similar concerns. The demand is for lesbians to be recognised as citizens 'not "in spite" of our lesbianism but simply regardless of it' (Phelan, 1995: 206), as equal members in a 'radical democracy' where the privilege of hegemonic identity is eliminated.

These ongoing debates over sexuality and citizenship status highlight the extent to which gendered understandings of the concept sexual or intimate citizenship are being used by some writers in contrast to 'gender-neutral' definitions used by others. To further illustrate the point we might, for example, ask of those campaigning for 'equal rights' for lesbians and gay men: to whom do gay men want to be equal, heterosexual women or heterosexual men? And is the same answer likely to be forthcoming from lesbians? These are complex questions, but we need to ask them if we are to have a clearer understanding of the social construction of sexual citizenship and its interconnections with gender.

6

THEORISING SEXUAL RIGHTS

What do we mean by 'sexual rights'?

In the previous Chapter I suggested that one way that we can think about
sexual citizenship is as a status entailing a number of different rights
claims, some of which are recognised as legitimate by the state and are
sanctioned. However, if we conceptualise sexual citizenship in this way, as
a set of rights and duties, then this prompts the question of what we define
as sexual rights. Although the concept is not new and is in common everyday usage, 'sexual rights' has no clear meaning and can be interpreted in a
variety of different ways. In part this reflects not only differences in how
sexuality is conceptualised, but also the fact that there is no singular agreed
definition of sexual citizenship. It is also a product of the times.
Increasingly demands are being made by a variety of social movements
and groups concerned with sexual issues, which are couched in the
language of sexual rights and citizenship.

With this increasing diversification, the language of sexual rights
becomes evermore diverse. For feminists, claims to rights in relation to sexuality have largely been about safety, bodily control, sexual self-definition,
agency and pleasure. Lesbian and gay movements have emphasised the
extension of specific sexual rights, including an equal age of consent, as
well as more broadly the right to freely choose consenting adult sexual
partners and the right to publicly recognised lesbian, bisexual or gay
identities and lifestyles. Some writers (e.g. Evans, 1993, 1995; Binnie, 1995)
also include in their discussion of sexual citizenship the right to consume
'sexual commodities', which can be defined as services and goods related
to sexual practices and identities. Such 'commodities' might include forms
of sex education, lesbian and gay magazines, contraceptives, abortion
services, prostitution and pornography.

In this chapter I want to examine this question of what is meant by the
term 'sexual rights'. How has rights language been used to articulate
demands in the field of sexuality? This is all the more important in a social
and political context where not only is the language of citizenship becoming more differentiated, it is also rapidly becoming the dominantspeak of
how we talk about sexuality and sexual politics. What this means in

practice is that at the same time as we are increasingly hearing and speaking the language of sexual rights, the meanings of the words we use are evermore complex, confused and contested.

Within sexual rights discourse it is possible to identify three broad areas of possible meaning: definitions of sexual rights which are related to conduct-based rights claims, definitions that are associated with identity-based rights claims and those that are connected to claims which are relationship-based. As a way of trying to structure the discussion, I will make use of these broad categories under the following headings: practice, identities and relationships. While I recognise that there is a certain artificiality in doing this, as if these were discrete rather than inter-related aspects of experience, I believe that it is a useful intellectual device to help make sense of the different ways of interpreting sexual rights. In addition, it provides a framework by which to try to clarify similarities and differences between both individual writers and social groups campaigning for social change in relation to sexuality. Most importantly, as will be illustrated below, it can also help to highlight where the boundaries of tolerance or rejection, inclusion or exclusion, are sometimes drawn.

Practice

Claims to rights which centre on sexual practice tend to fall into three main categories: those which are concerned with forms of social regulation which specify what one can and cannot do; those which are concerned not only with the right to participate in but also the right to enjoy sexual acts, commonly expressed as the right to sexual pleasure; and those which are concerned with rights of bodily self-control. I will consider each of these in turn.

The right to participate in sexual activity

At a fundamental level, the concept of sexual rights can be understood as the right to participate in sexual acts. Historically, the concept of rights has been linked to concepts of need and, in this context, such rights claims may be vindicated through definitions of sexuality as a physical need, integral to the status of being human. This is commonly referred to as an essentialist perspective; sexuality conceptualised as an innate sexual drive which seeks gratification through sexual activity (Richardson, 1997). A further assumption within this model is that the natural and normal aim of this sexual drive or instinct is reproduction. It is a heterosexual drive: ultimately sexuality is defined as the desire to engage in certain practices (vaginal intercourse) with particular individuals (partners of the 'opposite' sex). It is also largely constructed as a male drive, which, as will be demonstrated later, has important implications for female sexual citizenship.

This view of sexuality as a naturally given series of rights which

biology/God has created, has implications for understandings of responsibilities as well as rights. In relation to sexuality, the question of
responsibility has largely been concerned with establishing what are and
are not acceptable forms of expression of an assumed pregiven human
need. That is, how are needs to engage in sexual activity to be met, in
terms both of specific sexual practices and objects of desire? Having said
this, there are certain social groups where the assumption of sexuality as a
universal human 'need' appears to be challenged. Stereotypes of disability,
for example, include assumptions of asexuality and of lack of sexual potential. While historically there has been minimal discussion of the sexual
politics of disability, both within disability studies and work on sexuality,
in recent years attempts have been made to place sexual rights on the
political agenda of disability movements (see Shakespeare et al., 1996). A
particular focus has been the ways in which people with disabilities have
been denied the capacity for sexual feeling and rights to sexual expression.
This has been particularly apparent in the case of people with learning difficulties, for whom sex is not a right normally granted, but can only be
achieved by 'breaking the rules for their "kind"'(Brown, 1994).

The granting of sexual rights, formalised in age of consent legislation as
well as other laws and policies relating to sexual activity, should therefore
be viewed as a complex process, in which the context and form of expression of sexual behaviour are key factors. Another way of saying this, is that
recognition of the right to participate in sex, *where it is recognised*, should
not be confused with claims for the right of individuals to exercise personal
choice over the kinds of behaviours they engage in. Certain sexual acts
may be prohibited by law, reflecting views about what people have a right
to do with their bodies. For example, sexual intercourse between people of
the same sex is still illegal in almost half the states of the USA and in many
parts of the world (Moran, 1996; Bamforth, 1997). As I have already discussed in Chapter 4, prior to 1967 consensual sexual contact between men,
even in private, was illegal in England and Wales. After the 1967 Sexual
Offences Act, such practices remained unlawful unless the following conditions were met: both consenting adults were aged 21 and over and the
acts should take place in private.

It is important not to interpret such liberalisation of laws regulating
sexual contact between men as state recognition of the right to be homosexual. (This distinction will be discussed in more detail in the following
section.) What such changes in the law represent is the granting of the
right, under certain specific contexts, for one man to engage in sexual acts
with another man: a right which extends to all adult males, not only those
who identify as bisexual or gay.

Of particular importance in analysing the issues surrounding this and
other examples of sexual rights claims is the public/private binary. Indeed,
arguments for conduct-based rights claims have largely been based on
respect for privacy. Although, as I discussed in Chapter 2, in recent years
there has been a shift in this discourse, associated with the emergence of

new social movements, such as, for example, queer politics, which have emphasised the right to public forms of sexual expression (Bell, 1995; Ingram et al., 1997). This conceptual division between the public and the private is, nevertheless, fundamental to a liberal model of sexual citizenship, which has predominated in Britain since the 1960s. Thus, for example, those who wish to engage in sexual acts with members of their own gender are granted the right to be tolerated as long as they remain in the private sphere and do not seek public recognition: the 'I don't mind what they do in their own homes as long as I don't have to see or hear about it' argument. Similarly, justifications of the right to consume certain forms of pornography are frequently couched both in terms of individual civil liberties and a respect for privacy.

The justification for the right to engage in various forms of sexual conduct in terms of respect for privacy has not gone unchallenged and in some instances may be seen as illegitimate. In the example given above of the right to consume pornography, for instance, both moral right and certain feminist critiques reject the conceptualisation of the public and the private as distinct spheres, where what happens in the private is assumed to have no wider social effects, specifically in this case on male attitudes and behaviour towards women (Cameron and Frazer, 1993). Similarly, in the case of gay rights, respect for privacy may also be contested. For example, in the now famous Bowers versus Hardwick case in the USA, in 1986, the Supreme Court decided that individuals did not have a fundamental right to engage in 'homosexual sodomy' (see Currah, 1995). The plaintiff, Hardwick, challenged the court's decision, claiming that it violated his right to privacy since he was engaging in consensual sex with another adult male in the privacy of his own bedroom. The two men were 'discovered' by a police officer who, while delivering an unrelated arrest warrant, was inadvertently directed to Hardwick's bedroom. The Supreme Court's decision upheld the right of the State of Georgia to send individuals convicted of engaging in anal intercourse with someone of the same gender to prison for up to twenty years. At the same time, the court refused to rule on the constitutionality of laws that apply to 'heterosexual sodomy'.

What are the ideas and assumptions behind the denial of the right to perform certain sexual acts, even when conducted in private? Fundamentally important are institutionalised (hetero)sexual norms and practices, whereby heterosexuality is established as 'natural' and 'normal', an ideal form of sexual relations and behaviour by which all forms of sexuality are judged. Exclusions from the boundaries of sexual citizenship as practice, therefore, may be on the grounds of 'natural' disqualification. For example, the belief that the body should not be used for acts for which nature did not design it. This understanding of bodies within what Judith Butler (1993) refers to as a 'heterosexual matrix', which operates through naturalising a heterosexual morphology, is itself an important aspect of heterosexual ideology where the penis and the vagina are assumed to be a 'natural fit', unlike, for example, the penis and the anus. In addition to such dominant inscriptions of the body, the belief that vaginal intercourse is naturally the chief purpose of sexual behaviour is another 'norm' by which sexual practices have been judged to be more or less acceptable. For example, although the law has traditionally been much less hostile towards sexual conduct between men and women in both public and private settings, drawing on this view of what people should properly be engaging in sex for, it can prohibit certain heterosexual practices. It is, for instance, illegal for heterosexual couples to engage in oral sex in a number of states in the USA (Kaplan, 1997).

Lack of recognition of rights claims may also be on the grounds of moral inferiority, where again heterosexual ideology conflates a particular form of heterosexuality with propriety and moral worth. That is, if certain acts are categorised as immoral then the restrictions placed on the right to engage in them may be justified in terms of a moral threat posed to society. This is illustrated by the judgement in the 'Operation Spanner' case in Britain, in 1990, where eight adult men were convicted for engaging in consensual sado-masochistic acts in private. Following an appeal, the House of Lords upheld the decision that consensual sado-masochism was against the public interest and should therefore be found unlawful under the Offences Against the Persons Act 1861 (for an account of the case see R. v Brown, 1992, 1994). This was an interesting judgment in so far as it appeared to mark a reversal of the law's distinction, post-Wolfenden (see page 33 of this volume), between legality and morality; a distinction that was to be crucial to the recognition of future rights claims relating to the practice of, amongst other things, abortion and homosexuality. Indeed, echoing this view, those who dissented from the judgment claimed 'that questions of morality should not be presumed to fall within the remit of the criminal law unless explicitly stated by parliament' (Cooper, 1993: 194). The House of Lords decision was subsequently upheld at an appeal, in 1997, to the European Court of Human Rights in Strasbourg, who ruled that it was acceptable for the state to interfere in the 'right of privacy' where it is necessary for the protection of the nation's health or morals.

Health and welfare considerations in rights claims based on sexual conduct have been particularly apparent in relation to AIDS. An example of this from the early years of the epidemic was the calling for the (re)criminalisation of homosexuality as a sexual practice by moral right organisations in the USA (Altman, 1986). In both a US and a European context, by contrast, one of the demands of AIDS activists in organisations such as ACT UP has been the right to safer sexual practice through access to effective education about prevention of the sexual transmission of HIV, as well as health and welfare services which encourage safer sex, such as, for instance, the provision of condoms (Watney, 1991).

The right to pleasure

In the second category of rights claims associated with the right to sexual expression, the emphasis is more upon the right to gratification and enjoyment than simply the right to participate in various forms of sexual activity. Examples of this can be identified in claims for sexual liberation, as well as in some feminist demands. In the so-called sexual revolution of the 1960s, libertarians, in demanding freedom of sexual expression, emphasised sexual fulfilment as a right.

Demands for the right to sexual pleasure were also an important aspect of feminist politics earlier this century and, much more centrally, during the late 1960s and 1970s. Sexuality was identified as 'male-defined' and organised around male pleasure, with women's sexuality defined in terms of meeting male sexual needs. Feminists encouraged women to 'reclaim' their sexuality, a sexuality that many believed had been suppressed and denied them. They also sought to challenge the sexual double standard that favours men, granting them greater sexual rights and fewer responsibilities than women. In a sense, such claims were equal rights claims: equal rights to sexual citizenship, although such demands were not at that time couched in such terms. However, if it was equal rights to sexual pleasure and practice that feminists demanded, it was in the context of a different understanding of these. In particular, feminist writers challenged the centrality of intercourse in definitions of sexual practice and sexual pleasure (Koedt, 1974/1996).

Once again, how we understand and explain sexuality has important implications for claims for sexual rights. In this case, what is at stake is not just the right to engage in sexual practices, but the right to gratification of sexual desire. Whilst essentialist notions of sexuality as a reproductive drive may aid recognition of the former claim, in a heterosexual context at least, they are not necessarily supportive of the latter where the recognised aim of sex is individual pleasure. Indeed, these might be in contradiction. One might want to claim that there is no clear bounded right to sexual pleasure *per se* that is sanctioned by the state. However, in countries where, for instance, rape in marriage is not considered illegal, this may be interpreted as a state-sanctioned right of a man's access to a woman's body on the grounds of his rights to sexual fulfilment within marriage. In addition, the right to engage in non-reproductive sexual activities for pleasure can be seen to be linked to the extension of citizenship as consumption. Thus, by laying stress on individual liberty and on the citizen as consumer, the state does recognise various rights claims to consume sexual services and goods such as, for example, forms of prostitution and pornography.

For many feminists in the 1970s the demand for the right to sexual pleasure was not only about gaining greater personal authenticity and equal sexual rights with men, it was also about seeking empowerment in a much broader sense. That is, a connection was often made between sexual liberation and women's liberation. With hindsight, many feminists have since questioned this view (see, for example, Campbell, 1980; Jeffreys, 1990). Commenting on this period Jackson and Scott (1996: 4–5), for instance, point out that, in practice, sexual liberation had different consequences

for women and men: 'In retrospect many women felt that "sexual liberation" meant greater access for men to women's bodies and the removal of
their right to say "No" to sex, lest they be damned as "unliberated".' What
this highlights is that for women the right to sexual pleasure is complex
and inextricably linked to other rights of citizenship. For example, it is
difficult to envision what it would mean to speak of women's rights to
sexual pleasure, without at the same time recognising rights which enable
women's control over their sexuality and reproduction.

The right to sexual (and reproductive) self-determination

This leads on to the third aspect of conduct-based rights claims, which may
be analysed in terms of rights claims concerned with bodily autonomy
and integrity. Such claims, as I have already suggested, are particularly evident within feminist discourses, which have interpreted sexual rights in
terms not only of the right to sexual pleasure and agency, as described
above, but also of the right of control over one's body and to safety. This
latter focus, often characterised as the right to say no, is closely although
not exclusively associated with radical feminism. The emphasis is on the
right to engage in sex without fear, whether this be in terms of unwanted
pregnancy, sexually transmitted diseases, or male demands and force, and
includes claims to the right to freedom from sexual harassment, violence,
abuse and coercion, as well as rights of access to abortion and contraception.

Feminist debates over these issues have further demonstrated the gendered nature of sexual citizenship. For example, campaigns for changes in
policy and practice concerning sexual violence have highlighted how men
have traditionally been granted greater sexual rights than women, especially in marriage. In many countries the law decrees that rape in marriage
is not a crime (a view that was only overturned relatively recently in
England with the introduction, in 1991, of the Rape in Marriage Act).
Under such laws, a man's right of sexual access to his wife's body is privileged over her right to consensual sexual practice. He has the right to
take by force that which the law defines as rightfully his: sex within marriage and, more specifically, the act of vaginal penetration. An example of
what Tamsin Wilton (1992) refers to as 'rights of penetration', which she
claims, citing HIV/AIDS health promotion as evidence, frequently takes
precedence over other considerations, including rights to pleasure and
safety. Even in those countries and states where rape in marriage is recognised as a crime, it is often the case that 'the prosecution of offenders and
the success of these prosecutions is greatly reduced in comparison with
stranger rape, because socially it is not fully accepted as a crime' (Hanmer,
1997: 369). Translated into the language of rights, this means that men still
have greater social rights in relation to such forms of sexual practice.

Debates over HIV and AIDS have also been significant in the framing of
sexual rights in terms of the language of rights of safety, as well as for

reproductive rights of HIV positive women (Doyal et al., 1994). On the one hand, we have witnessed claims for the extension of sexual rights, such as the right to information about HIV and safer sex as part of rights recognised by the state to sex education in schools, as well as health education more generally (Watney, 1991). On the other hand, some responses to AIDS represent demands for the curtailment of rights to sexual expression which are justified in terms not of protection of public morals, but rather the protection of public health and the protection of the rights and freedoms (including the right to life) of others. Earlier I made reference to the example of calls for the (re)criminalisation of male homosexual conduct. Another illustrative case would be the suggestion that it should be a criminal offence for a person who is HIV infected to (knowingly) practise unsafe sex with a sexual partner without their informed consent (Sieghart, 1989). This is already the case in some countries. For example, in 1997, in Finland an American man who was HIV positive was sentenced to imprisonment for having unprotected intercourse with a series of women, some of whom became infected with HIV as a result.

Many of the conduct-based claims to sexual rights involve claims for civil rights, both in terms of the removal of laws which prohibit or try to restrict certain sexual acts – such as, for example, campaigns by gay rights groups over age of consent and other forms of discriminatory legislation – as well as the creation of new laws which penalise certain practices, such as the example I gave of feminist campaigns to outlaw rape within marriage. However, such rights claims go beyond protective civil rights. As I have argued above, they also include access to social rights, as is evidenced in feminist demands for the recognition of women's sexual needs, and the provision of welfare. For example, claims for the right to express oneself sexually without fear of unwanted pregnancy are informed by the right of access to education and health services in respect both of abortion and contraception.

Identity

In the 1970s and 1980s, a shift in emphasis occurred in the discourse of sexual rights. There was a partial move away from conduct-based claims, towards a concern with sexual identity rather than sexual practice as the basis for inclusion or exclusion from categories of citizenship. Having said this, we need to recognise the relationship between identity and conduct, in particular the ways in which a person's identity may be a mitigating variable in conduct-based claims. Thus, for example, a person may have differential access to the right to engage in certain forms of sexual activity depending upon whether they are defined as heterosexual or homosexual, as was evidenced in the Bower versus Hardwick case referred to earlier.

Perhaps the most illustrative case of this shift towards an identity-based approach to sexual rights was the emergence towards the end of the 1960s and the beginning of the 1970s, of gay liberation movements in the USA and Europe. Previous campaigns organised by and on behalf of 'homosexuals', such as, for example, the Homosexual Law Reform Society in Britain, had primarily focused on the removal of criminal laws that prohibited or restricted sexual activity between men. Gay Liberationist sets of demands went much further than this in challenging discrimination against people on the basis of a lesbian or gay 'identity'. These campaigns were not asking for the right to engage in same-sex activity couched in terms of respect for privacy, but were expressing opposition to social exclusion on the basis of sexual status through the language of the right to sexual freedom and liberation. This reflected an emphasis within this period of gay activism on the importance of being open about one's sexuality through 'coming out' and publicly identifying as lesbian or gay. Subsequently, and with varying degrees of success, gay campaigning groups have pressed for 'the repeal of hostile laws and for the creation of new laws offering protection against social hostility' (Bamforth, 1997: 3). However, it was not merely 'gay rights' in the civil rights meaning of the term that gay liberationists were claiming. In demanding the 'right of a person to develop and extend their character and explore their sexuality' (The Gay Liberation Front Demands cited in Jeffery-Poulter, 1991: 100–1), they were also claiming social and political rights. Thus, in the USA, for example, representatives of National Gay Liberation demanded that gays be represented in all governmental and community institutions. This marked a significant change in claims for sexual citizenship and, associated with this, the development of the notion of sexual rights.

The right to self-definition

At the most basic level, identity-based sexual rights claims include the right to sexual self-definition and the development of individual sexual identities. This is a model of sexual citizenship based upon notions of who the individual is, rather than what their sexual practices might involve – the right to identify with a specific sexual category defined in terms of a class of people, as distinct from the right to engage in specific sexual practices.

These demands are closely linked to notions of the right to self-ownership and self-determination. However, as in the case of conduct-based rights claims, assumptions and beliefs about sexuality are also extremely important. Thus, for example, a common justification of the right to sexual self-definition is the claim that one's sexuality is predetermined and that there is a natural or essential basis for sexual identities, usually explained in terms of genetics or prenatal hormonal influences on the structure of the brain. This is a view which persists, despite the weight of the social constructionist argument that sexual identities are socially and historically specific 'inventions' (Foucault, 1979; Weeks, 1990), as is evidenced by the considerable attention and debate generated by the research findings of Le

Vay (1991, 1996) and Hamer et al. (1993), who all claim to have discovered evidence of a biological basis to sexuality. Indeed, the arguments formulated by contemporary lesbian and gay political groups, especially in the USA, frequently draw upon essentialist notions of sexual categories as fixed and discrete, where one's sexuality is understood to be defined not by one's sexual practices but by one's underlying 'sexual orientation' and attendant identity. It is important to acknowledge that this form of political practice does not necessarily mean adherence to essentialist theories, in which case the term 'strategic essentialism' is more appropriate. Whether strategic or otherwise, within this model 'gay rights' claims to citizenship reproduce the discourse of minority civil rights, with lesbians and gays conceptualised as a legitimate minority group 'having a certain quasi-"ethnic" status' (Epstein, 1987: 12).

The assertion that homosexuality is not a chosen but an inborn orientation/identity constitutes an important aspect of the argument for civil and social rights for lesbians and gay men, as well as for many others campaigning for sexual rights. It has been a feature, for example, of the pursuit of rights by transvestites and transsexuals, as well as, albeit to a lesser extent, some bisexual and transgender activists. Its significance is that, within a liberal democracy, it should be possible to claim that discrimination on the basis of a personality trait that is believed to be unchangeable and beyond one's control should be regarded as unfair. However, it is important here to distinguish between conduct- and identity-based claims. Whilst such arguments may uphold the right to sexual self-definition, they do not necessarily support the right to express oneself sexually, on the grounds that, unlike identity, it may be assumed that a person can exercise a measure of control over their sexual conduct – although stereotypically less so in the case of men than women. An example of this is the official policy on homosexuality in the Church of England, which recognises the rights of participation of gay clergy, but does so only on the grounds that they abstain from 'homosexual acts'.

The right to self expression

The idea that being gay is a constructed identity has often been interpreted as less supportive of identity-based rights claims (although this need not necessarily be the case). An illustrative example of this was the debates surrounding the introduction of Section 28 of the 1988 Local Government Act in Britain, which sought to ban the 'promotion' of homosexuality and 'pretended' family relationships by local authority schools. Beyond these specific issues, Section 28 became a focus for discussion about the right to be lesbian and gay (Stacey, 1991). Speaking at the 1987 Conservative Party Conference, the then British Prime Minister Margaret Thatcher expressed such concerns when she remarked that: 'Children who need to be taught to respect traditional moral values are being taught that they have an inalienable right to be gay' (quoted in Evans, 1995: 126). Behind such concerns is not merely the issue of children possibly engaging in same-sex sexual activity (though that was still there), but also the issue of the right to 'choose' to identify with a specific category of people. The implication is that, where possible, the state should try to restrict the construction of such forms of sexual identification.

Arguably, the introduction of Section 28 represented both a recognition, as well as a restriction, of the social and civil rights of lesbians and gay men. By this, I mean that its proponents were motivated by what they perceived as a shift towards greater social acceptance of homosexuality which, as a consequence, fostered a belief in the necessity of introducing measures such as Section 28, which would help to keep or indeed return homosexuals to their proper place in society (i.e. within their own private spaces and communities). This is instructive in elucidating the legitimacy of identity-based rights claims. Beyond the right to sexual self-definition, claims for sexual citizenship include the right to public/social recognition of specific sexual identities. Thus, for example, although one may have the right to identify as a lesbian, one does not necessarily have the right to 'come out' and inform others of that identity. The 'Don't Ask / Don't Tell' policy in the US military is an illustration of this. Although a 'homosexual' identity is itself no longer a bar to military service, any public construction of oneself as lesbian or gay, including 'coming out' speech, constitutes grounds for discharge. In other words, one has the right to think one is gay, but not the right to say so. The effect of this policy, argues Currah (1995: 66), is to reinforce the public/private binary, leaving room 'only for a wholly private construction of a homosexual orientation'.

As I have already outlined, sexuality is commonly understood to belong to the 'private' sphere, but more especially so in the case of lesbian and gay relationships. For lesbians and gay men the private has been institution-alised as the boundary of sexual citizenship and social tolerance. Indeed, in terms of the sociology of rights, lesbian and gay rights claims have been primarily viewed in this way, as private individual rights rather than as human rights. Thus, for example, the right to recognition of lesbian and gay lifestyles and identities as a legitimate and equal part of social and cul-tural life is commonly understood as seeking 'a better deal' for particular sexual minority groups, rather than an extension of the right of freedom to choose one's sexual partner, and to identify as lesbian or gay, to all human beings.

The relative exclusion from the public does not only pertain to 'homo-sexual practices', then, but also to 'homosexuality' as a public identity and lifestyle. This raises important questions about claims to civil, social, polit-ical, as well as sexual citizenship. Indeed, if claims to rights are negotiated through public fora, then the negotiation of citizenship rights will be seri-ously restricted if one is disallowed from those fora, either formally or informally, through fear of stigmatisation or recrimination if one identifies publicly as a lesbian or gay man. The ability to be 'out' and publicly visi-ble is therefore crucial to the ability to claim 'sexual rights'.

At the same time, issues raised by the sexual politics of recent years have prompted the question of whether, alongside assertions of the right to be 'out'; people have the right not to be out about their sexuality as well. One way this has manifested itself is in the politics and practices of outing (see Johansson and Percy, 1994). Outing refers to the political practice of naming certain individuals as lesbian or gay, usually those in positions of power who are closeted and/or do not support lesbian and gay rights claims. It is a strategy closely associated with queer politics. As an example, in Britain activists in the organisation OutRage! have threatened to 'out' gay members of parliament who have opposed equal age of consent legislation, as well as those gay clergy deemed to be hypocritical for upholding the policy that lesbians and gay men may only be ministers in the church if they abstain from 'homosexual acts'. Such practices have been extremely controversial; however, the point I want to make here is that the political practice of outing challenges what has been a significant argument in the struggle for sexual rights, the right to privacy.

This is nothing new. As I have stated earlier, lesbian and gay politics over the last thirty years have been less about the right to privacy than about claims for the right not to have to be private. There is, however, an interesting paradox here, as Weeks (1998) also notes, in that it is through claiming rights to the public sphere that lesbians and gay men have sought to protect the possibilities of having private lives of their own choosing. This is further complicated by the influence of postmodern ideas about identity as fragmented and fluid, rather than fixed attributes which one may publicly declare or not. In this context, the right 'not to be out' can be conceptualised in a rather different sense to that above, as a right not to be defined in terms of a particular sexual identity.

The right to self realisation

Closely related to rights of expression of our identities, is the right to realise specific sexual identities. This may include the right to develop diverse sexual identities in an unhindered, if not state-assisted manner. It may also include claims to purchase individual sexual selves/lifestyles. The emergent debates on cultural citizenship (see Stevenson, 2000 and Chapter 4 in this volume) and the shift in recent years towards defining citizenship in terms of consumerism (Evans, 1993) are of relevance here. This is recognised by Pakulski (1997: 83), who argues that the concept of cultural citizenship involves 'the right to be "different", to re-value stigmatised identities, to embrace openly and legitimately hitherto marginalised lifestyles and to propagate them without hindrance'. Examples of this include claims concerning indigenous peoples' rights, as well as what might be termed more radical lesbian/feminist and gay rights campaigns who, recognising the problematic nature of the concept of tolerance, are concerned with restructuring the social institutions which support, maintain and reproduce the conditions of hegemonic (hetero)sexuality (Cooper,

1993; Wilson, 1993). More specifically, resistance to exclusion from popular culture and critical attention to negative media coverage have been an important focus of political activity.

What is important to emphasise, in the context of a discussion of sexual citizenship, is the distinction to be drawn between claims for tolerance of diverse identities and active cultivation and integration of these identities without 'normalising distortion'. The former can embrace the right to self-definition and, within the established boundaries of tolerance, a limited right to express one's identity as a tolerated 'minority'. The latter claims for sexual citizenship are, however, of a different order; they represent a demand for rights to enable the realisation of sexual diversity, for access to the cultural, social and economic conditions which will enable previously marginalised and stigmatised identities to develop and flourish as a legitimate and equal part of the 'cultural landscape'. There are, however, inherent problems in conceptualising sexual citizenship in this way. This is perhaps best illustrated by the question of the claims to sexual citizenship made by 'paedophiles' who identify as a socially excluded sexual minority. As Weeks (1998: 41) states: 'The emergence of "the paedophile", especially, indicates the limit case for any claim to sexual citizenship.'

The right to self-realisation of 'identity' can be linked with the shift towards defining citizenship in terms of consumerism. This use of citizenship as a concept which refers to access to the consumption of certain lifestyles, or membership of 'consumer communities' supportive of particular identities, has been viewed positively by some campaigning for sexual rights. For example Evans (1993), though critical of such developments, nonetheless suggests that the new commercial power of gay men and, to a lesser extent, lesbians is linked to access to sexual and other forms of citizenship (Evans, 1993).

Others take a more critical view of the power of the 'pink pound' to promote lesbian and gay rights (Binnie, 1995; Woods, 1995). Certainly one could argue that, as with other forms of citizenship, the dominant model is one of access to the right to consume within the boundaries of heterosexual tolerance. This is well illustrated by the fact that one of the largest sponsors of the 1997 Gay Pride festival in London, United Airlines, refused to extend partnership benefits to its lesbian and gay employees. United clearly recognises lesbian and gay consumer citizenship. In a full-page advertisement in the festival programme the company stated: 'We would be proud to fly you to Pride festivals around the world. It's the kind of things we do for you every day at United, rising to meet your needs, rising above your expectations'. Commenting on this at the time Peter Tatchell of the direct action campaigning group OutRage! remarked: 'United Airlines seems only interested in the Pride festival as a marketing opportunity. It wants gay customers but doesn't seem to give a damn about gay human rights' (*Time Out*, 2–9 July, 1997).

Relationships

Although the language of rights largely speaks to the freedoms and obligations of the citizen (Lister, 1997a), many citizenship rights are grounded in sexual coupledom rather than rights granted to us as individuals (Delphy, 1996). There are some exceptions; however, in most cases heterosexual relations in an 'idealised' marital form are the norm by which the rights of coupledom are measured. For example, in the case of social rights the questioning of the welfare rights of lone mothers who have children outside of marriage reflects the way access to and eligibility for benefits is often linked to normative assumptions about sexuality (Carabine, 1996a).

Claims to sexual rights which might be termed relationship-based cluster around three main strands: those which are concerned with the right of consent to sexual behaviours in personal relationships, those which are concerned with forms of regulation which specify who one can have as a consensual sexual partner, and those which are concerned with seeking public validation of various forms of sexual relations within social institutions.

The right of consent to sexual practice in personal relationships

In deciding to consider the right to consent to sexual behaviours under relationship rather than conduct-based rights claims, I want to make a distinction between the right to engage in forms of sexual practice and the right to participate in sexual acts with others. Age of consent legislation defines the age at which individuals are legitimately regarded as sexual citizens, with the right to engage in sexual conduct in personal relationships. Thus, even though dominant discourses of sexuality have defined sexuality as a pregiven need in all human beings, certain rights to sexual expression are also dependent upon the assumed capacity of the individual for self-determined sexual relations. In the case of children, cultural assumptions about when a child may be deemed to have reached a sufficient level of cognitive development and sexual maturity to be able to 'consent' to sex are the main considerations. Such judgments vary between countries. In the Netherlands, for example, the government decided in 1990 to allow 'heterosexual and homosexual intercourse' between those over the age of 12. Under British law, as a number of writers have detailed (Evans, 1993; Moran, 1996), the right to consent to sexual behaviours is not only set at a higher age, but is also both gendered and sexualised. The sexual status and rights of boys are recognised at an earlier age than girls, who are regarded as insufficiently mature to 'consent' to heterosexual acts under the age of 16. At the time of writing, a further sexual 'double standard' exists in so far as the law continues to recognise the right to consent to heterosexual acts before (male) homosexual relations.

Claims for the right to an equal age of consent have been an important aspect of lesbian and gay rights campaigns, with organisations like Stonewall lobbying for such legal reform. These can be distinguished from campaigns led by various paedophile organisations for legal recognition of 'cross-generational sex', such as, in the recent past in Britain, PIE (Paedophile Information Exchange) and, in the USA, NAMBLA (North American Man/Boy Love Association). As with child-liberationist objections to age of consent laws, though for somewhat different reasons, such organisations argue for the right of sexual self-determination for children. They are not, in other words, seeking equal rights in law with heterosexuals, but a reduction in the age children are granted sexual rights or the removal of age of consent laws altogether.

The right to freely choose our sexual partners

In discussing the right to freely choose one's partner I am not referring to the right to engage in various forms of consensual activity with another person. Although such rights may be influenced by who one's partner is, I am concerned here with the question of the right to express sexual feelings for members of specific social groups. That is to say, a person may have the right to sexual citizenship on reaching an age where s/he is considered old enough to be a sexual subject, but that does not then mean they automatically have the freedom to have sex with any consenting partner. In addition to laws governing age of consent, other restrictions exist on who one can legitimately have as a sexual partner. As with other aspects of sexual citizenship that have been considered, claims for the right of individuals to be free to choose who they have sex with have been an important aspect of lesbian and gay demands, as well as feminist politics – albeit with the recognition that 'choice' is a problematic term in this context. A similar set of demands can be observed in rights activism centred upon controls on inter-racial relationships.

Although a thorough analysis of restrictions on the rights to select sexual partners from groups defined as racially different from each other is beyond the scope of this chapter, it is well documented that many of these restrictions have been fuelled by a belief in white superiority and concerns about miscegenation. In the USA, for example, the outlawing of marriage between whites and people of colour has a long history. As Ruth Frankenberg (1993: 72) comments:

> The first antimiscegenation law (which is to say, law against marriage between white people and people of color) was enacted in Maryland in 1661, prohibiting white intermarriage with Native Americans and African Americans. Ultimately, over the next three hundred years, thirty-eight states adopted antimiscegenation laws. In the nineteenth century, beginning with western states, antimiscegenation statutes were expanded to outlaw marriages and sexual relationships between whites and Chinese, Japanese, and Filipino Americans. Not until 1967 did the US Supreme Court declare antimiscegenation laws to be unconstitutional.

Elsewhere in the world similar campaigns have been fought against restrictions on inter-racial sexual relationships. Under apartheid in South Africa, for instance, the prohibitions of the Mixed Marriages Act and Section 16 of the Immorality Act were designed to prevent miscegenation. These were among the first pieces of apartheid legislation to be introduced after the National Party came to power in 1948 (Weeks, 1986).

There are parallels with fears of miscegenation and eugenic concerns over maintaining 'purity of the race', in attempts to restrict the rights of people with disabilities to form sexual relationships. This has been evident in the social policies of various countries, including the United States, Sweden, Britain and Germany. For example, shortly after gaining power the Nazi Party introduced a number of laws for 'improving racial stock' which included the 1933 'Sterilisation laws'. Under the terms of this legislation, 'Germans suffering from physical malformation, mental retardation, epilepsy, imbecility, deafness or blindness were compulsorily sterilised' (Grunberger, 1987: 305). People who were sterilised were not allowed to marry and, if it were found out that they had done so illegally, their marriages were judicially annulled.

One might of course want to argue that despite legal prohibition of certain forms of consensual relationships, centred on the right to marry and have legitimate children, sexual relations still occurred. Such insistence on a restricted right to choose one's partner, however, must be understood in terms of the differential access of different social groups to forms of sexual citizenship. For example, it is also well documented that in the USA, in the context of colonialism and the slave economy, white men often assumed sexual rights over black women slaves who were their 'property'; those who resisted risked being tortured and punished (hooks, 1992). (There are parallels here with the way in which men have historically been granted rights of access to their wives, defined as their property within marriage.) By contrast, however, it was considered unthinkable that black men should have consensual sexual relations with white women. Indeed, black men were likely to be severely punished if they were even suspected of having made a 'sexual advance' to a white woman. As Rennie Simson (1984) points out, many black men were lynched and publicly castrated in the USA last century as a way of 'protecting white womanhood'. In other words, white men had social and economic rights which enabled them to engage in coercive non-consensual sex with non-white partners, at a time when black men were being denied the right to choose a consensual sexual partner 'across race lines'. What examples such as these clearly demonstrate is that sexual citizenship is not only closely associated with hegemonic heterosexual and gendered norms of sexual behaviour, but is also informed by, and informs, constructions of race.

The right to publicly recognised sexual relationships

The final aspect of relational-based rights claims that I want to consider are those which are concerned with the right to public recognition and validation of sexual relationships. Many groups are seeking to extend social legitimacy and institutional support to the relationships they have. Lesbian and gay rights movements, for example, have increasingly moved in this direction, most obviously in demanding the right to marry and access to the social and legal benefits accruing from being married. This issue is one that is extremely contentious, especially among feminists who have been critical of the marital model of relationships and rights (Delphy and Leonard, 1992). However, as Jenny Rankine (1997) points out in her examination of the current debates on same-sex marriage, feminist views are likely to differ in different countries, 'even if certain fundamental issues of political principle remain constant', reflecting differences in welfare systems. In the USA, for instance, where public health care is extremely limited, the issue of the right to entitlements to medical cover on one's married partner's insurance takes on a particular significance.

Although the right to marry and form family units is recognised in the UN Declaration of Human Rights, in most countries such rights are denied same-sex relationships which do not have, for example, the same immigration rights, pension rights, inheritance rights, next of kin status, and tax benefits as those accorded married heterosexual couples. At present, lesbian and gay partnerships are not legally recognised in Britain. However, in a number of other European countries, for example in Denmark and the Netherlands, partnership laws which recognise same-sex relationships have been introduced, which could have implications in future for citizens of other European Union member states. In the USA, same-sex marriages have been permitted in the state of Hawaii. However, the federal authorities, in 1996, passed the Defense of Marriage Act, which defines marriage as a relationship between a woman and a man.

It is important to recognise that even in countries that provide legal recognition of same-sex relationships, there may still be disparities with the rights granted to heterosexuals. Major focuses of such disparities are the rights of parenthood. In Norway, for example, lesbian and gay couples are denied the right to adopt children. In addition, lesbians who have had children through donor insemination 'find that their lifetime companions have no legal rights to the children, although their combined income is counted when the local county authorities calculate how much they should pay for day care' (Lindstad, 1996: 135).

Conclusion

Rights do not exist in nature; they are products of social relations and of changing historical circumstances. In the present social climate, as I have outlined in this chapter, we are witnessing more and more rights-based arguments concerned with sexual practices, identities and relationships. As we struggle to keep up with a rapidly evolving and broadening concept of 'sexual rights', we must also respond by extending and developing our frameworks for understanding the sexual rights discourse. We also need to recognise the wider social implications of such changes. In extending our definitions of what can be termed 'sexual rights', we are engaged in a process which potentially challenges not only what might be considered as a right, but the possible meanings attached to social practices and traditions such as marriage, family, kinship and parenting. This clearly represents a challenge to the current social/sexual order. However, in so far as such rights claims are for 'equality with heterosexuals', the question of how far this can be regarded as a displacement of heterosexuality as the privileged, institutionalised norm is quite a different matter.

PART 3

SEXUALITY, GENDER AND HIV/AIDS

7

FEMINISM AND THE CHALLENGE
OF AIDS

Introduction

It is one thing to say that AIDS is a 'women's issue', another to claim that it is a feminist issue. The latter demands that we ask not only how HIV/AIDS affects women specifically, but also how the social, political and economic conditions of women's lives may influence their risk status and experience of HIV/AIDS. How, and in what ways, do gendered power relations impact on the pattern of HIV infection in women and the implications this has for their lives? The question can also be asked in the other direction. Do the social and economic consequences of HIV/AIDS serve to reaffirm and reinforce gender inequalities?

Much has now been written about women and HIV and, although many of the issues HIV and AIDS raises for women continue to be marginalised, a great deal has been achieved globally on behalf of women living with HIV or its consequences (Wilton, 1994). Yet historically, in Britain, discussion of HIV and AIDS from a feminist perspective has been relatively limited, although there are some notable exceptions to this (see, for example, the collection edited by Doyal et al., 1994). Few writers have moved beyond acknowledging gender differences and outlining the specific ways in which HIV/AIDS affects women differently to men such as, for example, in the process of negotiating safer sex and the gender-specific issue of transmission of HIV during pregnancy and the process of birth.

That there has been relatively little analysis of the broader questions posed in my opening paragraph is surprising for a number of reasons. The development of feminist theory and practice in the area of health has been a major aspect of western feminism since the late 1960s and early 1970s. In addition, over the last thirty years sexuality has become a central political issue for feminists, who have developed analyses of a range of issues including, for example, pornography, sexual violence, prostitution, lesbianism and heterosexuality. Consequently, many of the issues connected with HIV/AIDS such as, for example, the ability to exercise control over one's sexuality, women's access to health care and reproductive rights, are ones that feminists are familiar with and have addressed in other contexts.

The relatively small number of women diagnosed with AIDS in Britain may seem an obvious explanation for the initial lack of feminist activism around AIDS. For example, as of October 1988 there were only 61 cases of AIDS in women reported, compared with 1,801 men (Department of Health and Social Security figures for 1988). However, this overlooks the fact that while the number of people affected may have been low, from 1987 onwards the increasing recognition of AIDS as a public health issue prompted a great deal of discussion and debate about sexuality. AIDS became a major focus for sexual politics, a site where various issues and 'truths' about sexuality were contested, in some cases leading to attempts to introduce new forms of social control over sexual practices. The failure of feminists to make a substantial contribution to this debate is difficult to explain. Commenting on this at the time, Sara Scott (1987: 13) conveys a sense of surprise:

> AIDS has created the biggest public debate on sexuality, sexual practice and sexual morality since the media recovered from the shock of the sixties; yet it is one to which feminists have yet to make a particular contribution. Our silence seems bizarre because the issues raised by AIDS are very much on our political patch.

What possible explanations are there for this? Why should HIV/AIDS have been perceived as a low priority issue for feminism? Was it a case of feminists failing to recognise certain issues in the context of HIV and AIDS? Did it reflect the importance (or lack of it) placed on sexuality and women's health within feminist theory and debate in the late 1980s and the 1990s? These and other possible reasons are considered in the following section.

For men only?

> Looking back over the 1980s it is clear that much of what has been said or written about AIDS has been coloured by an overwhelming, if unstated, assumption that AIDS is a disease of men. (Panos, 1990)

The focus on AIDS as a disease affecting (gay) men in early accounts, coupled with a dearth of information and lack of discussion about women and AIDS, may help to explain why, initially at least, many feminists did not identify AIDS as a politically relevant issue. This was notwithstanding the fact that, as 'homosexuals', lesbians were initially often perceived as 'high-risk'. (This is discussed in detail in Chapter 9.) There is another possible reason for the relative absence of feminist discourse on HIV/AIDS in the first decade of the epidemic, besides women's invisibility. Speaking about the situation in Australia in the early 1990s, Anne Mitchell (1992: 52) makes the point when she claims that when the number of women infected with HIV is low, these women not only suffer from marginalisation and a lack of appropriate services, '. . . they are also a group rightly fearful for their privacy, and an inevitable backlash against themselves and their children. Personal activism or energetic attempts to excite the ire of feminist advocates to act on their behalf can therefore be seen as threatening and out of the question.'

During the 1980s, the rapid response of the gay community to HIV/AIDS in designing and implementing HIV/AIDS education and information campaigns, and through its involvement in other forms of AIDS activism, tended to encourage a general perception that AIDS politics = gay politics. Since the early 1970s, lesbian/feminist and gay movements in Britain have developed mainly along separate lines. (For a discussion of the historical background to this, from a lesbian feminist perspective, see Stanley, 1982.) The dominance of a politics of AIDS seen as largely reflecting the interests and needs of gay men, I would therefore argue, helps to further explain the lack of motivation on the part of many lesbian/feminists to put their energies into the struggle against HIV/AIDS.

In the USA the history of both feminism and AIDS activism has been slightly different to that of Britain. Although there have also been separate lesbian and gay movements and organisations from the 1960s onwards, there is a more established history of lesbians and gay men working together which may, in part, account for the greater involvement in HIV/AIDS work by lesbian/feminists within the USA (Schneider, 1992).

In the 1990s the situation changed somewhat, as I discuss in Chapter 8, with a resurgence of 'mixed politics' in both the USA and Europe associated with AIDS and the emergence of queer. In this context, feminist and lesbian debate about HIV/AIDS did gradually begin to shape the agenda of AIDS politics, in demanding recognition of the need to address issues such as, for example, the kinds of difficulties women may experience in negotiating safer sex, the impact of HIV/AIDS on women as carers, reproductive rights issues raised by HIV/AIDS, and the lack of availability of HIV/AIDS-related services for women.

At the same time as this shift towards gendering AIDS as female was occurring in Britain, attempts were being made by certain sections of the gay male community to 're-gay' AIDS (see Watney, 1994). Such actions were an understandable and necessary response to the way in which gay men were becoming more and more invisible in the provision of government funded education and services around HIV and AIDS. Nevertheless, to a certain extent this also represented a 're-maleing' of AIDS which, as I have already suggested, has both hindered the recognition of how HIV/AIDS affects women and the development of links with feminism.

There was, then, an apparent tension between, on the one hand, attempts to challenge the construction of AIDS as a (gay) male disease and draw attention to women's specific concerns and, on the other hand, demands from sections of the gay male community that their needs be met. A tension that led in some cases to political disagreement and divisions between gay men and women asserting their respective need of AIDS resources. Commenting on this, AIDS activist Cindy Patton (1994: 148) remarks that: 'Unfortunately, the increase in attention to women's concerns has sometimes come at the cost of pushing the issues of gay men aside, resulting in both "de-gaying" and de-funding crucial existing projects'.

Another possible explanation for the relative lack of feminist involvement in AIDS politics is that HIV/AIDS has been perceived as low priority relative to wider health issues for women. For example, in Britain at present there are many more deaths in women as a result of breast and cervical cancer than are caused by HIV-related illness. There is another way of looking at this. Because many of the issues AIDS raises are ones that feminists have been tackling for a very long time, it potentially had less immediate impact and was in many ways a confirmation of past feminist concerns rather than a challenge to them. Arguably, AIDS lacked the power to repoliticise feminism in the way that it did gay politics. In this sense, feminist lack of attention to HIV/AIDS can be seen, in part, as the outcome of its assimilation to a broader political agenda rather than as an indicator of fashions in feminist thinking or simply the equating of AIDS politics with gay men.

Related to the fact that AIDS raises 'old' issues for feminism, is the suggestion that some feminists felt angered by the attention that has been given to HIV and AIDS when other serious health issues for women such as, for example, breast cancer, have never received the same level of funding or interest (Winnow, 1992). They may also have felt angry because previously feminists raising similar issues to those prompted by HIV/AIDS, albeit in a different context, have often been ignored or marginalised. For example, commenting on the first governmental HIV/AIDS public education campaigns introduced in Britain towards the end of 1987, Ros Coward claimed that there were some 'cruel ironies' for feminists in observing the ways in which the government, media and medical profession were responding to the 'AIDS crisis':

> We have to watch general pressure mounting to transform sexual innuendo in advertising yet feminist campaigns against sexism in adverts have largely failed. Especially cruel is the conclusion of the British Government AIDS leaflet: 'Ultimately, defence against the disease depends on all of us taking responsibility for our own actions.' The feminist call for men to do just that has been something of a voice in the wilderness in the past. (Coward, 1987: 21)

In this section I have briefly considered some of the possible reasons why in the first decade of the epidemic HIV/AIDS received relatively little attention within feminism in Britain. Equally important is that we ask what the possible consequences of this may have been on social responses to, and conceptualisations of, HIV/AIDS.

A lack of feminist input?

Arguably, one of the most important consequences is that the contribution of feminist theory could have more effectively informed the policy-making process and influenced the development of the provision of services for women. The view of men as 'the norm' in the first decade of the AIDS crisis not only helped to render women invisible to researchers and those involved in the diagnosis and treatment of HIV and AIDS, it also shaped the development of educational, housing, health and social services policies. Not surprisingly, such policies often failed to meet women's specific needs. For example, the development of effective health and social services to care for and support people with AIDS or other HIV-related illness, and those looking after them, requires some understanding of the extent of women's unpaid work in the home, in particular their primary responsibility for the care of family members. Housing policies also need to recognise both women's position in the labour market and the fact that they frequently bear disproportionate responsibility for childcare. It is, in part, insufficient attention to these sorts of issues which has, in the past, prevented women from receiving adequate information and services.

HIV/AIDS health education policies are also unlikely to be effective unless they acknowledge the sorts of problems confronted by feminist and other research on (hetero)sexuality. As a number of studies have demonstrated (Holland et al., 1990, 1994a, 1998; Ingham et al., 1992; Lees, 1993), analysing the gendered power relations embedded in (hetero)sexual relations helps to explain how and why women can find the process of negotiating safer sex difficult. For example, on the basis of a detailed empirical study of young women and men's understanding of HIV/AIDS, their conceptions of risk and danger in sexual activity, their approaches to relationships and their responsibility within them and their ability to communicate effectively their ideas on safety within sexual relationships, Janet Holland, Caroline Ramazanoglu, Sue Sharpe and Rachel Thomson (1998: 31–2) conclude that:

> From a feminist perspective, negotiating condom use is not just a question of individuals making rational choices about personal safety. It is the outcome of a social encounter between potentially unequal partners in which this inequality is hidden in linguistic and social conventions that take masculinity and femininity (and the relations between them) to be the natural opposites . . . Women's choices about whether or how to engage in sexual activity with men are always constrained, in some cases by sexual pressure and violence, but more often by less explicit pressures.

Yet the majority of health education campaigns aimed at heterosexuals, in emphasising individual choice and personal responsibility, have tended to ignore the contribution of feminist theory to understandings of sexuality. Only very rarely, for instance, have they explicitly addressed the dynamics of power in (hetero)sexual relations. Paradoxically, given the findings of studies carried out by Holland et al. (1998) and others, the emphasis in HIV/AIDS education has tended to be on female rather than male sexual responsibility, especially in relation to insisting on the dominant safe (hetero)sex message 'Always use a condom'. At the same time, there has been little acknowledgement of the various constraints on women, which can make negotiating safer (hetero)sex difficult and, in some circumstances, dangerous. Not only does this limit how effective HIV/AIDS education campaigns are likely to be, it can also lead to women's difficulties in translating safer sex advice into practice being understood at the level of individual 'excuses', with potentially important implications for attributions of blame.

Feminist work has been ignored in other ways. To listen to what many have had to say about AIDS since it was first reported you could be forgiven for assuming that sex had never before been 'risky'. In the 'moral panic' that was a part of the cultural narratives for understanding AIDS in the first decade of the epidemic, sex became another aspect of 'risk society' (Beck, 1992). Within the majority of safer sex education and promotion materials aimed at heterosexuals, albeit in a much more muted manner than those directed at gay and bisexual men, there was an implicit 'fun morality'. By that I mean an assumption that the basis for effective safer sex promotion is to stress the erotic potential of safer sex. (For a more detailed discussion see Wilton, 1997, who analyses differences in HIV/AIDS health education and promotion targeted at gay men, heterosexual women, lesbians and heterosexual men.) A kind of tit for tat reasoning was apparent. We would be encouraged into practising safer sex through emphasising that enjoyment and pleasure could still be had, which would compensate for something that had apparently been lost. It almost seemed as if sex pre-AIDS had been all fun and games, a glorious time when sex could be spontaneous and you didn't have to worry about the possible risks to oneself or one's partner.

This is a gendered account of the significance of HIV/AIDS for contemporary understandings of sexuality. Moreover, it is one that fails to recognise the contribution of feminist accounts of sexual risk and safety prior to the emergence of AIDS. Feminists, both earlier this century and more recently, have campaigned for 'safer sex'; especially in relation to the prevention of unwanted pregnancy, reducing the health risks associated with certain forms of contraception and abortion, and opposing sexual violence and abuse. Many nineteenth-century feminists, for example, drew attention to the ways in which (hetero)sex could be 'risky' to women; in particular through the debilitating effect of repeated pregnancies and infection from venereal diseases such as syphilis (see Jeffreys, 1985). Also, as I discussed in Chapter 1, during the 1970s and early 1980s criticism of heterosexuality as a form of sexual practice was an important aspect of feminist debates. In particular, feminists challenged the centrality of vaginal intercourse in heterosexual relations as often unsatisfying for women, legitimising other ways of obtaining sexual pleasure through non-penetrative means (Koedt 1974/1996). Feminists, in other words, have had a great deal to say about 'safer sex' long before HIV appeared on the scene.

Arguably, in largely ignoring feminist analyses of sexuality, the construction of a concept of safer sex that now predominates tends to marginalise more traditional feminist concerns about sexual practice. According to Debbie Cameron (1992: 44):

> The whole question of what constitutes 'safer sex' has come to be defined in terms of whether a particular sexual practice is more or less likely to transmit HIV: the sense in which pornography and phone sex might actually threaten the physical or psychological safety of women, or be open to criticism on other grounds, is glossed over in this discourse where safer sex is better and 'safer' means 'carrying lower HIV risk'.

As I have outlined above, from a feminist perspective the concept of safer sex incorporates much broader concerns than HIV/AIDS. It is also about not getting other sexually transmitted diseases, avoiding unplanned pregnancy, reducing the health risks associated with certain forms of contraception and preventing cervical cancer. In addition, as Cameron suggests, there are all sorts of reasons why sex for women may be experienced as unsafe for emotional as well as physical reasons. Studies such as those I referred to earlier have demonstrated that women often feel pressurised into having sex to please their partner, which can damage their self-esteem and leave them feeling used and exploited. 'Safer sex is about sex we enjoy and feel good about. It is about sex on our terms; sex that reduces the risks to our minds as well as our bodies' (Richardson, 1990: 34–5). From this perspective, it is possible to critique the promotion of certain practices as 'safer sex' *despite* their involving little or no risk of transmission of HIV.

Another argument put forward for the need for greater feminist engagement with HIV/AIDS, which I referred to at the beginning of this chapter, is that AIDS became a major focus for public debates about sexuality and 'the family'. As Sontag (1983) has argued, AIDS has served as a metaphor, one which during the 1980s helped to revitalise a conservative sexual politics that seeks to situate sexuality within a reproductive, marital context, associating other forms of sexuality – homosexuality, prostitution and promiscuity in particular – with sin and disease. Alongside and in part as a response to this renewed sexual conservatism, a very different form of politics emerged towards the end of the 1980s out of especially gay organisations involved in AIDS activism, such as, for example, ACT UP. Feminist theory and politics also contributed to the discourse on the 'sexual politics of AIDS' but, as I have already outlined, to a rather limited extent. This was seen by some feminist writers at the time as a major cause for concern, primarily because many of the issues raised in connection with HIV/AIDS are of central importance to feminism (Segal, 1987b, 1989). In a more positive vein, some writers warned that feminists were 'missing the boat' in so far as HIV/AIDS afforded opportunities to redefine sexuality and negotiate new meanings (Coward, 1987; Richardson, 1987/1989). The gradual recognition during the 1980s that, globally, HIV was primarily a (hetero)sexually transmitted disease could, for instance, be seen as contesting what has commonly been understood as 'natural' or 'normal' about sexuality, in particular the focus on 'sex' as vaginal intercourse. More fundamentally, what I have elsewhere referred to as 'the challenge of AIDS' (Richardson, 1987/1989), provided feminism with an opportunity to highlight the role that sexuality plays in men's control over women and the need for changes in sexual discourse which will enable the social transformation of heterosexual relationships. Sara Scott (1987: 18) clearly recognised this:

> Ironically, AIDS has promoted the open discussion of sexual practice on an unprecedented scale. We should seize the opportunity to get into the debate, proposing alternatives to a penetrative heterosexual morality and place a radical feminist analysis of sexuality firmly on the agenda.

In addition to considering the contribution feminist theory can make to how we understand and respond to HIV and AIDS, we can also ask: 'What are the implications for feminist theory and practice of the HIV/AIDS epidemic?' HIV/AIDS has reminded us, in case we needed reminding, that sexuality is still a central concern and that, even in supposedly postmodern western societies, as Tamsin Wilton (1994: 4) has commented: '. . . unequal relations of power between women and men are not simply of academic interest. In the context of HIV/AIDS they are literally life or death issues, for men as well as for women'.

Research on how women are placed at risk and how they feel able – or not – to protect themselves and their partners, highlights how men's power over women, economically and socially, affects sexual relationships and constrains women's options for HIV prevention, as well as for safer sex more generally. Furthermore, HIV/AIDS not only highlights the potential dangers of heterosexuality as a form of sexual practice, it also underlines the importance of the current ordering of heterosexuality to understanding women's subordination more broadly. This can be evidenced in a number of ways, for example in the way that women outside of 'normal' married, heterosexual relations have often been represented within the AIDS discourse. Motherhood is another important aspect of the institution of heterosexuality, and here again many of the reproductive rights issues connected with HIV/AIDS can be seen as attempts at preventing HIV transmission through the control of women's fertility.

In the following two chapters I will examine these and related issues in an attempt to illustrate how feminist theory and practice, as well as being validated in certain respects, might also be developed in the light of our understanding of HIV/AIDS and how it impacts on women's lives.

8

IN/VISIBLE WOMEN AND
DIS/APPEARING MEN

Cultural constructions of AIDS and HIV infection influence the formation of HIV policy and education, research paradigms and media accounts as well as individual understandings of risk and safety. More specifically, they invoke and constitute particular ideas about gender and sexuality, which inform representations of women and men in discourses on AIDS, in particular in HIV policy and health education. This chapter will examine constructions of gender in the context of HIV/AIDS and, related to this, consider how (hetero)sexuality is conceptualised. In so doing, I hope to illustrate some of the contradictions that exist in the representation of women, men and heterosexuality within AIDS discourse.

Gendering AIDS

> In the AIDS crisis, *women are most of the time completely invisible*, . . . face severe and sometimes insurmountable obstacles to coming out with a positive HIV status, have almost no research done about them, have little money, are rarely provided with adequate care, and have to take care of the most people. (The ACT UP / New York Women and AIDS Book Group, 1990: 243, my italics)

From 1981, when the first cases of AIDS were reported in the United States, AIDS was firmly constructed in the west as a disease affecting male bodies, more specifically the bodies of gay men. The initial linking of AIDS with gay men, reified in the naming of the new disease Gay Related Immune Deficiency (GRID), reflected the assumption on the part of medical researchers that this was a disease that was associated with the lifestyles and behaviours of 'homosexuals'. The media also played a significant role in constructing this view, frequently referring to AIDS as the 'gay disease' or the 'gay plague' (Crimp, 1989; Watney, 1994).

Popular and scientific narratives for the understanding of AIDS, in addition to being gendered and sexualised, have also drawn substantially on ideas about race. In this early context, it was the image of the *white* gay man who represented the major source of 'contagion'. However, the racialisation of the body affected by AIDS as white was soon to be disrupted by accounts of cases of AIDS among black groups in the USA, in particular Haitian and African immigrants. By the mid-1980s, as writers began to focus on the occurrence of AIDS in Africa and the possibility that the disease had originated there – drawing on highly racist beliefs about differences in sexual and other forms of possible 'risk practices' (see, for example, Chirimuuta and Chirimuuta, 1987; Sabatier, 1988) – AIDS also increasingly became associated with the bodies of black (heterosexual) men and women.

These early accounts have had a significant and long-standing effect on shaping responses to HIV and AIDS individually, socially and politically. Most obviously, the initial gendering of the body affected by AIDS as male decreased the likelihood of HIV infection being perceived as significant to women (Wilton, 1997). This was compounded by the association of AIDS with 'homosexuality', a social category also usually gendered as male. Sexualising the HIV-infected body as gay also encouraged the view that heterosexual men were also not at risk and, by implication, 'safe'. The construction of discrete sexual constituencies within the medical and health education literature, as well as in the social imagination more generally, was (and still is) important to this understanding of risk, as has been the dominant representation of AIDS as a sexually transmitted disease.

The 'gay/male-ing' of AIDS not only influenced individual women's perceptions of HIV risk – in particular, who may or may not pose a risk to them – it also shaped women's experiences of living with HIV/AIDS. As I pointed out in the previous chapter, development of models of service provision and support networks were initially based primarily upon the needs of young gay men living in urban communities, often single and mostly without children. Available treatments were frequently tested on male-only samples, which meant that, as a consequence, they were often difficult for women to access because of medical fears of possible unknown risks both to them but more especially to any future child they might have. Many women experienced crucial delays in diagnosis because doctors often failed to think of HIV/AIDS as affecting female bodies. This situation was compounded by the fact that until 1993, when the US Centers for Disease Control altered its criteria for a diagnosis of AIDS and HIV-related illness to include gynaecological symptoms, diagnostic categories of AIDS/HIV-related illness were constructed almost entirely on the basis of studies of the effects of HIV infection on men.

A further consequence of the initial 'gay/male-ing of AIDS' was that HIV/AIDS was linked with stigmatised and deviant practices (Patton, 1994). The association of risk of HIV infection and 'deviance', which emerges as a strong theme in AIDS discourse, has been highly significant in constructing ways of thinking about women and HIV/AIDS, in particular who is in/visible. Both HIV/AIDS education and media reports of AIDS have frequently relied on traditional constructions of 'woman' as white, heterosexual and middle class. More specifically, the term 'woman' typically represents the 'ordinary', 'innocent' and *heterosexual* 'victim', against which other 'women at risk' are constructed as 'deviations' who appear as a danger to others. In particular, as women whose bodies are a risk to men and to possible future children.

In/visible women

Cindy Patton (1994: 2) is right to challenge the 'often circulated idea that women were "invisible" in the first decade of the epidemic', as the quote at the beginning of this chapter claims. Although it is true to say that until the early 1990s researchers, policymakers and governments largely ignored how HIV/AIDS affects women specifically, certain groups of women were clearly visible in AIDS discourse. In the early stages of the epidemic women at risk were usually represented as women sex workers, lesbians, black African women, women who injected drugs, and 'promiscuous' women. (The inclusion and exclusion of lesbians in AIDS discourse is explored more fully in the next chapter.)

This division between visible and invisible women in AIDS discourse is characterised by Kitzinger (1994) as a form of the good woman/bad woman, madonna/whore dichotomy which is a common feature of representations of women. However, it is not simply a case of the figure of 'bad woman' being depicted, in all her various forms, within AIDS discourses, while the figure of 'good woman' fails to materialise. For instance, within HIV/AIDS education aimed at promoting safer sex among heterosexuals, as I discussed briefly in Chapter 7, the focus has been upon the need for women to take control in sexual encounters, in particular through encouraging condom use. This is one of the main ways in which 'woman' is visible in AIDS discourse as a symbol of normality, as distinct from 'woman' as deviant other. 'Woman' as protector of the nation's sexual health and safety.

Other common representations of women as responsible/good citizens in AIDS discourse are 'woman' as carer and, interconnected with this, 'woman' as mother. Although much of the early literature on women, HIV and AIDS concentrated on women as possible sources of HIV infection, in particular on female prostitutes, attention was also given to women as carers of people with AIDS (Richardson, 1987/1989). Although it is women who provide much of the day-to-day care of the sick in public health care settings, the focus was primarily upon care within domestic settings by women as wives of men perceived as 'victims' of the disease (most commonly men who had received HIV-infected blood or blood products) or as mothers, usually of gay men (Moffat, 1986). In both of these contexts traditional notions of 'woman' as wife and mother, providing care within the home for male partners and for children, are invoked.

In contrast to this, we can observe a very different conceptualisation of motherhood in AIDS discourse, which arguably comes within the boundaries of the 'bad woman' category. This is the woman who has apparently failed her duties as a mother, for instance by rejecting a child who has HIV or AIDS or, more commonly, through transmitting HIV to her infant, *especially* if she was aware of her HIV status prior to becoming pregnant. We need to understand such responses in the context of the public health advice that has been offered to women. Because of the possible risk of transmission of HIV during pregnancy and delivery, women were initially advised that if they thought they may have been at risk of infection they should take an HIV test and, if the result was positive, delay having a child until more was known about the effects of HIV on pregnancy. The recommendation for women who were already pregnant and tested positive was that they be considered for and counselled about a termination of the pregnancy. Some doctors went further than this in advocating 'directive counselling' as a way of 'persuading' HIV positive women to forgo future childbearing altogether (Arrras, 1989). As a consequence, concerns were expressed about the 'reproductive rights' of HIV positive women who, it was claimed, were at risk of being pressurised into having 'forced abortions' or sterilisation (for a fuller discussion see Richardson, 1993).

As the numbers of women reported to be HIV positive have steadily increased, so has public concern over mother to child transmission. The dominant message in most HIV/AIDS campaigns and health education has continued to be one of preventing women from passing HIV to a child during pregnancy, the process of birth and, in the west, through breast-feeding if they have already had a baby. (Breastfeeding has been shown to be a route of HIV transmission and therefore, where it is a safe and economic option, bottle-feeding is recommended (Dunn et al., 1992; Newell et al., 1997).) The risk of a baby acquiring HIV from its mother ranges from 15% to 25% in industrialised countries and from 25% to 45% in developing countries – a difference that can, in part, be explained by the fact that breastfeeding is more likely to be practised in the latter. Evidence suggests that the risk of transmission is likely to be higher when the mother has recently been infected with HIV or is in an advanced stage of HIV-related disease, or if the baby is exposed to the mother's bodily fluids during the birth (European Collaborative Study, 1992; Peckham and Gibb, 1995; UNAIDS, 1999).

In many countries concern about mother to child transmission has led to the introduction of routine testing of pregnant women in antenatal clinics, with the option of termination for those who test positive or treatment and interventions during antenatal care to reduce the risk of transmission of HIV if they decide to go ahead with the pregnancy. Routine testing of pregnant women in antenatal clinics has been recommended in high HIV prevalence areas in the UK since 1994. By the 1990s the social context of taking an HIV test had changed from the early years of the epidemic, when HIV testing offered no recourse to cure or treatment. In the west, with economic resources to support medical research and treatment programmes for the prevention of HIV/AIDS, the pros and cons of taking a test gradually changed as medical interventions became available which, despite the disadvantage of various side effects, appeared to ameliorate HIV-related disease. In addition, studies identified a number of interventions that if applied in the case of women who are aware of their HIV positive status can reduce their risk of having an HIV-infected baby. These include treatment with antiretroviral drugs such as AZT during the pregnancy and labour and administration to the infant after birth, delivery by caesarean section and avoiding breastfeeding. If all of these are followed then, in the west, research suggests that the risk of infection can be reduced from 25% to 5%. (Connor et al., 1994; Duong et al., 1999). The long-term picture of disease progression in children with HIV is unknown, as are the implications of treatment with antiretroviral drugs (Havens et al., 1997). However, in the west currently about a fifth of children with HIV die before the age of one. After this, disease progression is slower, but by the age of six 30% to 40% of HIV-infected children will have developed AIDS or other HIV related disease (Department of Health, 1999).

The introduction of routine testing of pregnant women in antenatal clinics raises numerous ethical issues, including the need to ensure voluntary and informed consent and the issue of whose interests are being served by such testing (Sherr, 1999). This is highlighted in the case of women who decide not to be tested, with some centres such as, for example, in New York, mandating antenatal testing or insisting on the infant being tested, which would mean that the mother would eventually know her own HIV status (Beder and Beckerman, 1996; Cooper, 1996). The argument that is often put forward as a justification for such measures is in terms of the rights of the 'unborn child', as against the rights of women. It is also almost always the woman who is tested and not her male partner, if she has one. This is despite the fact that a woman could be infected by heterosexual transmission during pregnancy. Here we have a good example of 'old' issues for feminism resurfacing, albeit in a different context. In many developing countries this is thrown into starker relief by the fact that having identified HIV pregnant women through antenatal testing, their access to antiviral drugs is often limited to the period of pregnancy and labour. This has prompted the question of whether women are being treated for the sake of the baby alone. (There are parallels here with the decision in the west to offer routine testing of women in antenatal clinics but not, say, in abortion clinics.) The response of organisations such as UNAIDS is that such questions are based on an 'erroneous perception'; the use of such drugs should not be seen as 'treatment' but as a 'vaccine' for the infant (UNAIDS, 1999). This is notwithstanding the fact that elsewhere in the world such drugs are used as a treatment for HIV-infected women and men.

In recent years, AIDS researchers have made significant advances in the prevention of mother to child transmission of HIV, and the number of cases in children infected has declined in many countries as a result. In the United States, for example, where antiretroviral therapy is widely used to reduce perinatal transmission, the number of reported children with AIDS has gone down dramatically, by 80% (Lindegren et al., 1999). Numbers have also declined in many European countries. In the UK, however, the number of infants with HIV infection has not declined and, in 1997, was higher than in countries such as France and Italy that have significantly more HIV-infected adults (Nicoll et al., 1999). As a consequence, the Department of Health, in 1999, announced a change of policy that *all* pregnant women should be offered and recommended an HIV test along with other antenatal screening tests with the aim of reducing mother to baby transmission of HIV by 80% by the year 2002 (Department of Health, 1999). The expectation was that more HIV positive pregnant women would be diagnosed at a sufficiently early stage in the pregnancy to be offered either a termination or treatment and interventions during antenatal care to reduce the chances of the baby's being infected.

Within this general framework it is important to acknowledge that during the 1990s some moves were made towards accepting the HIV positive mother. This, in part, reflects the better medical prognosis for any children they might have, both in terms of advances in treatments which lower the risks of mother to child transmission and the life expectancy of the child if infection does occur. Much more controversial is the idea that HIV positive women should be positively supported in their desire to have children, for instance through access to infertility treatments. In the UK, this was evidenced when Lord Robert Winston agreed to provide IVF (in vitro fertilisation) treatment to a woman known to be HIV positive.

The HIV positive pregnant woman represents a different version of the female body as a source of possible infection and danger; it is women's reproductive potential that is perceived as a risk factor as distinct from women as bodies which personify sexual danger. Risk reduction is once again sought largely through control of the female body, in this case by rendering it incapable of reproduction either temporarily, through contraceptive use or a termination, or permanently, through sterilisation. In countries where abortion is illegal, such as Ireland, the latter option may be attractive to some practitioners and policy makers who wish to affirm their concern with the future health of children whilst leaving unchallenged the view that abortion is morally wrong whatever the circumstances.

The representation of certain groups of women as at risk has, then, largely been in terms of the danger they pose to others; it is through them that HIV may be transmitted to men and their 'heterosexual partners', and to children. Such understandings also draw attention to the ways in which constructions of woman as sexually risky/safe are interpreted through the interacting categories of class and race. Historically, the sexuality of working-class women *and* men has often been portrayed as more lascivious, animal, free and liberated (read sexually available) than that of middle-class women and men, representing the threat of both immorality and disease (Hawkes, 1996). Similarly, racist stereotypes of black men *and* women as highly sexed, promiscuous and immoral (Collins, 1996), in part, help to explain the focus on black Africans as the original source of HIV infection (Chirimuuta and Chirimuuta, 1987). The interconnections between race and gender, however, mean that the racialisation of sexual ideologies has somewhat different implications for black women than for black men. Discussing representations of black female sexuality, bell hooks (1992) highlights how the association of black women with a heightened (hetero)sexuality leads to an association between black female sexuality and sexual deviancy – in particular, an association between black female sexuality and prostitution.

These constructions of black female sexuality have important implications for how black women's bodies are perceived as potentially dangerous to (white) heterosexual males and, interestingly, their female sexual partners. Men's fears of women may reflect such racist stereotyping. For example, Jenny Kitzinger (1994) reports that some of the white heterosexual male participants interviewed in the AIDS Media Research Project made explicit reference to the dangers of black women. This is also a good example of how the bodies of (white) heterosexual men come to be positioned as 'at risk', rather than posing a risk to their partners. Indeed, in this scenario it is through the body of a deviant and dangerous other acting on their male partner that 'ordinary (white) heterosexual women' are put at risk.

In the case of women perceived as being in 'ordinary heterosexual relationships', this has encouraged a belief in their invulnerability and safety. This view is also influenced by the social construction of female sexuality as 'passive', so that in AIDS discourse heterosexual women are generally understood to be sexual partners of men rather than as sexual agents in their own right. Indeed, if women are sexually assertive in heterosexual encounters they potentially run the risk of losing their 'heterosexual respectability' and becoming labelled as deviant/at risk.

Dis/appearing men

The construction of the heterosexual man in AIDS discourse as primarily someone who is at risk from others, in particular from certain categories of women who may tempt him, or from predatory gay or bisexual men, raises a number of interesting contradictions. For example, between traditional notions of male sexual agency and the situating of the (white) heterosexual male as a body which is acted on, a 'passive victim' to the sexual power of the other who seeks to tempt or seduce him. There is also clearly a tension here between the perception of heterosexual men as 'victims' of strong sexual urges, which may lead them into dangerous liaisons with 'deviant' women/men, and the relative invisibility of heterosexual men as a possible source of HIV infection and a potential danger to others. In this respect one might want to argue that the emphasis within HIV/AIDS prevention campaigns and health education on encouraging condom use not only

1e possibility of 'normal' so-called heterosexual intercourse
fe, but also the male body, in so far as it is men who wear con-
eir penises and women who are being targeted at encouraging

One of the consequences of the representation of women primarily as a
potential source of HIV infection within much of the published work on
HIV/AIDS in the past, is that it helped to render invisible possible risks to
women themselves. Arguably, this resulted in educators and policy-makers
marginalising the issues relating to how and why women become infected.
The underlying concern would appear to have been how to protect the
health of men and children, rather than addressing women's health needs.

As I have already indicated, much of the health education aimed at
heterosexuals in the USA, Britain, Australia and elsewhere, was initially
targeted at women (Wilton, 1997). For example, in Britain in March 1989
the Health Education Authority (HEA) launched their first major advertising campaign targeted at (heterosexual) women, with the aim of
encouraging women to ask their male partners to use a condom.
Unfortunately, what the HEA did not do was run a parallel campaign
directed at heterosexual men, thereby reinforcing the belief that it is
women who are primarily responsible for safer sex and, by implication,
heterosexual transmission of HIV. Since then the Health Education
Authority has made some attempts to specifically target heterosexual
men – such as, for instance, in the television campaign it ran in 1992,
which had men talking about how they had become infected through heterosex.

One could argue that such examples are evidence of HIV/AIDS health
education colluding with dominant discourses of sexuality, in which it is
commonly assumed that men are 'naturally' less able to exercise self-control in sexual encounters than are women. However, there is a
contradictory message in expecting girls and young women, who are often
positioned as 'passive' (hetero)sexual partners, both to carry condoms and
encourage their use. Such contradictions are clearly felt by many young
women themselves. In Holland et al.'s (1998) study, for example, concern
about the negative implications of being seen as sexually assertive was an
important factor in inhibiting women from carrying condoms or insisting
on their use. Research on heterosexual men suggests that women's fears of
being labelled by their male partners in negative ways if they carry condoms, for example as 'easy' or a 'slag', are well founded (e.g. Kitzinger,
1994; Holland et al., 1994b, 1998).

A parallel can be drawn here with the concerns expressed by some politicians and policymakers since the late 1980s over the so-called problem of
teenage pregnancy, notably in Britain, which has the highest rates in
Europe, and in the United States (Millar, 1994). For example, the construction of pregnancy as a deliberate and wilful act by young single girls in
order to jump housing queues and qualify for welfare benefits seemingly
ignores the various problems young women often face in negotiating

sexual encounters with their male partners, which a number of studies have highlighted (Holland et al., 1990, 1998; Ingham et al., 1992; Lees, 1993). Furthermore, as is the norm in AIDS discourse, the heterosexual male is largely invisible in such accounts, with the emphasis on controlling female bodies. Even the labelling of the 'problem' as teenage pregnancy rather than teenage conception reveals the way in which it is female bodies and behaviour, rather than men's, which are under public scrutiny; it is almost as if women became pregnant through parthenogenesis.

The lack of discussion of men's contribution to reproduction in accounts which problematise 'teenage pregnancy' could be seen as somewhat contradictory in a British context, given the government's apparent concern with male responsibility in introducing the 1991 Child Support Act. The Act, implemented from 1993, represents an attempt to reduce the amount paid in welfare benefits to the growing number of single mothers by making men financially liable for any children they biologically father. However, the primary focus has been on how to ensure payment rather than how to ensure men's involvement in avoiding an unwanted pregnancy. More recently, under a Labour government, recommendations that boys should have their pocket money reduced if they father a child (Social Exclusion Report, 1999) reflect a similar approach, one that focuses on economic liability rather than seeking to encourage 'safer' sexual and reproductive practices in teenage boys.

As I have previously argued, similar issues are raised in the context of HIV and AIDS. For instance, although in 1993 the World Health Organisation (WHO) identified (heterosexual) men's reluctance to make changes in their sexual behaviour as an important factor in the global transmission of HIV, the 'highest priority' was given to encouraging 'woman controlled' methods to prevent HIV transmission, including research into vaginal virucides (WHO, 1993). Although the development of such products, including, for example, the female condom which was launched in Britain in 1992, can be seen as offering women greater control, such proposed 'solutions' are nevertheless focused upon the manipulation of female bodies, leaving male risk behaviours seemingly unchallenged.

Heteronormativity

The omission of critiques of heterosexuality in debates about teenage pregnancy and in health education campaigns aimed at HIV/AIDS prevention not only fails to acknowledge heterosexuality as a powerful dynamic in the social control of women, but to some extent also serves to construct heterosexuality as exempt from the need to change, particularly in the case of heterosexual males. This differs from HIV/AIDS health education and promotional materials targeted at gay men, many of which have insisted on the importance of using condoms during anal penetration, at the same time managing to convey the message that gay men are expected to

alternatives to anal intercourse or even give it up altogether
1996). The 'ON ME, NOT IN ME' slogan used in some of the safer
rmation designed for gay men in the USA in the 1980s is an example of this. This is perhaps unsurprising; social policy is socially
constructed on the basis of normative assumptions about sexuality, and
central to this is the notion of heterosexuality as normal, appropriate and
acceptable sexual behaviour (Carabine, 1996a). Furthermore, the association of risk for HIV infection and social 'deviance', to which I have already
referred, makes it difficult to see those involved in relationships defined as
socially acceptable and 'normal' as at risk.

In line with dominant constructions of risk and AIDS, the context in
which heterosexuality *is* likely to be perceived as unsafe or risky in relation
to HIV infection is when it is 'deviant heterosexuality', or some might
prefer to use the term 'queer heterosexuality'. This can be interpreted in a
number of different ways: for instance, where the deviancy is 'promiscuous
(hetero)sex', sex where heterosexuality is challenged by the identity of one
or more of the partners, or as specific forms of sexual practice. The first two
are gendered understandings. It is primarily heterosexual women, not
men, who are likely to be deemed to be deviant/at risk through being
labelled as 'promiscuous'. Whereas, in the second example, as the person
identified in normative heterosexual narratives as the 'active' partner, it is
the identity of the man as sexually 'different', not the woman, which is
most likely to influence the perception of their partner being at risk. This is
evidenced in the way that the characterisation of bisexuals as posing a
threat to society, by acting as a 'bridging group' by which HIV can spread
into the 'general population' (i.e. 'ordinary' heterosexual women and men),
primarily refers to bisexual men. As Wilton (1997: 26) states: 'It is non-
sense to suggest that bisexual *women* are "likely to have sex with
homosexual men" or that they will then "spread HIV into the heterosexual
community" by having sex with a heterosexual woman. Bisexuality, then,
is *male* sexuality.' This is reflected in HIV/AIDS health education strategies.
Although HIV/AIDS educational materials have targeted bisexual men,
very little safer sex information has been addressed to bisexual women
specifically.

Finally, the association of AIDS with certain kinds of sexual practice, anal
sex in particular, relates to the linking of HIV/AIDS with gay men and the
stereotyping of 'gay sex' as anal intercourse (i.e. penile penetration of the
rectum). Deviant heterosexuality, in this sense, can include the practice of
what are commonly construed as 'homosexual' practices. Attempts to
understand the occurrence of AIDS among heterosexuals have appealed to
such understandings of 'deviant heterosexuality'. For instance, in the mid-
1980s many writers sought to explain the wider occurrence of HIV
infection and AIDS among heterosexuals in Africa by suggesting that anal
intercourse was more commonly practised in Africa than in the west,
mainly as a cheap method of birth control (see, for example, Leibowitch,
1985).

In situating particular acts (anal intercourse) and individuals (promiscuous women/bisexual men) as deviant/risky the normative boundaries of heterosexual inclusion are firmly constructed and, by implication, those of safe/normal sex. That is to say, the construction of heterosexuality within AIDS discourse reinforces the idea of heterosexuality being associated with specific practices. A more interesting question perhaps is whether it also increases the likelihood of a heterosexual identification.

Recent attempts to theorise heterosexuality by feminist and queer theorists have included discussion of the (de)construction of heterosexual identities and greater specification of the social and political meanings attached to heterosexuality as an identity (Jackson 1996a, b; Smart, 1996a, b). Some writers have also queried the contexts under which such hegemonic ways of being and behaving are disrupted. For example, (some) feminist gatherings may be one context where (some) heterosexual women may feel 'part of a marginal fringe as heterosexuals' (Lips and Freedman, 1993). The question I am raising here is how far responses to HIV/AIDS can be regarded as providing a context in which the 'heterosexual person' is in the process of being produced? Certainly, the initial conflation of AIDS with 'gay man' both gendered and sexualised the disease in a way that provided a context where heterosexual men could declare themselves as not at risk because *they* were heterosexual. For heterosexual women, the potential impact of stereotyping lesbians as, initially, 'high-risk', and then subsequently as women who are unaffected by HIV/AIDS, is diminished by the relative absence of lesbians in literature on HIV and AIDS.

Such constructions rely, at least in part, on the association of risk with certain social groups, which was evident in early AIDS educational strategies that employed the idea of specific 'risk-groups'. The concept of 'risk groups' has been used to stereotype and categorise people who are seen as outside the parameters of 'the general population'. Thus, 'heterosexual' has tended to be equated with the general public, as distinct from other groups categorised as 'at risk' such as, for example, gay or bisexual men, intravenous (IV) drug users, or sex workers.

By the late 1980s, it was evident that there had been a shift in HIV/AIDS health education policy away from talking about risk groups to emphasising risk behaviours. From this perspective, it is possible to argue that rather than encouraging a new (hetero)sexual categorisation, AIDS had the potential to disrupt the notion of distinct sexual categories of people – for example, heterosexual, lesbian, gay – through an emphasis on routes of transmission rather than on group identities. However, the fact that this distinction between risk group and risk behaviour is only partial in HIV/AIDS health education would seem to counter such possibilities. Indeed, the (contradictory) emphasis within governmental HIV/AIDS campaigns on partner selection as a risk reduction strategy – the need to 'Choose Your Partner Carefully' – is one possible reason for the continued association of risk with particular individuals rather than specific practices.

Conclusion

In this chapter I have argued that HIV/AIDS health education, more especially information and advice about safer sex, has relied on culturally dominant notions of gender and sexuality. However, it is also the case that within AIDS discourse there are numerous contradictions in the representation of women, men and (hetero)sexuality. For example, much of the (heterosexual) safer sex discourse appears to have reaffirmed rather than challenged the notion of 'sex' as vaginal intercourse, even though vaginal and anal intercourse are associated with 'high-risk' (Campbell, 1987; Wilton, 1997). It is, I would argue, the privileged construction of heterosexuality and heterosexual (vaginal) intercourse as 'safe by nature' (Patton, 1994: 118), that gives rise to such contradictions. A contradiction that is thrown into starker relief when one considers that, as I have stated earlier, the dominant message in health education policies aimed at targeting gay men has been on the dangers associated with anal intercourse, and the need to avoid such risks by engaging in other, less risky, non-penetrative sexual practices.

There are other contradictions within AIDS discourse which threaten to disrupt how gender and sexuality are traditionally conceptualised. For example, as I have already indicated, although AIDS has been firmly constructed as a 'male disease', at least in the west, the heterosexual male is largely invisible in AIDS discourse. This is evident when one examines HIV/AIDS health education campaigns aimed at heterosexuals, most of which have been targeted at women. Thus, while the construction of normative female sexuality as 'passive' and male as 'active' is reinforced in certain aspects of AIDS discourse, for instance in representing heterosexual women as the sexual 'partners' of men and in the association of female sexual agency with deviancy, it is elsewhere threatened by the allocation of responsibility for negotiating sexual practices to women and the demand that they take active control of the (hetero)sexual encounter. Similarly, the construction of (white) heterosexual male bodies as safe, at risk from dangerous/deviant women/men as sexual agents, further threatens the active male/passive female binaries. Such elaborations are important not only because they highlight how particular ideas about gender and sexuality are represented in HIV/AIDS policy and education, but also because they help illustrate how gender and (hetero)sexuality are constructed through HIV/AIDS policy-making.

9

SEXUALITY, IDENTITY AND RISK

In recent years there has been greater recognition of issues relating to women, HIV and AIDS, yet lesbians and bisexual women are among the least studied and least understood populations affected by HIV/AIDS. However, while questions of difference and exclusion are central to understanding the position of lesbians in media and medical accounts of HIV/AIDS, it is not true to say that lesbians have been absent from such discourses. The position of lesbians is characterised, at least in Britain and the United States, by three main phases which reveal the ways in which lesbians have been both excluded *and* included in debates about AIDS. I have described these three phases in the following terms: 'High-Risk' Women (from 1981 to the mid-1980s), Lesbians Are Safe (from the mid- to late-1980s) and, finally, Addressing Women's Actual Risk (from the mid-1980s in the USA and 1990 in the UK). With some degree of overlap, each of these phases represents a significant shift in the history of the AIDS epidemic.

In this chapter I intend to analyse these shifts through an examination of each of these three phases. Although this will highlight how lesbians as a specific social group have been addressed in the context of responses to HIV/AIDS, my aims are somewhat broader than this. In using the interesting case example of lesbians, a group whose risk status has undergone a number of changes, I want to address the question of how meanings of risk are mediated by sexual status, in particular through the effects on attributions of 'risky' and 'non-risky' to both partners and practices.

'High-risk' women

The initial stereotyping of AIDS as a 'gay disease', particularly by the media, resulted in a resurgence of public homophobia, an increase in hostility towards the 'gay community' that was directed at lesbians as well as gay men. Also like gay men, lesbians were often perceived as 'high-risk'; as HIV/AIDS 'carriers'. The American Red Cross in 1982–3, for example, advised lesbians to defer donating blood, as gay men were urged to do (Crimp, 1989). In Britain, the question of whether it was safe for lesbians to

d was still being debated by the medical profession in the pages
cet as late as 1986. That same year the Blood Transfusion Service
r city in England refused to accept a woman's donated blood
~~...~~ ~~...~~ told them that she was a lesbian. Shortly afterwards she received
a letter stating the Service's policy of not accepting blood of known lesbians, because of the supposed risk of it being infected with HIV
(Richardson, 1987/1989). Campaigns by local lesbian groups subsequently
led to this policy's being changed.

The inclusion of lesbians in early accounts of AIDS is interesting for a
number of reasons. As was outlined in the previous chapter, in the west
AIDS was initially gendered as a 'male disease', so much so that until the
late 1980s in Britain a common response to attempts to discuss the topic of
women and AIDS was 'Do women actually get AIDS?' The representation
of lesbians was, however, informed by two other important aspects of the
conceptualisation of AIDS that counterbalanced this: the association with
'homosexuality' and risk of HIV infection with social/sexual 'deviance'. It
is as 'deviant' individuals, subsumed under the category 'homosexual',
that lesbians could be perceived as 'at risk'.

The inclusion of women identified as lesbians as a 'high-risk' group for
exposure to HIV is further evidence of how, despite very little attention
being given to women and AIDS until the late 1980s, neither AIDS nor
homosexuality were entirely gendered as male in the early stages of the
epidemic. On the other hand, as I discussed in Chapter 8, we need to
recognise that the category 'woman' has been employed as an exclusive
category in AIDS discourse, symbolically excluding large proportions of
the female population who fall into so-called 'high-risk' populations
(Kitzinger, 1994). In this phase the lesbian body is constructed as a source
of possible HIV infection as distinct from the construction of 'women's
bodies', equated with a normalised and naturalised heterosexuality, as
unaffected by AIDS. Conceptualising lesbians as 'deviant other', as not
'real women' in either body or mind, therefore enabled the potential disruption to the perception of AIDS as a disease affecting male bodies to be
partially resisted.

The idea of the 'homosexual' body (both male and female) as diseased,
and a source of possible contagion and danger, has a long history in medical and psychiatric accounts (Terry, 1995). The association with disease is
further compounded by the representation of certain forms of female
sexual practice as leading to the spread of sexually transmitted disease.
This has been particularly evident in relation to female prostitutes who, as
was the case with syphilis during the nineteenth century (Walkowitz,
1992), have been represented as a source of HIV infection and a danger to
'innocent male victims' (Brandt, 1985). More generally, women who are
labelled sexually 'promiscuous' have also been portrayed as a vector
through which sexually transmitted diseases infiltrate wider society.
Significantly, it is promiscuity in women and not (heterosexual) men that
is seen as problematic. Underlying such characterisations is a concern with

sexual behaviour which transgresses the normative boundaries of female sexuality – specifically, women's autonomous sexuality and sexual agency. In this context, it is not difficult to see how lesbians and bisexual women also come to represent sexualities that threaten to infiltrate and contaminate.

Lesbians are safe

The picture of how lesbians related to the emerging AIDS epidemic is more complex, however, than an overemphasis on (homo)sexual identity and an underemphasis on the gendered dimensions of 'risk'. In direct contrast to the initial construction of lesbians as 'high risk', from the mid- to late-1980s the dominant biomedical interpretation was that lesbians were among those *least* at risk for HIV infection and AIDS. As a consequence, lesbians were gradually excluded from and rendered invisible within AIDS discourses. A comprehensive report from the National Research Council in the United States, for example, referred to lesbians only in terms of their recruitment for blood donors to help protect the safety of the blood supply (Miller et al., 1990).

This shift towards lesbians becoming increasingly invisible in AIDS discourse is all the more interesting when one considers that it occurred at a time when there was a rapid increase in the incidence of HIV infection in women, especially in the USA, and, related to this, a growing awareness of how HIV/AIDS affects women. The year 1987 was particularly significant in terms of public recognition of AIDS as a women's health issue. Prior to then, there had been very little written about women and AIDS. However, in 1987 the Centers for Disease Control in the United States produced its first published report on women and AIDS and a number of books and articles were published in North America and Europe which specifically addressed AIDS-related issues which affected women (e.g. Kaplan, 1987; Norwood, 1987; Patton and Kelly, 1987; Richardson, 1987/1989).

What are some of the possible reasons for this shift in notions of 'risk' as applied to lesbians? The appearance of women in epidemiological accounts, as well as the emergence of other 'risk-groups' such as haemophiliacs and injecting drug users, provoked, in 1982, the renaming of the syndrome as Acquired Immune Deficiency Syndrome (rather than GRID). Despite this, the fact that the majority of people reported to have AIDS in the west were gay or bisexual men meant that the association between homosexuality and AIDS still continued. Gradually, however, as research and epidemiological data from other countries emerged, it became clear that AIDS affected both individuals and communities in a multiplicity of different ways (Doyal, 1994). In particular, in a number of African countries the almost equal numbers of men and women infected with HIV led to claims that 'heterosexual intercourse' was the most common route for transmission of HIV. The global epidemic of HIV, therefore, challenged the western perception of AIDS as a 'homosexual disease' and forced a closer examination of patterns of sexual behaviour that recognised the complex relationship between sexual identity and practice. This has since been described as a 'de-gaying' of AIDS (Watney, 1994), a process which potentially weakens the original connection of lesbians, as female 'homosexuals', to the epidemic.

Changes in public health policy within the USA and in Britain were also significant in creating the conditions by which lesbians could gradually be excluded from AIDS discourse. By the late 1980s, the notion of 'risk' within HIV health education policy had undergone a number of changes. Of particular importance was the *partial* shift in HIV health education policy away from talking about 'risk groups' to risk behaviours. In the case of sexual transmission of HIV, this meant a focus on sexual acts, in particular anal and vaginal intercourse as 'high-risk', rather than specific sexual identities. This is significant in terms of the perception of lesbians as 'at risk', given that the basis for including lesbians and gay men within one category as 'homosexuals' is sexual partner choice, rather than specific sexual practices.

Particular sexual acts have been assigned a key definitive status in the construction of lesbian, gay and heterosexual identities. As I have discussed elsewhere in this volume, anal intercourse is commonly constructed as a gay male practice, with consequences for the recognition of heterosexuals who may also engage in such practices (Wilton, 1995). The construction of 'normative' gay male sexuality is also distinct from that of lesbian sexuality. Whereas anal penetration has been constituted as the 'definitive and paradigmatic gay male act', it is oral sex which is commonly associated with lesbianism (Wilton, 1997: 27). This is reflected in safer sex campaigns and information, where advice on the use of dental dams during cunnilingus has been almost exclusively addressed to lesbians. The shift towards conceptualising 'risk' in behavioural terms therefore undermines the use of the term homosexual as a category that is applicable to both gay men and lesbians. The exclusion of lesbians is, in this sense, connected to the perception of *difference* from gay men, as well as from heterosexual women.

In addition to the gradual decoupling of homosexuality and AIDS, as well as the categories lesbian and gay man, the identification of lesbians as a social group who do not engage in risk practices is a further key factor in the exclusion of lesbians in popular conceptions of AIDS. This is not only informative of definitions of lesbianism and lesbian sexuality, it also illuminates the socially constructed nature of the concept of risk itself. In this case 'risk' is defined almost exclusively in sexual terms; lesbians are seen as low risk because it is presumed they do not have sex with men. Cultural norms about gender and sexuality have also played an important role in this respect. As we saw in Chapter 8, one of the main ways that women have been represented within AIDS discourse has been as a source of infection, in particular to male sexual partners and to any children they may have. The marking of lesbian bodies as non-reproductive, the idea that lesbians do not become mothers, and as non-heterosexual, in terms of assumed sexual practice, helps to further explain the construction of the lesbian body as invisible and 'safe'.

The dominant construction of lesbianism as a monolithic and socially and sexually discrete category, ignores the plurality of lesbian lifestyles that currently exist. In addition to this, the emphasis on female–female sexuality in defining lesbians as a social group has meant that where questions of risk *have* been raised they have largely been about sexual transmission of HIV. The focus is on female–female transmission; the possibility of other risk factors affecting this population, such as, for example, practices associated with injecting drug use, was largely ignored by researchers until the early 1990s.

To date, only a very few cases of possible female-to-female transmission of HIV during sexual activity have been reported (Sabatini et al., 1984; Marmor et al., 1986; Monzon and Capellan, 1987; Perry et al., 1989) and, although almost no research has been carried out, the medical construction of risk in sexual encounters between women is that it is negligible. This is a view many lesbians appear to share. In the context of institutionalised exclusion from AIDS discourse, many lesbians appear to believe that they will not acquire HIV, irrespective of their behaviour (Cole and Cooper, 1991; Magura et al., 1992; Young et al., 1992; Stevens, 1994; Perry, 1995). This social construction of immunity is based on two different notions of 'risk': one defined in terms of risk behaviours and the other in terms of social group membership. That is, the belief that HIV infection is not a relevant concern may be based upon both a construction of sex between women as 'safe' and the belief that lesbians are a low or no risk group. Although these may be inter-related, it is theoretically important to make a distinction if we are to understand HIV risk perceptions and behaviours. In formulating notions of personal HIV risk, a woman may either rely on notions of the safety of 'lesbian sex' (see Hart, 1986), or she may emphasise identity over behaviour.

Some have argued, on the basis of studies of HIV risk perception and prevention among lesbians, that partner selection practices are the most salient factor in the mediation of understandings of 'risk' (Patton, 1994). Indeed, in one community-based intervention project on HIV prevention education for lesbians and bisexual women, situated in San Francisco, constricting choice of partner was an important risk reduction strategy. Significantly, the exclusion of lesbians from AIDS discourse appeared to reinforce the belief that lesbians were a 'no-risk group', whereas women who identified as bisexual were often considered to be less 'safe' as sexual partners because they were presumed to have sex with men. On this basis, some women stated they would not have sex with bisexual women at all. Others, whilst they did not restrict their sexual partners only to lesbians, practised safer sex with women who identified as bisexual and not with those who identified as lesbian, irrespective of what their partners' actual

behaviours were, because they believed that lesbians were 'safe'. In a similar vein, some women believed that they were not at risk in sharing
needles to inject drugs because they only shared with other lesbians
(Stevens, 1994). Interestingly, 'risk' here is not only being defined in terms
of a woman's sexual identity, but also the presumed relationship of that
identity with sexual practice. Women who were identified as lesbian were
generally thought to be 'safe' because they were presumed not to be
having sex with men.

The assumption that lesbians are not at risk of HIV infection is further
strengthened by a lack of epidemiological data. Unlike reports of male
cases, which usually distinguish between men in terms of sexual orientation, governmental statistics rarely classify cases of AIDS or HIV infection
in women according to whether they are heterosexual, bisexual or lesbian.
The term 'woman' is employed as a homogeneous category, which in practice means that lesbians (and bisexual women), as a defined population,
remain unidentified within official statistics on AIDS and HIV infection.
There have been attempts to guesstimate the number of lesbians in the
United States who are seropositive (Schneider, 1992), and the Centers for
Disease Control (CDC) has provided some information on lesbians and
AIDS. Analysing national surveillance data from June 1980 through to
1991, more than 100 cases of HIV infection and 164 cases of AIDS were
reported in women classified as lesbian, 0.9% of the total number of
women with AIDS (Chu et al., 1992). This should not be regarded as an
accurate record of lesbians and bisexual women with AIDS in the USA at
that time; rather the figures represent those women who were known by
the CDC to have had sexual relationships with other women. In general,
women were not asked if they had sex with other women, and if they did
not say otherwise they were classified as heterosexual (Leonard, 1990).
Under-reporting of HIV among lesbians therefore seems likely, especially
as studies indicate that women who have sexual relationships with other
women are usually very reluctant to acknowledge this to their doctor
(Stevens, 1992).

Relatively little is known about levels of HIV risk among lesbians and
bisexual women. The limited body of research that currently exists supports the view that female-to-female sexual transmission of HIV is
probably rare (Raiteri et al., 1994; Bevier et al., 1995; Lemp et al., 1995).
However a significant number of lesbians appear to be at risk for HIV
infection, in particular through engaging in unprotected vaginal or anal
intercourse with men and risk practices associated with injection drug use
such as needle sharing (Dicker, 1989; Cole and Cooper, 1991; Sasse et al.,
1992; Bevier et al., 1995; Friedman et al., 1992; Hunter et al., 1992; Iardino
et al., 1992; Magura et al., 1992; Reardon et al., 1992; Young et al., 1992;
Cohen et al., 1993). Intravenous drug use, more than high-risk sexual practices with men, has been identified as the most likely means of HIV
transmission. Almost all of the women in the CDC study, for example,
were reported to have become HIV infected through risk practices

associated with injecting drugs. The remainder were women with a history of blood transfusion (Chu et al., 1992).

However we need to examine this last statement a little more closely, both in terms of how risk categories are constructed and what this means in terms of lesbian visibility in the context of AIDS. For example, in the CDC study the definition of a lesbian was a woman who reported having had sexual relations exclusively with women since 1977. Effectively, this meant that if a woman who identified as a lesbian had had sex with a man after 1977, however infrequently, she would most likely be counted as a 'partner' of a heterosexual man. This also reflects the fact that the CDC, like most other surveillance organisations, uses a hierarchy of categories of risk for exposure to HIV: intravenous drug use, receipt of blood products, heterosexual contact with a partner having HIV infection or a specified risk for infection, and no identified risk. Women with multiple risks are assigned to only one exposure category, the category accorded highest risk, unlike men, who may be placed into multiple risk categories if they have more than one possible exposure, for example gay male/injecting drug user. The reported pattern of infection may, in part, therefore, reflect the hierarchical classification of transmission routes which ranks risks associated with injection drug use above other risk behaviours (Bevier et al., 1995). In addition, this means that in the United States if a lesbian uses or has injected drugs, even if she never shared needles, or if she has had sex with a man since 1977, it is likely she will be classified under the category female injecting drug user or, in the latter case, heterosexual contact. There is no specific category for female-to-female exposure. Any woman who insists that her only risk factor is female-to-female transmission is assigned to the category 'other' or 'unknown' risk. This expresses the medical view that female–female transmission is rare. Epidemiological categories of risk behaviour may mean, therefore, that information about possible routes of transmission is not recorded. As Bloor (1995: 55) points out: '. . . these schemes have a self-fulfilling character. The ways of seeing that are endorsed by the adoption of particular classificatory schemes become themselves the basis for the everyday interpretative acts of those who compile and construct the statistical tables.'

The association of risk of HIV infection and 'deviance' which, as I discussed in Chapter 8, emerges as a very strong theme in AIDS discourse, makes the lesbian invisibility I have outlined all the more interesting, not to say contradictory. As I have argued, from the mid- to late-1980s lesbians are presumed to be at 'low or no risk' and therefore not 'dangerous' to others, at least in relation to the spread of HIV infection. However, lesbians still have deviant status, in common with gay and bisexual men and other groups of women such as sex workers and women who inject drugs. The exclusion of lesbians from risk is not then as 'ordinary women', against which other 'women at risk' are constructed, but as a 'deviant group' defined by their sexuality yet whose 'deviance', paradoxically, is not to engage in 'real' sex. Having said this, it is also important to acknowledge that the perception of lesbians as a low- or no-risk group derives less from a monolithic construction of lesbian sex as not 'real or risky sex', than from competing notions of lesbian identity and sexual practice, some of which are highly sexualised and constituted as dangerous and others which are desexualised (Richardson, 1992). Arguably, it is, in part, this ambiguity and lack of clarity over what counts precisely as lesbian 'sex', both with respect to dominant as well as lesbian cultures, which has led to lesbians being excluded from sexual health concerns.

The assumption that lesbians, as a group, are not at risk has important implications for the prevention of HIV infection amongst women who identify as lesbian and may be engaging in behaviours that put them at risk of HIV infection. On a theoretical level it also raises interesting and important questions about the social construction of sex, lesbianism, risk, and safer sex, as well as differences between the category 'lesbian', 'gay' and 'homosexual'. It tells us, for instance, a great deal about the way in which lesbians are defined. It begs the question: 'What is a lesbian?' Presumably, a lesbian is someone who does not and never will inject drugs and share needles, someone who does not and will not have unprotected sex with men, someone who does not get sexually abused or raped, and who does not try to become pregnant. The dominant construction of lesbians as a homogenous social group defined by their sexuality means that the dominant perception of lesbians is as women who sexually desire and have sex with women, and little else. This point is vitally important to grasp if we are to understand the resistance to demands for HIV/AIDS prevention efforts amongst lesbians. The construction of lesbians as essentially sexual, in combination with the assumption that woman-to-woman transmission of HIV is extremely unlikely, leads many to conclude that lesbians are neither at risk of HIV/AIDS nor, therefore, in need of information about risk.

Assessing women's actual risk

The third response to understanding lesbians and risk that I have identified can be characterised as a recognition of the fact that lesbians can and do become infected with HIV. The challenge to the erroneous notion that lesbians are not at risk for HIV infection or don't get AIDS has come largely from within lesbian communities, prompted in part by the emergence of a small but gradually increasing number of lesbians who have 'come out' as HIV positive. In addition, during the late 1980s and early 1990s, a number of books and articles were published which discussed various issues that HIV/AIDS raises for lesbians, including some which provided safer sex guidelines (see, for example, Patton and Kelly, 1987; Richardson, 1987/1989; Patton, 1990; O'Sullivan and Parmar, 1993), as well as personal accounts by HIV positive women (O'Sullivan and Thomson, 1992). The publication of a number of studies in the medical literature, some of which

I referred to in the previous section, also helped to highlight women's actual risk.

Evidence suggests that it is not only limited knowledge about lesbians and bisexual women and HIV, but also the lack of HIV prevention programmes specifically aimed at lesbians which militates against perceptions of risk and the need to adapt behaviours where risk of exposure to HIV exists (Stevens, 1994). In the main, HIV/AIDS health education and promotion efforts have ignored both lesbians themselves, as well as the complexity of lesbian lives and the diversity of lesbian communities (Richardson, 1994; Wilton, 1997). (Other groups who have been ignored include people with disabilities, elders, and heterosexual men.) Presumably this is because of the dominant perception, outlined in the previous section, that lesbians are at little or no risk for HIV infection. As a consequence, lesbians are thought not to need health promotion materials relating to sexual risk/safety. One could also argue that what this highlights is the privileging of a concept of safer sex defined primarily in terms of HIV transmission and unplanned pregnancy, which marginalises other concerns about sexual practice. Although it is unclear whether the presence of HIV in menstrual blood, vaginal and cervical secretions means that it can be passed on during sex from one woman to another, other sexually transmitted infections such as herpes and chlamydia can be transmitted (Rose, 1993). As was discussed in Chapter 7, from a feminist perspective the concept of safer sex incorporates much broader concerns, and it is therefore perhaps not surprising that attempts to provide safer sex guidelines for lesbians have come largely from the lesbian/feminist community.

Lesbian and gay organisations have been producing HIV/AIDS education materials for lesbians since the early years of the epidemic. Although it is also the case that certain sections of both the lesbian and gay community have expressed resistance to acknowledging HIV/AIDS as a relevant health issue for lesbians (Hart, 1986; O'Sullivan and Parmar, 1993). In part, this may reflect the fact that HIV/AIDS raises issues that historically have been taboo and difficult to talk openly about within lesbian communities such as, for example, injecting drug use and having sex with men. For different reasons, some gay men have also been critical of lesbians wanting to discuss how AIDS and HIV affects them, on occasion going so far as to describe this as lesbians having 'virus envy'. Commenting on this, Sue O'Sullivan and Pratibha Parmar (1993: 23–4) make the point that:

> . . . some gay men are now claiming that lesbians working in HIV and AIDS are taking up valuable resources at a point where gay men continue to be the main group affected in Britain and other northern European countries. Within this scenario, lesbians are criticised simply for pointing out the lack of knowledge about women and HIV.

In the USA one of the first organisations to provide information specifically addressed to lesbians was the San Francisco AIDS Foundation. Their leaflet *Lesbians and AIDS: What's the Connection?*, published in July 1986, included information on risk practices, pregnancy and donor insemination, as well as safe sex guidelines that are fairly typical of the kind of advice that has been offered to lesbians and bisexual women. These guidelines describe Safe, Possibly Safe and Unsafe Sex Practices. Included in the latter category is unprotected cunnilingus (especially during menstruation), unprotected rimming (anal-oral contact), fisting (unprotected hand in vagina or rectum) and sharing sex toys that have contact with body fluids. The leaflet does not distinguish between risk to women in terms of who is doing what to whom such as, for example, whether during cunnilingus the risk lies in going down on a woman or having this done to you. However, it does recommend using a thin piece of latex to reduce any risk of infection during cunnilingus, or rimming, as well as the use of disposable rubber gloves or finger cots for vaginal or anal penetration. (Dental dams, which are thin squares of latex originally designed for use in dental surgery, are also often recommended for oral sex.) Although the leaflet recognises the possibility that lesbians may be at risk because they may have sex with men, it offers only the following limited advice to women in these circumstances: 'If you have sex with men in high risk groups, learn about, and always use, a condom.' Interestingly, the assumption would seem to be that women's having sex with men would involve unsafe penetrative sex. Other possibilities of engaging in heterosex, many of which are listed in the menu of safer sex for women having sex with women, are not mentioned.

A number of other AIDS organisations in the USA, such as, for example, Gay Men's Health Crisis in New York and the Women's AIDS Project in Los Angeles, published similar sorts of AIDS health education materials for lesbians around this time. Representation of lesbians within safer sex campaigns in Britain, however, emerged at a slightly later point in the history of the epidemic. The London-based organisation the Terence Higgins Trust was one of the first to produce an information leaflet about HIV and AIDS for lesbians, towards the end of 1990. Since then the Trust has produced a variety of HIV/AIDS educational materials for lesbians including, in 1992, a controversial advertising campaign aimed at informing women about the relative risks of HIV infection in 'lesbian sex'. The campaign claimed that lesbians are at very low risk in oral sex and should 'ditch those dental dams'. This was seen by some to be irresponsible as so few studies have examined risk behaviour among lesbians, in particular the possibility of female-to-female sexual transmission of HIV.

HIV/AIDS educational materials for lesbians soon began to appear elsewhere in Britain and other parts of Europe during the 1990s. In Holland, in 1991, for example, the lesbian and gay organisation the COC produced a booklet *Lesbian Women and AIDS*, and in Italy similar pamphlets also appeared. In Britain, the Sheffield AIDS Education Project produced a leaflet *LESBIANS, HIV and AIDS: ARE YOU SERIOUS?*, whose title imaginatively captured the moment of transition that such interventions represented: namely, a shift away from a belief that AIDS is not an issue for lesbians, to one of a growing recognition that lesbians 'should not be excluded from issues around sexual health' and that 'neither should we exclude ourselves'.

Conclusion

This account illustrates some of the ways in which sexual identity, in conjunction with medical notions of risk, can inform and authorise individual assessments of HIV risk which, in certain situations, may mean that lesbians and bisexual women are at risk for contracting HIV. Some of the issues it raises may be applicable to understandings of risk in other contexts. Research on lesbians' assessment of the risks of breast cancer and cervical cancer, for example, suggests similar processes may be at work. In particular, it has been suggested that the dominant construction of cervical cancer as heterosexually transmitted 'may lead lesbians and medical practitioners to believe that lesbians are at low risk' (Fish, 1997). More generally, it is important to recognise that the conflation of identity and immunity is not restricted to lesbians nor is it only a problem in relation to HIV, rather it is an issue in almost all health promotion contexts and with many different groups.

REFERENCES

Abbot, Pam and Wallace, Claire (1996) *An Introduction to Sociology: Feminist Perspectives*, 2nd edn. London: Routledge.

The ACT UP / NY Women & AIDS Book Group (1990) *Women, AIDS & Activism*. Boston: South End Press.

Adkins, Lisa and Leonard, Diana (1997) *French Radical Feminism*. London: Taylor & Francis.

Alcoff, Lisa (1988) 'Cultural feminism versus post-structuralism: the identity crisis in feminist theory', *Signs: A Journal of Women in Culture and Society*, 13 (3): 405–36.

Alexander, M. Jacqui (1994) 'Not just (any) body can be a citizen: the politics of law, sexuality and postcoloniality in Trinidad and Tobago and the Bahamas', *Feminist Review*, 48: 5–23.

Altman, Dennis (1986) *AIDS in the Mind of America*. New York: Doubleday.

Amnesty International United Kingdom (1997) *Breaking The Silence: Human Rights Violations Based on Sexual Orientation*. London: Amnesty International United Kingdom.

Anderson, Benedict (1991) *Imagined Communities*. London: Verso.

Anthias, Floya and Yuval-Davis, Nira (1992) *Racialized Boundaries: Race, Nation, Gender, Colour and Class, and the Anti-Racist Struggle*. London: Routledge.

Arendt, Hannah (1958) *The Human Condition*. Chicago: University of Chicago Press.

Arras, J.D. (1989) 'HIV infection and reproductive decisions'. Paper presented at the Fifth International Conference on AIDS, Montreal, 4–7 June.

Atkinson, Ti-Grace (1974) *Amazon Odyssey*. New York: Links Books.

Ault, Amber (1996) 'The dilemma of identity: bi women's negotiations', in Steven Seidman (ed.), *Queer Theory/Sociology*. Oxford: Blackwell.

Baciu, Ingrid, Cimpeanu, Vera and Nicoara, Mona (1996) 'Romania', in Rachel Rosenbloom (ed.), *Unspoken Rules. Sexual Orientation and Women's Human Rights*. London: Cassell.

Bamforth, Nicholas (1997) *Sexuality, Morals and Justice: A Theory of Lesbian and Gay Rights Law*. London: Cassell.

Banks, Amy and Gartrell, Nanette K. (1995) ' Hormones and sexual orientation: a questionable link', *Journal of Homosexuality*, 28 (3/4) : 247–68.

Bartky, Sandra (1988) 'Foucault, femininity, and the modernization of patriarchal power', in Irene Diamond and L. Quinby (eds), *Feminism and Foucault: Reflections on Resistance*. Boston, MA: Northeastern University Press.

Beam, Joseph (ed.) (1986) *In the Life: A Black Gay Anthology*. Boston, MA: Alyson Publications.

Beck, Ulrich (1992) *Risk Society: Towards a New Modernity*. London: Sage.

Beder, J. and Beckerman, N. (1996) 'Mandatory screening in newborns: the issues and a programmatic response'. Paper presented at XI International Conference on AIDS, Vancouver, 1996, Abstract ThC 4613.

Beechey, Veronica (1986) 'Introduction', in Veronica Beechey and Elizabeth Whitelegg (eds), *Women in Britain Today*. Milton Keynes: Open University Press.

Bell, David (1995) 'Perverse dynamics, sexual citizenship and the transformation of intimacy', in David Bell and Gill Valentine (eds), *Mapping Desire. Geographies of Sexualities*. London: Routledge.

Bell, David and Binnie, Jon (2000) *The Sexual Citizen: Queer Politics and Beyond*. Oxford: Polity Press.

Bell, David and Valentine, Gillian (eds) (1995) *Mapping Desire: Geographies of Sexualities*. London: Routledge.

Bell, Diane and Klein, Renate (eds) (1996) *Radically Speaking: Feminism Reclaimed*. Melbourne: Spinifex Press.

Bennett, Catherine (1994, May 28) 'Interview with Catharine MacKinnon', *Weekend Guardian*, 20–7.

Berlant, Lauren (1997) *The Queen of America Goes to Washington City: Essays on Sex and Citizenship*. Durham and London: Duke University Press.

Berlant, Lauren and Freeman, Elizabeth (1993) 'Queer nationality', in Michael Warner (ed.), *Fear of a Queer Planet: Queer Politics and Social Theory*. Minneapolis: University of Minnesota Press.

Bersani, Leo (1987) 'Is the rectum a grave?', *October*, 43: 197–222.

Berube, Allan and Escoffier, Jeffrey (1991) 'Queer/Nation', *Out/Look: National Lesbian and Gay Quarterly*, 11: 13–15.

Bevier, Pamela Jean, Chiasson, Mary Ann, Hefferman, Richard T. and Castro, Kenneth G. (1995) 'Women at a sexually transmitted disease clinic who reported same-sex contact: their HIV seroprevalence and risk behaviours', *American Journal of Public Health*, 85: 1366–71.

Bhavnani, Kum-Kum (1997) 'Women's studies and its interconnection with "race", ethnicity and sexuality', in Victoria Robinson and Diane Richardson (eds), *Introducing Women's Studies: Feminist Theory and Practice*, 2nd edn. London: Macmillan.

Binnie, Jon (1995) 'Trading places: consumption, sexuality and the production of queer space', in David Bell and Gill Valentine (eds), *Mapping Desire. Geographies of Sexualities*. London: Routledge.

Bloor, M. (1995) *The Sociology of HIV Transmission*. London: Sage.

Boffin, Tessa (1990) 'Fairy tales, "facts" and gossip: lesbians and AIDS', in Tessa Boffin and Sunil Gupta (eds), *Ecstatic Antibodies: Resisting the AIDS Mythology*. London: Rivers Oram Press.

Brandt, Alan M. (1985) *No Magic Bullet: a Social History of Venereal Disease in the United States Since 1880*. Oxford: Oxford University Press.

Brown, H. (1994) '"An ordinary sexual life?": a review of the normalisation principle as it applies to the sexual options of people with learning disabilities', *Disability and Society*, 9 (2): 123–44.

Brownmiller, Susan (1976) *Against Our Will*. Harmondsworth: Penguin.

Bryson, Valerie (1992) *Feminist Political Theory: An Introduction*. Basingstoke: Macmillan.

Burns, Jan (1992) 'The psychology of lesbian health care', in Paula Nicolson and Jane Ussher (eds), *The Psychology of Women's Health and Health Care*. London: Macmillan.

Bury, Judy, Morrison, Val and McLachlan, Sheena (eds) (1992) *Working with Women and AIDS: Medical, Social and Counselling Issues*. London: Routledge.

Butler, Judith (1990) *Gender Trouble*. London: Routledge.

Butler, Judith (1993) *Bodies that Matter: On the Discursive Limits of 'Sex'*. London: Routledge.

Butler, Judith (1997a) 'Critically queer', in Shane Phelan (ed.), *Playing With Fire: Queer Politics, Queer Theories*. London: Routledge.

Butler, Judith (1997b) *Excitable Speech: A Politics of the Performative*. London: Routledge.

Byne, William (1995) 'Science and belief: psychobiological research on sexual orientation', *Journal of Homosexuality*, 28 (3/4): 303–44.

Cameron, Deborah (1992) 'Old het?', *Trouble and Strife*, 24: 41–5.

Cameron, Deborah (1993) 'Telling it like it wasn't', *Trouble and Strife*, 27: 11–15.

Cameron, Deborah and Frazer, Elizabeth (1993) 'On the question of pornography and sexual violence: moving beyond cause and effect', in Catherine Itzen (ed.), *Pornography: Women, Violence and Civil Liberties*. Oxford: Oxford University Press.

Campbell, Beatrix (1980) 'A feminist sexual politics: now you see it, now you don't', *Feminist Review*, 5: 1–18.

Campbell, Beatrix (1987) 'Taking the plunge', *Marxism Today*, December: 9.

Caprio, Frank (1954) *Female Homosexuality: A Psychodynamic Study of Lesbianism*. New York: The Citadel Press.

Carabine, Jean (1992) 'Constructing women: women, sexuality and social policy', *Critical Social Policy*, 34: 23–37.

Carabine, Jean (1995) 'Invisible sexualities: sexuality, politics and influencing policy-making', in Angelia R. Wilson (ed.), *A Simple Matter of Justice? Theorizing Lesbian and Gay Politics*. London: Cassell.

Carabine, Jean (1996a) 'Heterosexuality and social policy', in Diane Richardson (ed.), *Theorising Heterosexuality*. Buckingham: Open University Press.

Carabine, Jean (1996b) 'A straight playing field or queering the pitch: centring sexuality in social policy', *Feminist Review*, 54: 31–64.

Cavin, Susan (1985) *Lesbian Origins*. San Francisco: ism Press.

Central Statistical Office (CSO) (1995) *Social Trends, 25*. London: HMSO.

Chirimuuta, Richard and Chirimuuta, Rosalind (1987) *Aids, Africa and Racism*.

Chu, S.Y., Hammett, T.A., Buehler, J.W. (1992) 'Update: epidemiology of reported cases of AIDS in women who reported sex only with other women, United States, 1980–91', *AIDS*, 6: 509–22.

Citizen's Charter: Raising the Standard (1991) Cmnd 1599, July. London: HMSO.

Clark, Danae (1993) 'Commodity lesbianism', in Henry Abelove, Michele Aina Barale and David M. Halperin (eds), *The Lesbian and Gay Studies Reader*. London: Routledge.

Cohen, Henry, Marmor, Michael, Wolfe, Hannah and Ribble, Denise (1993) 'Risk assessment of HIV transmission among lesbians', *Journal of Acquired Immune Deficiency Syndrome*, 6: 1173–4.

Cole, Rebecca and Cooper, Sally (1991) 'Lesbian exclusion from HIV/AIDS education. Years of low-risk identity and high-risk behaviour', *SIECUS Report*, December 1990 / January 1991: 18–23.

Collins, Patricia Hill (1996) 'Black women and the sex/gender hierarchy', in Stevi Jackson and Sue Scott (eds), *Feminism and Sexuality: a Reader*. Edinburgh: Edinburgh University Press.

Colomina, Beatriz (ed.) (1992) *Sexuality and Space*. Princeton, NJ: Princeton Architectural Press.

Connell, Robert W. (1995) *Masculinities: Knowledge, Power and Social Change*. London: Polity Press.

Connor, E.M., Sperling, R.S., Gelber, R., Kiselev, P., Scott, G., O'Sullivan, M.J., et al. (1994) 'Reduction of maternal–infant transmission of human immunodeficiency virus type-1 with zidovudine treatment', *New England Journal of Medicine*, 331: 1173–80.

Cooper, Davina (1993) 'An engaged state: sexuality, governance and the potential for change', in Joseph Bristow and Angelia R. Wilson (eds), *Activating Theory: Lesbian, Gay and Bisexual Politics*. London: Lawrence and Wishart.

Cooper, Davina (1994) *Sexing the City. Lesbian and Gay Politics Within the Activist State*. London: Rivers Oram Press.

Cooper, Davina (1995) *Power in Struggle: Feminism, Sexuality and the State*. Buckingham: Open University Press.

Cooper, E. (1996) 'Mandatory HIV testing of pregnant delivering women and new-borns – a legal, ethical and pragmatic assessment'. Paper presented at XI International Conference on AIDS, Vancouver, 1996, Abstract WeD 491.

Cottingham, Laura (1996) *Lesbians Are so Chic . . . that We Are not Really Lesbians at All*. London: Cassell.

Coveney, Lal, Jackson, Margaret, Jeffreys, Sheila, Kaye, Leslie and Mahony, Pat (1984) *The Sexuality Papers: Male Sexuality and the Social Control of Women*. London: Hutchinson.

Coward, Rosalind (1987) 'Sex after AIDS', *New Internationalist*, March: 20–1.

Crimp, Douglas (ed.) (1989) *AIDS: Cultural Analysis / Cultural Activism*. Cambridge, MA: MIT Press.

Currah, Paisley (1995) 'Searching for immutability: homosexuality, race and rights discourse', in Angelia R. Wilson (ed.), *A Simple Matter of Justice? Theorizing Lesbian and Gay Politics*. London: Cassell.

Daly, Mary (1978) *Gyn/Ecology: The Metaethics of Radical Feminism*. Boston: Beacon Press.

Davis, Tim (1995) 'The diversity of queer politics and the redefinition of sexual identity and community in urban spaces', in David Bell and Gill Valentine (eds), *Mapping Desire. Geographies of Sexualities*. London: Routledge.

de Lauretis, Teresa (1991) 'Queer Theory: lesbian and gay sexualities: an introduction', *differences: a Journal of Feminist Cultural Studies*, 3 (2): iii–xviii.

de Lauretis, Teresa (1994) 'The essence of the triangle or, taking the risk of essentialism seriously: feminist theory in Italy, the U.S., and Britain', in Naomi Schor and Elizabeth Weed (eds), *the essential difference*. Bloomington and Indianapolis: Indiana University Press.

Delphy, Christine (1984) *Close to Home: a Materialist Analysis of Women's Oppression*. London: Hutchinson.

Delphy, Christine (1996) 'The private as a deprivation of rights for women and children'. Paper given at the International Conference on Violence, Abuse and Women's Citizenship, Brighton, UK, November 1996.

Delphy, Christine and Leonard, Diana (1992) *Familiar Exploitation: a New Analysis of Marriage in Contemporary Western Societies*. Cambridge: Polity Press.

D' Emilio, John (1984/1993) 'Capitalism and gay identity', in Ann Snitow, Christine Stansell and Sharon Thompson (eds), *Desire: The Politics of Sexuality*. London: Virago. Reprinted in Henry Abelove, Michele Aina Barale and David M. Halperin (eds), *The Lesbian and Gay Studies Reader*. New York: Routledge.

Denfeld, R. (1995) *The New Victorians: a Young Woman's Challenge to the Old Feminist Order*. New York: Simon and Schuster.

Denny, Elaine (1994) 'Liberation or oppression? radical feminism and in vitro fertilisation', *Sociology of Health and Illness: a Journal of Medical Sociology*, 16 (1): 62–80.

Department of Health (1999) *Targets Aimed at Reducing the Number of Children Born with HIV: Report From an Expert Group*.

Dhavernas, Marie-Jo (1996) 'Hating masculinity not men', in Claire Duchen (ed.), *French Connections*. London: Unwin Hyman. Reprinted in Stevi Jackson and Sue Scott (eds), *Feminism and Sexuality: a Reader*. Edinburgh: Edinburgh University Press.

Dicker, B.G. (1989) 'Risk of AIDS among lesbians', *American Journal of Public Health*, 79: 1569.

Doan, Laura (ed.) (1994) *The Lesbian Postmodern*. New York: Columbia University Press.

Donovan, Catherine, Heaphy, Brian and Weeks, Jeffrey (1999) 'Citizenship and same sex relationships', *Journal of Social Policy*, 28 (4): 689–709.

Douglas, Carol Anne (1990) *Love and Politics: Radical Feminist and Lesbian Theories*. San Francisco: ism Press.

Doyal, Lesley (1994) 'HIV and AIDS: putting women on the global agenda', in Lesley Doyal, Jennie Naidoo and Tamsin Wilton (eds), *AIDS: Setting a Feminist Agenda*. London: Taylor & Francis.

Doyal, Lesley, Naidoo, Jennie and Wilton, Tamsin (eds) (1994) *AIDS: Setting a Feminist Agenda*. London: Taylor & Francis.

DuBois, Ellen C. and Gordon, Linda (1984) 'Seeking ecstasy on the battlefield: danger and pleasure in nineteenth-century feminist thought', in Carole S. Vance (ed.), *Pleasure and Danger: Exploring Female Sexuality*. London: Pandora Press.

Duggan, Lisa (1995) 'Queering the state' in Lisa Duggan and Nan Hunter, *Sex Wars: Sexual Dissent and Political Culture*. New York: Routledge.

Duggan, Lisa and Hunter, Nan D. (1995) *Sex Wars: Sexual Dissent and Political Culture*. New York: Routledge.

Duncan, Nancy (ed.) (1996a) *Bodyspace: Destabilizing Geographies of Gender and Sexuality*. London: Routledge.

Duncan, Nancy (1996b) '(Re) negotiating gender and sexuality in public and private spaces', in Nancy Duncan (ed.), *Bodyspace: Destabilizing Geographies of Gender and Sexuality*. London: Routledge.

Dunn, D.T., Newell, M.L., Ades, A.E. and Peckham, C.S. (1992) 'Risk of HIV type-1 transmission through breastfeeding', *Lancet*, 340: 585–8.

Dunn, Sara (1995) 'Teenage mutant big-haired feminists', *Diva*, June, 46–7.

Duong, T., Ades, A.E., Gibb, D.M., Tookey, P.A. and Masters, J. (1999) 'Vertical transmission rates for HIV in the British Isles: estimates based on surveillance data', *British Medical Journal*, 319: 1227–9.

Durham, Martin (1991) *Sex and Politics: The Family and Morality in the Thatcher Years*. Basingstoke: Macmillan.

Dworkin, Andrea (1981) *Pornography: Men Possessing Women*. London: The Women's Press.

Dworkin, Andrea (1987) *Intercourse*. New York: Free Press and Macmillan.

Dworkin, Andrea (2000) *Scapegoat: Jews, Israel and Women's Liberation*. London: Virago.

Dyer, Richard (1990) *Now You See It. Studies on Lesbian and Gay Film*. London: Routledge.

Echols, Alice (1989) *Daring To Be Bad: Radical Feminism in America 1967–1975*. Minneapolis: University of Minnesota Press.

Edelman, Lee (1992) 'Tearooms and sympathy, or, the epistemology of the water closet', in Andrew Parker, Mary Russo, Doris Sommer and Patricia Yaeger (eds), *Nationalisms and Sexualities*. London: Routledge.

Eisenstein, Hester (1984) *Contemporary Feminist Thought*. London: Unwin.

Eisenstein, Zillah (1997) 'Women's publics and the search for new democracies', *Feminist Review*, 57: 140–67.

Ellis, Caroline (1991) 'Sisters and citizens', in Geoff Andrews (ed.), *Citizenship*. London: Lawrence and Wishart.

Epstein, Steven (1987) 'Gay politics, ethnic identity: the limits of social constructionism', *Socialist Review*, 93/94: 9–54.

European Collaborative Study (1992) 'Risk factors for mother-to-child transmission of HIV-1', *Lancet*, 339: 1007–12.

Evans, David (1993) *Sexual Citizenship: The Material Construction of Sexualities*. London: Routledge.

Evans, David (1995) '(Homo)sexual citizenship: a queer kind of justice', in Angelia R. Wilson (ed.), *A Simple Matter of Justice? Theorizing Lesbian and Gay Politics*. London: Cassell.

Faderman, Lillian (1992) *Surpassing the Love of Men: Romantic Friendship and Love Between Women from the Renaissance to the Present*. Harmondsworth: Penguin.

Faderman, Lillian (1993) 'The return of the butch and femme: a phenomenon in lesbian sexuality of the 1980s and 1990s', in J. Fout and M.S. Tantillo (eds), *American Sexual Politics: Sex, Gender and Race since the Civil War*. Chicago: University of Chicago Press.

Feminist Review (1997) *Citizenship: Pushing the Boundaries*. (Issue 57). London: Routledge.

Ferguson, Ann (1989) *Blood at the Root: Motherhood, Sexuality and Male Dominance*. London: Pandora Press.

Findlen, B. (ed.) (1995) *Listen Up. Voices From The Next Feminist Generation*. Seattle: Seal Press.

Firestone, Shulamith (1970) *The Dialectic of Sex: The Case for Feminist Revolution*. London: Jonathan Cape.

Fish, Julie (1997) 'Lesbians' assessments of the risks of breast and cervical cancer'. Paper presented at the 10th Annual Women's Studies (UK) Network Conference, Institute of Education, London, 14–17th July, 1997.

Foucault, Michel (1979) *The History of Sexuality, Volume One*. London: Allen Lane.

Frankenberg, Ruth (1993) *White Women, Race Matters: The Social Construction of Whiteness*. London: Routledge.

Friedan, Betty (1965) *The Feminine Mystique*. Harmondsworth: Penguin.

Friedman, S.R., Des Jarlais, D.C., Deren, S., Jose, B. and Neaigus, A. (1992) 'HIV seroconversion among street-recruited drug injectors in 14 United States cities'. Paper presented at Eighth International Conference on AIDS, July 19–24, Amsterdam. Abstract PoC 4251.

Fuss, Diana (1990) *Essentially Speaking: Feminism, Nature and Difference*. London: Routledge.

Fuss, Diana (ed.) (1991) *Inside/Out: Lesbian Theories, Gay Theories*. London: Routledge.

Fuss, Diana (1993) 'Freud's fallen women: identification, desire, and "A case of homosexuality in a woman"', in Michael Warner (ed.), *Fear of a Queer Planet: Queer Politics and Social Theory*. Minneapolis: University of Minnesota Press.

Gagnon, John H. and Simon, William (eds) (1967) *Sexual Deviance*. New York: Harper &Row.

Gagnon, John H. and Simon, William (1973) *Sexual Conduct*. London: Hutchinson.

Gamson, Joshua (1996) 'Must identity movements self-destruct?: a queer dilemma', in Steven Seidman (ed.), *Queer Theory/Sociology*. Oxford: Blackwell.

Gates, Henry Louis Jr (1993) 'The black man's burden', in Michael Warner (ed.), *Fear of a Queer Planet: Queer Politics and Social Theory*. Minneapolis: University of Minnesota Press.

Geltmaker, T. (1992) 'The queer nation acts up: health care, politics, and sexual diversity in the County of Angels', *Environment and Planning D: Society and Space*, 10: 609–50.

Giddens, Anthony (1992) *The Transformation of Intimacy: Sexuality, Love and Eroticism in Modern Societies*. Cambridge: Polity Press.

Goldsby, Jackie (1993) 'Queen for 307 days: looking b(l)ack at Vanessa Williams and the sex wars', in Arlene Stein (ed.), *Sisters, Sexperts, Queers: Beyond the Lesbian Nation*. New York: Plume.

Griffin, Susan (1981) *Pornography and Silence: Culture's Revenge Against Nature*. New York: Harper & Row.

Griggers, Cathy (1993) 'Lesbian bodies in the age of (post)mechanical reproduction', in Laura Doan (ed.), *The Lesbian Postmodern*. New York: Columbia University Press.

Grunberger, Richard (1987) *A Social History of the Third Reich*. London: Penguin.

Halberstam, Judith (1997) 'Sex debates', in Andy Medhurst and Sally R. Munt (eds), *Lesbian and Gay Studies: A Critical Introduction*. London: Cassell.

Hall, Stuart and Held, David (1989) 'Citizens and citizenship', in Stuart Hall and Martin Jacques (eds), *New Times: The Changing Face of Politics in the 1990s*. Buckingham: Open University Press.

Halley, Janet E. (1993) 'The construction of heterosexuality', in Michael Warner (ed.), *Fear of a Queer Planet: Queer Politics and Social Theory*. Minneapolis: University of Minnesota Press.

Hamer, D.H., Hu, S., Magnuson, V.L., Hu, N. and Pattatucci A.M.L. (1993) 'A linkage between DNA markers on the X chromosome and male sexual orientation', *Science*, 26: 321–27.

Hanmer, Jalna (1997) 'Women and reproduction', in Victoria Robinson and Diane Richardson (eds), *Introducing Women's Studies: Feminist Theory and Practice*, 2nd edn. Basingstoke: Macmillan.

Harding, Sandra (1992) *Whose Science? Whose Knowledge?* Buckingham: Open University Press.

Harper, Phillip Brian (1993) 'Eloquence and epitaph: black nationalism and the homophobic impulse in responses to the death of Max Robinson', in Michael Warner (ed.), *Fear of a Queer Planet: Queer Politics and Social Theory*. Minneapolis: University of Minnesota Press.

Hart, John (1981) 'Theoretical explanations in practice', in John Hart and Diane Richardson, *The Theory and Practice of Homosexuality*. London: Routledge & Kegan Paul.

Hart, Vada (1986) 'Lesbians and AIDS', *Gossip: a Journal of Lesbian Feminist Ethics*, 2.

Havens, P., Cuene, B. and Holtgrare, D. (1997) 'Lifetime costs of care for children with human immunodeficiency virus infection', *Paediatric Infectious Diseases Journal*, 16: 607–10.

Hawkes, Gail (1996) *A Sociology of Sex and Sexuality*. Buckingham: Open University Press.

Hemmings, Susan (1980) 'Horrific practices: how lesbians were presented in the newspapers of 1978', in Gay Left Collective (eds), *Homosexuality: Power and Politics*. London: Allison and Busby.

Herman, Didi (1993) 'The politics of law reform: lesbian and gay rights struggles into the 1990s', in Joseph Bristow and Angelia R.Wilson (eds), *Activating Theory: Lesbian, Gay, Bisexual Politics*. London: Lawrence and Wishart.

Herman, Didi (1994) *Rights of Passage: Struggles for Lesbian and Gay Equality*. Toronto: University of Toronto Press.

Herman, Didi (1995) 'A jurisprudence of one's own? Ruthann Robson's lesbian legal theory', in Angelia R. Wilson (ed.), *A Simple Matter Of Justice? Theorizing Lesbian and Gay Politics*. London: Cassell.

Holland, Janet, Ramazanoglu, Caroline, Scott, Sue, Sharpe, Sue and Thomson, Rachel (1990) '"Don't Die of Ignorance" – I Nearly Died of Embarrassment': Condoms in Context (WRAP PAPER 2). London: the Tufnell Press.

Holland, Janet, Ramazanoglu, Caroline, Scott, Sue and Thomson, Rachel (1994a) 'Desire, risk and control: the body as a site of contestation', in Lesley Doyal, Jennie Naidoo and Tamsin Wilton (eds), *AIDS: Setting a Feminist Agenda*. London: Taylor & Francis.

Holland, Janet, Ramazanoglu, Caroline, Sharpe, Sue and Thomson, Rachel (1994b) 'Achieving masculine sexuality: young men's strategies for managing vulnerability', in Lesley Doyal, Jennie Naidoo and Tamsin Wilton (eds), *AIDS:Setting a Feminist Agenda*. London: Taylor & Francis.

Holland, Janet, Ramazanoglu, Caroline, Thomson, Rachel (1996) 'In the same boat? The gendered (in)experience of first heterosex', in Diane Richardson (ed.), *Theorising Heterosexuality*. Buckingham: Open University Press.

Holland, Janet, Ramazanoglu, Caroline, Sharpe, Sue and Thomson, Rachel (1998) *The Male in the Head: Young People, Heterosexuality and Power*. London: the Tufnell Press.

Hollway, Wendy (1993) 'Theorizing heterosexuality: a response', *Feminism and Psychology*, 3 (3): 412–17.

Hollway, Wendy (1996) 'Recognition and heterosexual desire', in Diane Richardson (ed.), *Theorising Heterosexuality*. Buckingham: Open University Press.

hooks, bell (1989) *Talking Back: Thinking Feminist – Thinking Black*. London: Sheba.

hooks, bell (1992) *Black Looks: Race and Representation*. Boston, MA: South End Press.

Hotaling, Norma (1996) 'Prostitution: getting women out'. Paper presented at the International Conference on Violence, Abuse and Women's Citizenship, November, Brighton, U.K.

Humm, Maggie (ed.) (1992) *Feminisms: a Reader*. London: Harvester Wheatsheaf.

Hunt, Margaret (1990) 'The de-eroticization of women's liberation: social purity movements and the revolutionary feminism of Sheila Jeffreys', *Feminist Review*, 34: 23–46.

Hunter, J., Rotheram-Borus, M.J., Reid, H. and Rosario, H. (1992) 'Sexual and substance abuse acts that place lesbians at risk for HIV'. Paper presented at Eighth International Conference on AIDS, July 19–24, Amsterdam. Abstract PoD 5208.

Iardino, R. et al. (1992) 'Potential routes of HIV transmission among women'. Paper presented at Eighth International Conference on AIDS, July 19–24, Amsterdam.

Ingham, R., Woodcock, A. and Stenner, K. (1992) 'The limitations of rational decision-making as applied to young people's sexual behaviour', in Peter Aggleton, Peter Davies and Graham Hart (eds), *AIDS: Rights, Risks and Reason*. London: Falmer Press.

Ingram, Gordon Brent, Bouthillette, Anne-Marie and Retter, Yolanda (eds) (1997) *Queers in Space: Communities/Public Places/Sites of Resistance*. Seattle: Bay Press.

Isin, Engin and Wood, Patricia (1999) *Citizenship and Identity*. London: Sage.

Jackson, Stevi (1992) 'The amazing deconstructing woman: the perils of postmodern feminism', *Trouble and Strife*, 25: 25–31.

Jackson, Stevi (1996a) 'Heterosexuality and feminist theory', in Diane Richardson (ed.), *Theorising Heterosexuality: Telling it Straight*. Buckingham: Open University Press.

Jackson, Stevi (1996b) 'Heterosexuality as a problem for feminist theory', in Lisa Adkins and Vicky Merchant (eds), *Sexualising the Social: Power and the Organisation of Sexuality*. London: Macmillan.

Jackson, Stevi (1996c) 'Heterosexuality, power and pleasure', in Stevi Jackson and Sue Scott (eds), *Feminism and Sexuality: a Reader*. Edinburgh: Edinburgh University Press.

Jackson, Stevi (1997) 'Taking Liberties', *Trouble and Strife*, 34: 36–43.

Jackson, Stevi (1997) 'Women, marriage and family relationships', in Victoria Robinson and Diane Richardson (eds), *Introducing Women's Studies: Feminist Theory and Practice*, 2nd edn. Basingstoke: Macmillan.

Jackson, Stevi (1999) *Heterosexuality in Question*. London: Sage.

Jackson, Stevi and Scott, Sue (1996) 'Sexual skirmishes and feminist factions: twenty-five years of debate on women and sexuality', in Stevi Jackson and Sue Scott (eds), *Feminism and Sexuality: a Reader*. Edinburgh: Edinburgh University Press.

Jeffery-Poulter, Stephen (1991) *Peers, Queers and Commons: The Struggle for Gay Law Reform from 1950 to the Present*. London: Routledge.

Jeffreys, Sheila (1985) *The Spinster and Her Enemies: Feminism and Sexuality 1880–1930*. London: Pandora Press.

Jeffreys, Sheila (1990) *Anticlimax: a Feminist Perspective on the Sexual Revolution*. London: The Women's Press

Jeffreys, Sheila (1994) *The Lesbian Heresy: a Feminist Perspective on the Lesbian Sexual Revolution*. London: The Women's Press.

Jeffreys, Sheila (1996) 'Heterosexuality and the desire for gender', in Diane Richardson (ed.), *Theorising Heterosexuality*. Buckingham: Open University Press.

Jeffreys, Sheila (1997) *The Idea of Prostitution*. Melbourne, Victoria: Spinifex Press.

Jenkins, Richard (1996) *Social Identity*. London: Routledge.

Johansson, W. and Percy, W.A. (1994) *Outing: Shattering the Conspiracy of Silence*. Binghampton, NY: Harrington Park Press.

Johnson, Jill (1973) *Lesbian Nation: The Feminist Solution*. New York: Touchstone.

Johnson, Jon (1994) 'Politics and passion or pilsner and porn?', *Rouge*, 16: 14.

Kaplan, Helen Singer (1987) *The Real Truth About Women and AIDS: How to Eliminate the Risks Without Giving Up Love and Sex*. New York: Simon and Schuster.

Kaplan, Morris B. (1997) *Sexual Justice: Democratic Citizenship and the Politics of Desire*. New York: Routledge.

Kelly, Liz (1988) *Surviving Sexual Violence*. Oxford: Polity Press.

Kelly, Liz (1992) 'Sex exposed: sexuality and the pornography debate', *Spare Rib*, 237 (August–September): 19–20.

Kitzinger, Celia and Wilkinson, Sue (1994) 'Virgins and queers: rehabilitating heterosexuality?, *Gender and Society*, 8 (3): 444–63.

Kitzinger, Jenny (1994) 'Visible and invisible women in AIDS discourses', in Lesley Doyal, Jennie Naidoo and Tamsin Wilton (eds), *AIDS: Setting a Feminist Agenda*. London: Taylor & Francis.

Koedt, Anne (1974/1996) 'The myth of the vaginal orgasm', in The Radical Therapist Collective (eds), *The Radical Therapist*. Harmondsworth: Penguin. Reprinted in Stevi Jackson and Sue Scott (eds), *Feminism and Sexuality: a Reader*. Edinburgh: Edinburgh University Press.

Kotz, Liz (1993) 'Anything but idyllic: lesbian filmaking in the 1980s and 1990s', in Arlene Stein (ed.), *Sisters, Sexperts, Queers: Beyond the Lesbian Nation*. New York: Plume.

Lamos, Colleen (1994) ' The postmodern lesbian position: on our backs', in Laura Doan (ed.), *The Lesbian Postmodern*. New York: Columbia University Press.

Leeds Revolutionary Feminist Group (1981) 'Political lesbianism: the case against heterosexuality', in Onlywomen Press (eds), *Love Your Enemy? The Debate Between Heterosexual Feminism and Political Lesbianism*. London: Onlywomen Press.

Lees, Sue (1993) *Sugar and Spice: Sexuality and Adolescent Girls*. London: Penguin.

Lees, Sue (2000) 'Sexuality and citizenship', in Madeleine Arnot and Jo-Anne Dillabough (eds), *Challenging Democracy*. London: Routledge.

Leibowitch, J. (1985) *A Strange Virus of Unknown Origin*, trans. R. Howard. New York: Ballantine.

Lemp, George F., Jones, Melissa, Kellogg, Timothy A., Guiliano, N. Nieri., Anderson, Laura, Withum, David and Katz, Mitchell (1995) 'HIV seroprevalence and risk behaviours among lesbians and bisexual women in San Francisco and Berkeley, California', *American Journal of Public Health*, 85: 1549–52.

Leonard, Zoe (1990) 'Lesbians in the AIDS crisis', in The ACT UP / New York Women and AIDS Book Group (eds), *Women, AIDS and Activism*. Boston: South End Press.

Le Vay, Simon (1991) 'A difference in hypothalamic structure between heterosexual and homosexual men', *Science*, 253: 1034–7.

Le Vay, Simon (1996) *Queer Science: The Use and Abuse of Research into Homosexuality*. Cambridge, MA: MIT Press.

Lindegren, M., Byers, R.H., Thomas, P., Davis, S.F., Caldwell, B., Rogers, R., et al. (1999) 'Trends in perinatal transmission of HIV/AIDS in the United States', *Journal of the American Medical Association*, 282: 531–8.

Lindstad, Gro (1996) 'Norway', in Rachel Rosenbloom (ed.), *Unspoken Rules: Sexual Orientation and Women's Human Rights*. International Gay and Lesbian Human Rights Commission. London: Cassell.

Lips, Hilary and Freedman, Susan Alexandra (1993) 'Heterosexual feminist identities: private boundaries and shifting centers', in Sue Wilkinson and Celia Kitzinger (eds), *Heterosexuality: a Feminism and Psychology Reader*. London: Sage.

Lister, Ruth (1990) 'Women, economic dependency and citizenship', *Journal of Social Policy*, 19 (4): 445–68.

Lister, Ruth (1996) 'Citizenship engendered', in David Taylor (ed.), *Critical Social Policy: a Reader*. London: Sage.

Lister, Ruth (1997a) *Citizenship: Feminist Perspectives*. London: Macmillan.

Lister, Ruth (1997b) 'Citizenship: towards a feminist synthesis', *Feminist Review*, 57: 28–48.

Lovell, Terry (ed.) (1990) *British Feminist Thought*. Oxford: Blackwell.

Luff, Donna (1996) 'Sisters or enemies: women in the British moral lobby and feminisms', unpublished PhD thesis, University of Sheffield.

MacKinnon, Catharine A. (1982) 'Feminism, Marxism, method and the state: an agenda for theory', *Signs*, 7(3): 515–44.

Mack-Nataf, Isling (1992) quote in Cherry Smyth, *Lesbians Talk Queer Notions*. London: Scarlet Press.

Magura, Stephen, O'Day, Joanne and Rosenblum, Andrew (1992) 'Women usually take care of their girlfriends: bisexuality and HIV risk among female intravenous drug users', *The Journal of Drug Issues*, 22: 179–90.

Marcuse, Herbert (1970) *Eros and Civilisation*. London: Allen Lane.

Marmor, M. Weiss, L.R., Lyden, M. et al. (1986) 'Possible female to female transmission of human immunodeficiency virus', *Annals of Internal Medicine*, 105: 969.

Marshall, T.H. (1950) *Citizenship and Social Class*. Cambridge: Cambridge University Press.

Marshall, T. H. (1977) *Class, Citizenship and Social Development*. Chicago and London: University of Chicago Press.

Marshment, Margaret (1997) 'The picture is political: representation of women in contemporary popular culture', in Victoria Robinson and Diane Richardson (eds), *Introducing Women's Studies: Feminist Theory and Practice*, 2nd edn. Basingstoke: Macmillan.

Massey, Doreen (1994) *Space, Place and Gender*. Oxford: Polity Press.

Maynard, Mary (1995) 'Beyond the "Big Three": the development of feminist theory into the 1990s', *Women's History Review*, 4 (3): 259–81.

Maynard, Mary and Winn, Jan (1997) 'Women, violence and male power', in Victoria Robinson and Diane Richardson (eds), *Introducing Women's Studies: Feminist Theory and Practice*, 2nd edn. Basingstoke: Macmillan.

McClintock, Anne (1995) *Imperial Leather: Race, Gender and Sexuality in the Colonial Contest*. London: Routledge.

McIntosh, Mary (1968/1996) 'The homosexual role', *Social Problems*, 16(2): 182–92. Reprinted in Steven Seidman (ed.), *Queer Theory/Sociology*. Oxford: Blackwell.

McIntosh, Mary (1993) 'Queer Theory and the war of the sexes', in Joseph Bristow and Angelia R. Wilson (eds), *Activating Theory: Lesbian, Gay and Bisexual Politics*. London: Lawrence and Wishart.

Millar, Jane (1994) 'Lone mothers', *Feminist Review*, 48: 25–39.

Miller, H.G., Turner, C.F. and Moses, L.E. (eds) (1990) *AIDS: The Second Decade*. Washington, DC: National Academy Press.

Miller, Neil (1993) *Out in the World. Gay and Lesbian Life from Buenos Aires to Bangkok*. New York: Vintage Books.

Millett, Kate (1970) *Sexual Politics*. London: Abacus.

Mitchell, Anne (1992) 'Women and AIDS activism in Victoria, Australia', *Feminist Review*, 41: 52–7.

Moffatt, Betty Clare (1986) *When Someone You Love Has AIDS*. Santa Monica, CA: IBS.

Monzon, O. and Capellan, J.M.B. (1987) 'Female-to-female transmission of HIV', *Lancet*, ii: 40–1.

Moraga, Cherrie and Anzaldua, Gloria (eds) (1981) *This Bridge Called My Back: Writings by Radical Women of Color*. Watertown, MA: The Persephone Press.

Moran, Leslie J. (1996) *The Homosexual(ity) of Law.* London: Routledge.

Morrison, David and Tracey, Michael (1979) *Whitehouse.* London: Macmillan.

Mort, Frank (1995) 'Essentialism revisited? Identity politics and late twentieth-century discourses of homosexuality', in Jeffrey Weeks (ed.), *The Lesser Evil and the Greater Good: The Theory and Politics of Social Diversity.* London: Rivers Oram Press.

Nestle, Joan (1988) *A Restricted Country.* London: Sheba Press.

Newell, M.L., Gray, G. and Bryson, T.J. (1997) 'Prevention of mother to child transmission of HIV-1 infection', *AIDS*, 11(suppl A): 5165–72.

Nichols, Margaret (1987) 'Lesbian sexuality: issues and developing theory', in Boston Lesbian Psychologies Collective (eds), *Lesbian Psychologies.* Chicago: University of Illinois Press.

Nicholson, Linda J. (1984) 'Feminist theory: the private and the public', in C.C. Gould (ed.), *Beyond Domination: New Perspectives on Women and Philosophy.* USA: Rowman and Littlefield.

Nicholson, Linda (1994) 'Interpreting gender', *Signs: Journal of Women in Culture and Society*, 20(11): 79–105.

Nicoll, A., Steele, R. and Mortimer, P. (1999) 'Pregnant women and testing for HIV', *Practising Midwife*, 2 (8): 34–7.

Norwood, Chris (1987) *Advice for Life: a Woman's Guide to AIDS Risks and Prevention.* New York: Pantheon Books.

Onlywomen Press (eds) (1981) *Love Your Enemy? The Debate Between Heterosexual Feminism and Political Lesbianism.* London: Onlywomen Press.

O'Sullivan, Sue and Parmar, Pratibha (1993) *Lesbians Talk (Safer) Sex.* London: Scarlet Press.

O'Sullivan, Sue and Thomson, Kate (eds) (1992) *Positively Women: Living With AIDS.* London: Sheba.

Pakulski, Jan (1997) 'Cultural citizenship', *Citizenship Studies*, 1 (1): 73–86.

Palmer, Anya (1995) 'Lesbian and gay rights campaigning: a report from the coalface', in Angelia R. Wilson (ed.), *A Simple Matter of Justice? Theorizing Lesbian and Gay Politics.* London: Cassell.

Panos (1990) *Triple Jeopardy: Women and AIDS.* London: The Panos Institute.

Patton, Cindy (1990) *Inventing AIDS.* New York: Routledge.

Patton, Cindy (1993) 'Tremble, hetero swine!', in Michael Warner (ed.), *Fear of a Queer Planet: Queer Politics and Social Theory.* Minneapolis: University of Minnesota Press.

Patton, Cindy (1994) *Last Served? Gendering the HIV Pandemic.* London: Taylor & Francis.

Patton, Cindy (1996) *Fatal Advice: How Safe-Sex Education Went Wrong.* Durham: Duke University Press.

Patton, Cindy and Kelly, Jancis (1987) *Making It: A Woman's Guide to Sex in the Age of AIDS.* Ithaca, NY: Firebrand Books.

Peckham, C.S. and Gibb, D. (1995) 'Mother-to-child transmission of the human immunodeficiency virus', *New England Journal of Medicine*, 333: 298–302.

Penelope, Julia (ed.) (1994) *Out of the Class Closet: Lesbians Speak.* Freedom, CA: The Crossing Press.

Perry, S., Jacobsberg, L. and Fogel, K. (1989) 'Orogenital transmission of human immunodeficiency virus (HIV)', *Annals of Internal Medicine*, 11: 951.

Perry, Susanna M. (1995) Lesbian alcohol and marijuana use: correlates of HIV risk behaviours and abusive relationships', *Journal of Psychoactive Drugs*, 27: 413–19.

Peters, J.S. and Wolper, A. (1995) *Women's Rights, Human Rights: International Feminist Perspectives*. London: Routledge.

Phelan, Shane (1994) *Getting Specific: Postmodern Lesbian Politics*. Minneapolis: University of Minnesota Press.

Phelan, Shane (1995) 'The space of justice: lesbians and democratic politics', in Angelia R. Wilson (ed.), *A Simple Matter of Justice? Theorizing Lesbian and Gay Politics*. London: Cassell.

Phillips, Anne (1991) 'Citizenship and feminist theory', in Geoff Andrews (ed.), *Citizenship*. London: Lawrence and Wishart.

Plummer, Kenneth (1975) *Sexual Stigma: An Interactionist Account*. London: Routledge & Kegan Paul.

Plummer, Kenneth (1981) 'Going gay: identities, life cycles and lifestyles in the male gay world', in John Hart and Diane Richardson, *The Theory and Practice of Homosexuality*. London: Routledge & Kegan Paul.

Plummer, Kenneth (1995) *Telling Sexual Stories. Power, Change and Social Worlds*. London: Routledge.

Plummer, Kenneth (2000) 'Intimate Citizenship', in Diane Richardson and Steven Seidman (eds), *Handbook of Lesbian and Gay Studies*. London: Sage.

Radicalesbians (1970) 'The woman-identified woman', in Anne Koedt, Ellen Levine and Anita Rapone (eds), *Radical Feminism*. New York: Quadrangle Books.

Raiteri, R., Fora, R., Gioannini, P., Russo, R., Lucchini, A., Terzi, M.G., Giacobbi, D., Sinicco, A. (1994) 'Seroprevalence, risk factors and attitude to HIV-1 in a representative sample of lesbians in Turin', *Genitourinary Medicine*, 70 (3): 200–5.

Ramazanoglu, Caroline (1993) 'Theorizing heterosexuality: a response to Wendy Hollway', in Sue Wilkinson and Celia Kitzinger (eds), *Heterosexuality: a Feminism and Psychology Reader*. London: Sage.

Ramos, Juanita (ed.) (1987) *Compañeras: Latina Lesbians: an anthology*. New York: Latina Lesbian History Project.

Rankine, J. (1997) 'For better or for worse?', *Trouble and Strife*, 34: 5–11.

Reardon, J., Wilson, M.J., Lemp, G.F., Gaudino, J., Snyder, D., Elcock, M.E. and Nguyen, S. (1992) 'HIV-1 infection among female injection drug users (IDUs) in the San Francisco Bay Area, California, 1989–1991: increased seroprevalence rates for IDUs who are lesbian/bisexual, racial/ethnic minorities or cocaine injectors'. Paper presented at Eighth International Conference on AIDS, July 19–24, Amsterdam, Abstract ThC 1553.

Reich, Wilhelm (1962) *The Sexual Revolution*. New York: Farrar, Straus and Giroux.

Reider, Ines and Ruppelt, Patricia (eds) (1989) *Matters of Life and Death: Women Speak about AIDS*. London: Virago.

Reinhold, Susan (1994) 'Through the parliamentary looking glass: "real" and "pretend" families in contemporary British politics', *Feminist Review*, 48: 61–79.

Reyes, Nina (1990) 'Queerly speaking', *Outweek*, August 15, 59: 40–5.

Rich, Adrienne (1977) *Of Woman Born: Motherhood as Experience and Institution*. London: Virago.

Rich, Adrienne (1980) 'Compulsory heterosexuality and lesbian existence', *Signs*, 5 (4) : 631–60.

Richardson, Diane (1981) 'Theoretical perspectives on homosexuality', in John Hart and Diane Richardson, *The Theory and Practice of Homosexuality*. London: Routledge & Kegan Paul.

Richardson, Diane (1987/1989) *Women and the AIDS Crisis*. London: Pandora Press, 2nd edn.

Richardson, Diane (1990) *Safer Sex: The Guide for Women Today*. London: Pandora Press.

Richardson, Diane (1992) 'Constructing lesbian sexualities', in Kenneth Plummer (ed.), *Modern Homosexualities: Fragments of Lesbian and Gay Experience*. London: Routledge.

Richardson, Diane (1993) 'AIDS and reproduction', in Peter Aggleton, Peter Davies and Graham Hart (eds), *AIDS: Facing the Second Decade*. London: Falmer Press.

Richardson, Diane (1994) 'AIDS: issues for feminism in the U.K.', in Lesley Doyal, Jennie Naidoo and Tamsin Wilton (eds), *AIDS: Setting a Feminist Agenda*. London: Taylor & Francis.

Richardson, Diane (ed.) (1996a) *Theorising Heterosexuality: Telling it Straight*. Buckingham: Open University Press.

Richardson, Diane (1996b) 'Heterosexuality and social theory', in Diane Richardson (ed.), *Theorising Heterosexuality*. Buckingham: Open University Press.

Richardson, Diane (1997) 'Sexuality and feminism', in Victoria Robinson and Diane Richardson (eds), *Introducing Women's Studies: Feminist Theory and Practice*, 2nd edn. Basingstoke: Macmillan.

Richardson, Diane (1998) 'Sexuality and citizenship', *Sociology*, 32 (1): 83–100.

Richardson, Diane (2000a) 'Extending citizenship: cultural citizenship and sexuality', in Nick Stevenson (ed.), *Culture and Citizenship*. London: Sage.

Richardson, Diane (2000b) 'Claiming citizenship? Sexuality, citizenship and lesbian/feminist theory', *Sexualities*, 3 (2): 271–88.

Richardson, Diane and May, Hazel (1999) 'Deserving victims? Sexual status and the social construction of violence', *Sociological Review*, 47 (2): 308–31.

Robinson, Victoria (1993) 'Heterosexuality: beginnings and connections', in Sue Wilkinson and Celia Kitzinger (eds), *Heterosexuality: a Feminism and Psychology Reader*. London: Sage.

Robinson, Victoria (1996) 'Heterosexuality and masculinity: theorising male power or the male wounded psyche?', in Diane Richardson (ed.), *Theorising Heterosexuality*. Buckingham: Open University Press.

Robson, Ruthann (1992) *Lesbian (Out)Law: Survival Under the Rule of Law*. Ithaca, NY: Firebrand.

Rodgerson, Gillian and Wilson, Elizabeth (eds) (1991) *Pornography and Feminism by Feminists Against Censorship*. London: Lawrence and Wishart.

Roiphe, Katie (1994) *The Morning After: Sex, Fear and Feminism*. London: Hamish Hamilton.

Roscoe, Will (ed.) (1992) *Living the Spirit: A Gay American Indian Anthology*. New York: St. Martin's Press.

Rose, P. (1993) 'Out in the open?', *Nursing Times*, 89: 50–2.

Rosenbloom, Rachel (ed.) (1996a) *Unspoken Rules. Sexual Orientation and Women's Human Rights*. London: Cassell.

Rosenbloom, Rachel (1996b) 'Introduction', in Rachel Rosenbloom (ed.), *Unspoken Rules. Sexual Orientation and Women's Human Rights*. London: Cassell.

Rowbotham, Sheila (1990) *The Past is Before Us: Feminism in Action Since the 1960s*. Harmondsworth: Penguin.

Rowland, Robyn (1996) 'Politics of intimacy: heterosexuality, love and power', in Diane Bell and Renate Klein (eds), *Radically Speaking: Feminism Reclaimed*. Melbourne: Spinifex.

Rubin, Gayle (1984/1993) 'Thinking sex; notes for a radical theory of the politics of sexuality', in Carole S. Vance (ed.), *Pleasure and Danger: Exploring Female Sexuality*.

London: Routledge & Kegan Paul. Reprinted in Henry Abelove, Michele Aina Barale and David M. Halperin (eds), *The Lesbian and Gay Studies Reader*. New York: Routledge.

Rudd, Andrea and Taylor, Darien (eds) (1992) *Positive Women: Voices of Women Living with AIDS*. Toronto: Second Story Press.

Russo, Vito (1981) *The Celluloid Closet: Homosexuality in the Movies*. New York: Harper & Row.

R. vs Brown (1992) 1 QB 491.

R. vs Brown (1994) AC 212.

Sabatier, Renee (1988) *Blaming Others*. London: Panos Institute.

Sabatini, M.T., Patel, K. and Hirschman, R. (1984) 'Kaposi's sarcoma and T-cell lymphoma in an immunodeficient woman: a case report', *AIDS Research*, 1: 135–7.

Sanderson, Terry (1995) *Mediawatch: The Treatment of Male and Female Homosexuality in the British Media*. London: Cassell.

Sasse, H., Iardino, R., Codice, A., Gherardi, C., Farchi, F. and Chiarotti, F. (1992) 'Potential for transmission of HIV virus among homo/bisexual women'. Paper given at the Second European Conference on Homosexuality and HIV: HIV Policy, Prevention, Care and Research: a Gay and Lesbian Perspective, February 14–16, Amsterdam.

Schneider, Beth E. (1992) 'Lesbian politics and AIDS work', in Kenneth Plummer (ed.), *Modern Homosexualities: Fragments of Lesbian and Gay Experience*. London: Routledge.

Scott, Sara (1987) 'Sex and danger: feminism and AIDS', *Trouble and Strife*, 11: 13–18.

Sedgwick, Eve Kosofosky (1990) *Epistemology of the Closet*. Berkeley: University of California Press.

Sedgwick, Eve Kosofsky (1993) 'How to bring your kids up gay', in Michael Warner (ed.), *Fear of a Queer Planet: Queer Politics and Social Theory*. Minneapolis: University of Minnesota Press.

Segal, Lynne (1987a) *Is the Future Female? Troubled Thoughts on Contemporary Feminism*. London: Virago.

Segal, Lynne (1987b) 'AIDS is a feminist issue', *New Socialist*, April.

Segal, Lynne (1989) 'Lessons from the past: feminism, sexual politics and the challenge of AIDS', in Erica Carter and Simon Watney (eds), *Taking Liberties: AIDS and Cultural Politics*. London: Serpent's Tail.

Segal, Lynne (1990) *Slow Motion: Changing Masculinities Changing Men*. London: Virago.

Segal, Lynne (1994) *Straight Sex: Rethinking the Politics of Pleasure*. London: Virago.

Segal, Lynne (1999) *Why Feminism? Gender, Psychology, Politics*. Oxford: Polity Press.

Seidman, Steven (ed.) (1996) *Queer Theory/Sociology*. Oxford: Blackwell.

Seidman, Steven (1997) *Difference Troubles: Queering Social Theory and Sexual Politics*. Cambridge: Cambridge University Press.

Shakespeare Tom, Gillespie-Sells, K. and Davies, D. (1996) *The Sexual Politics of Disability: Untold Desires*. London: Cassell.

Sharp, Joanne P. (1996) 'Gendering nationhood: a feminist engagement with national identity', in Nancy Duncan (ed.), *Bodyspace: Destabilizing Geographies of Gender and Sexuality*. London: Routledge.

Sherr, Lorraine (1999) 'Counselling and HIV testing', in Rebecca Bennett and Charles A. Erin (eds), *HIV and AIDS: Testing, Screening and Confidentiality*. New York: Oxford University Press.

Shotter, John (1993) 'Psychology and citizenship: identity and belonging', in Bryan S. Turner (ed.), *Citizenship and Social Theory*. London: Sage.

Sibley, David (1995) *Geographies of Exclusion. Society and Difference in the West*. London: Routledge.

Sieghart, P. (1989) *AIDS & Human Rights: a UK Perspective*. London: British Medical Foundation for AIDS.

Simson, Rennie (1984) 'The Afro-American female: the historical context of the construction of sexual identity', in Ann Snitow, Christine Stansell and Sharon Thompson (eds), *Desire: The Politics of Sexuality*. London: Virago.

Sinfield, Alan (1995) 'Diaspora and hybridity: queer identities and the ethnicity model'. Paper presented at the Changing Sexualities Conference, Middlesex University, UK, July 1995.

Smart, Carol (1996a) 'Collusion, collaboration and confession: on moving beyond the heterosexuality debate', in Diane Richardson (ed.), *Theorising Heterosexuality*. Buckingham: Open University Press.

Smart, Carol (1996b) 'Desperately seeking post-heterosexual woman', in Janet Holland and Lisa Adkins (eds), *Sex, Sensibility and the Gendered Body*. Basingstoke: Macmillan.

Smith, Anna-Marie (1995) *New Right Discourse on Race and Sexuality: Britain, 1968–90*. Cambridge: Cambridge University Press.

Smyth, Cherry (1992) *Lesbians Talk Queer Notions*. London: Scarlet Press.

Snitow, Ann, Stansell, Christine and Thompson, Sharon (eds) (1984) *Desire:The Politics of Sexuality*. London: Virago.

Social Exclusion Report (1999) 'Teenage pregnancy', Social Exclusion Unit, June 1999, Cm 4342. London: HMSO.

Sontag, Susan (1983) *Illness as a Metaphor*. Harmondsworth: Penguin.

Squires, Judith (1994) 'Ordering the city: public spaces and political participation', in Jeffrey Weeks (ed.), *The Lesser Evil and the Greater Good: The Theory and Politics of Social Diversity*. London: Rivers Oram Press.

Stacey, Jackie (1991) 'Promoting normality: Section 28 and the regulation of sexuality', in Sarah Franklin, Celia Lury and Jackie Stacey (eds), *Off Centre: Feminism and Cultural Studies*. London: Unwin Hyman.

Stacey, Jackie (1993) 'Untangling feminist theory', in Diane Richardson and Victoria Robinson (eds), *Introducing Women's Studies: Feminist Theory and Practice*. London: Macmillan.

Stacey, Jackie (1997) 'Feminist Theory: capital F, capital T', in Victoria Robinson and Diane Richardson (eds), *Introducing Women's Studies: Feminist Theory and Practice*. 2nd edn. London: Macmillan.

Stanley, Liz (1982) '"Male Needs": the problems and problems of working with gay men', in Scarlet Friedman and Elizabeth Sarah (eds), *On the Problem of Men: Two Feminist Conferences*. London: The Women's Press.

Stanley, Liz and Wise, Sue (1993) *Breaking Out Again: Feminist Ontology and Epistemology*. London: Routledge.

Stein, Arlene (ed.) (1993) *Sisters, Sexperts, Queers: Beyond The Lesbian Nation*. New York: Plume.

Stein, Arlene and Plummer Ken (1996) '"I can't even think straight": "queer" theory and the missing sexual revolution in sociology', in Steven Seidman (ed.), *Queer Theory/Sociology*. Oxford: Blackwell.

Stevens, Patricia E. (1992) 'Lesbian health care research: a review of the literature from 1970 to 1990', *Health Care For Women International*, 13: 91–120.

Stevens, Patricia E. (1994) 'HIV prevention education for lesbians and bisexual women: a cultural analysis of a community intervention', *Social Science and Medicine*, 39: 1565–78.

Stevenson, Nick (ed.) (2000) *Culture and Citizenship*. London: Sage.

Stychin, Carl (1998) *A Nation by Rights: National Cultures, Sexual Identity Politics, and the Discourse of Rights*. Philadelphia: Temple University Press.

Taylor, David (1996) 'Citizenship and social power', in David Taylor (ed.), *Critical Social Policy: a Reader*. London: Sage.

Terry, Jennifer (1995) 'Anxious slippages between "us" and "them": a brief history of the scientific search for homosexual bodies', in Jennifer Terry and Jacqueline Urla (eds), *Deviant Bodies: Critical Perspectives on Difference in Science and Popular Culture*. Bloomington and Indianapolis: Indiana University Press.

Thompson, Denise (1991) *Reading Between the Lines: a Lesbian Feminist Critique of Feminist Accounts of Sexuality*. Sydney: Lesbian Studies and Research Group, The Gorgon's Head Press.

Thomson, Rachel (1994) 'Moral rhetoric and public pragmatism: the recent politics of sex education', *Feminist Review*, 48: 40–61.

Torres, Sasha (1993) 'Prime time lesbianism', in Henry Abelove, Michele Aina Barale and David M. Halperin (eds), *The Lesbian and Gay Studies Reader*. London: Routledge.

Torton Beck, Evelyn (ed.) (1982) *Nice Jewish Girls: a Lesbian Anthology*. Boston, MA: Beacon Press.

Tsoulis, Anthena (1987) *Spare Rib*, (June) 179.

Tucker, Scott (1995) *Fighting Words: an Open Letter to Queers and Radicals*. London: Cassell.

Turner, Bryan S. (1993a) *Citizenship and Social Theory*. London: Sage.

Turner, Bryan S. (1993b) 'Contemporary problems in the theory of citizenship', in Bryan S. Turner (ed.), *Citizenship and Social Theory*. London: Sage.

Turner, Bryan S. (1993c) 'Outline of the theory of human rights', in Bryan S. Turner (ed.), *Citizenship and Social Theory*. London: Sage.

Turner, Bryan S. (1994) 'Postmodern culture / modern citizens', in B.V. Steenbergen (ed.), *The Condition of Citizenship*. London: Sage.

Turner, Bryan (1999) 'Cosmopolitan virtue: citizenship, reactive nationalism and masculinity'. Paper presented at the Rethinking Citizenship: Critical Perspectives For The 21st Century conference, University of Leeds, 29–30th June, 1999.

Turner, Bryan S. (2000) 'Outline of a general theory of cultural citizenship', in Nick Stevenson (ed.), *Culture and Citizenship*. London: Sage.

UNAIDS (1999a) 'Questions and answers: mother-to-child transmission (MTCT) of HIV', www.unaids.org: 1–17.

UNAIDS (1999b) *AIDS Epidemic Update*. December 1999. Geneva.

Ussher, Jane (1991) *Women's Madness: Misogyny or Mental Illness?* London: Harvester Wheatsheaf.

VanEvery, Jo (1995) *Heterosexual Women Changing the Family: Refusing to be a Wife!* London: Taylor & Francis.

VanEvery, Jo (1996) 'Heterosexuality and domestic life', in Diane Richardson (ed.), *Theorising Heterosexuality*. Buckingham: Open University Press.

Voet, R. (1998) *Feminism and Citizenship*. London: Sage.

Walby, Sylvia (1990) *Theorising Patriarchy*. Oxford: Blackwell.

Walby, Sylvia (1994) 'Is citizenship gendered?', *Sociology*, 28 (2): 379–95.

Walby, Sylvia (1997) *Gender Transformations*. London: Routledge.

Walkowitz, Judith (1992) *City of Dreadful Delight: Narratives of Sexual Danger in Late-Victorian London*. London: Virago.

Walter, Natasha (1998) *The New Feminism*. London: Little, Brown.

Walter, Natasha (ed.) (1999) *On the Move: Feminism for a New Generation*. London: Virago.

Warner, Michael (1993a) 'Introduction', in Michael Warner (ed.), *Fear of a Queer Planet: Queer Politics and Social Theory*. Minneapolis: University of Minnesota Press.

Warner, Michael (ed.) (1993b) *Fear of a Queer Planet: Queer Politics and Social Theory*. Minneapolis: University of Minnesota Press.

War On Want (1996) *Pride World-Wide. Sexuality, Development and Human Rights*. London: War on Want.

Watney, Simon (1989) 'The spectacle of AIDS', in Douglas Crimp (ed.), *AIDS: Cultural Analysis / Cultural Activism*. Cambridge, MA: MIT Press.

Watney, Simon (1991) 'Citizenship in the age of AIDS', in Geoff Andrews (ed.), *Citizenship*. London: Lawrence and Wishart.

Watney, Simon (1994) *Practices of Freedom: Selected Writings on HIV/AIDS*. London: Rivers Oram Press.

Weedon, Chris (1987) *Feminist Practice and Post-Structuralist Theory*. Oxford: Blackwell.

Weeks, Jeffrey (1977/1990) *Coming Out: Homosexual Politics in Britain from the Nineteenth Century to the Present*. London: Quartet.

Weeks, Jeffrey (1986) *Sexuality*. London: Ellis Horwood/Tavistock Publications.

Weeks, Jeffrey (1990) *Sex, Politics and Society*, 2nd. edn. London: Longman.

Weeks, Jeffrey (1991) *Against Nature: Essays on History, Sexuality and Identity*. London: Rivers Oram Press.

Weeks, Jeffrey (1995) *Invented Moralities: Sexual Values in an Age of Uncertainty*. Oxford: Polity Press.

Weeks, Jeffrey (1998) 'The sexual citizen', *Theory, Culture and Society*, 15 (3–4): 35–52.

Weston, Kath (1993) 'Parenting in the Age of AIDS', in Arlene Stein (ed.), *Sisters, Sexperts, Queers: Beyond the Lesbian Nation*. New York: Plume.

Wiegman, Robyn (1994) 'Introduction: mapping the lesbian postmodern', in Laura Doan (ed.), *The Lesbian Postmodern*. New York: Columbia University Press.

Wilkinson, Sue and Kitzinger, Celia (eds) (1993) *Heterosexuality: a Feminism & Psychology Reader*. London: Sage.

Wilkinson, Sue and Kitzinger, Celia (1996) 'The queer backlash', in Diane Bell and Renate Klein (eds), *Radically Speaking: Feminism Reclaimed*. Melbourne: Spinifex.

Williams, Fiona (1989) *Social Policy: a Critical Introduction*. Cambridge: Polity Press.

Wilson, Angelia R. (1993) 'Which equality? Toleration, difference or respect', in Joseph Bristow and Angelia R. Wilson (eds), *Activating Theory: Lesbian, Gay, Bisexual Politics*. London: Lawrence and Wishart.

Wilson, Angelia R. (1995) 'Their justice: heterosexism in a theory of justice', in Angelia R. Wilson (ed.), *A Simple Matter of Justice? Theorizing Lesbian and Gay Politics*. London: Cassell.

Wilson, Elizabeth (1993) 'Is transgression transgressive?', in Joseph Bristow and Angelia R. Wilson (eds), *Activating Theory: Lesbian, Gay, Bisexual Politics*. London: Lawrence and Wishart.

Wilton, Tamsin (1992) 'Desire and the politics of representation: issues for lesbians and heterosexual women', in Hilary Hinds, Ann Phoenix and Jackie Stacey (eds), *Working Out: New Directions for Women's Studies*. London: Falmer Press.

Wilton, Tamsin (1994) 'Silences, Absences and Fragmentation', in Lesley Doyal, Jennie Naidoo and Tamsin Wilton (eds), *AIDS: Setting a Feminist Agenda*. London: Taylor & Francis.

Wilton, Tamsin (1995) *Lesbian Studies: Setting an Agenda*. London: Routledge.

Wilton, Tamsin (1996) 'Which one's the man? The heterosexualisation of lesbian sex', in Diane Richardson (ed.), *Theorising Heterosexuality*. Buckingham: Open University Press.

Wilton, Tamsin (1997) *EnGendering AIDS: Deconstructing Sex, Text and Epidemic*. London: Sage.

Winnow, Jackie (1992) 'Lesbians evolving health care: cancer and AIDS', *Feminist Review*, 41: 68–76.

Wittig, Monique (1979) 'The straight mind', *Feminist Issues*, 1(1): 103–11.

Wittig, Monique (1981) 'One is not born woman', *Feminist Issues*, I (2): 47–54.

Wittig, Monique (1992) *The Straight Mind and Other Essays*. Brighton: Harvester Wheatsheaf.

Witz, Anne (1997) 'Women and work', in Victoria Robinson and Diane Richardson (eds), *Introducing Women's Studies: Feminist Theory and Practice*, 2nd edn. Basingstoke: Macmillan.

Wolfenden, John (1957) Report of the Departmental Committee on Homosexual Offences and Prostitution, Cmnd 247. London: HMSO.

Women and Geography Study Group (1997) *Feminist Geographies: Explorations in Diversity and Difference*. Harlow: Longman.

Woods, Chris (1995) *State of the Queer Nation: A Critique of Gay and Lesbian Politics in 1990s Britain*. London: Cassell.

Woolf, Virginia (1928/2000) *A Room of One's Own*. Harmondsworth: Penguin Classics.

World Health Organization (WHO) (1993) *Women and AIDS: Research Priorities. Global Programme on AIDS, ACA (1)/93.8*. Geneva: WHO.

Young, Rebecca M., Weissman, Gloria and Cohen, Judith B. (1992) 'Assessing risk in the absence of information: HIV risk among women injection-drug users who have sex with women', *AIDS and Public Policy Journal*, 7: 175–83.

Yuval-Davis, Nira (1993) 'The (dis)comfort of being "hetero"', in Sue Wilkinson and Celia Kitzinger (eds), *Heterosexuality: a Feminism and Psychology Reader*. London: Sage.

Yuval-Davis, Nira (1997) 'Women, citizenship and difference', *Feminist Review*, 57: 4–27.